MW01204709

Living In The Word
A Devotional Journey
Through the New Testament

"For the word of God is living and powerful, and sharper than any two-edged sword. piercing even to the division of soul and spirit, and of joints and marrow, and is a discerner of the thoughts and intents of the heart."
Hebrews 4:12

by Mike & Terri Rodriguez

Living In The Word
A Devotional Journey Through the New Testament

© 2004 by Mike & Terri Rodriguez

Published by Calvary Chapel Corona
130 W. Chase Dr.
Corona, CA 92882
1-951-278-0600
Livingintheword@calvarycorona.org

ISBN 978-0-9724679-1-9
Library of Congress Control Number: 2004099011

First printing -- November 2004
Second printing -- November 2006

Book Cover designed by Daniel Peterson @ VPD
(www.visionphotodesign.com)
and Jeff & Andee Wright - photography
Edited by Robin Ronkes, Mike Rodriguez
and Debbie Parise

Printed in the United States by Morris Publishing
3212 East Highway 30
Kearney, NE 68847
1-800-650-7888

Dedication

*I*t is with great joy and respect that this Devotional is dedicated to Pastor Chuck and Kay Smith, whom we <u>all</u> love.

"And He Himself gave some to be apostles, some prophets, some evangelists, and some pastors and teachers, for the equipping of the saints for the work of the ministry."
Ephesians 4:11,12

A Pastor To Pastors
A Pastor to Pastors is what you are
Calvary Chapels are everywhere
It started when leaving Corona in faith
God blessed you more than You ever dreamed
He saw all the years that you toiled and gave
He said, "I will use Chuck and Kay
In an extraordinary way!"
From City to City and State to State
Over the ocean and far away
Pastors are preaching and teaching God's Word
Because you believed God and took "A Venture in Faith"
Tonight we are honored to have you here
To dedicate our building in a place you once were
We thank Jesus for allowing us to be
Part of the work of Calvary.

This poem was inspired by God and presented to Pastor Chuck and Kay Smith on August 20th, 2003 when they came to Calvary Chapel Corona to dedicate our new facility.

Acknowledgement

We give special thanks to our Great God and Savior, Jesus Christ; we are nothing without You. Thank You for the fresh whispers from your heart that have inspired us daily through Your Word.

A project like this simply cannot be accomplished without a team of people who share the vision and then make it happen by contributing their individual gifts.

Special thanks to Debra Parise and Robin Ronkes for sharing the vision of <u>Living In The Word</u>. Your time and talent are a treasure to us and are woven throughout every page of this devotional. Words fail to express our appreciation for your labor of love.

Special thanks to Sheldon and Stew Ivester from "Vision Photo Design." Your talent invites people to come and look inside and to see "what's behind the cover." You are always there for us, and only God knows how many times you have worked until the eleventh hour. (We see some hockey tickets in your future!)

Special thanks to Jeff and Andee Wright for opening your hearts and home to so many, and blessing us with your photography skills.

Finally, special thanks to our family. You are the best cheerleaders we know, and a great support and inspiration to us. To the church family at Calvary Chapel Corona, we are blessed, honored, and privileged to serve in such a loving body of believers who truly desire to live in God's Word.

Introduction

Living in God's Word is choosing to live daily in His presence and subjecting ourselves to His heart. So often people say, "I don't seem to hear from God. How is it that He speaks to you?" He communicates to us through His written Word, the Bible. As we read through the Word of God, we can expect Him to speak to our hearts and inspire us. He never fails to offer us something to hold onto, something to take with us. We can expect that He will reveal Himself in an extraordinary way.

Living in God's Word cuts to the deepest parts of our souls, searches our hearts, and transforms us into His Image. His Word is truly living, powerful and full of promise: *"So shall My word be that goes forth from My mouth; it shall not return to Me void, but it shall accomplish what I please, and it shall prosper in the thing for which I sent it." (Isaiah 55:11 NKJV)*

As we journey through the New Testament, God will accomplish great things. His desire is to transform us and bring out the best in us. But in order to do so, we must surrender our lives to Him. As we live daily in His Word, the Lord's character will be developed within us. This will lead to a radical change in our outlook and actions, and we will bear the image of Jesus Christ. As you seek and devote your heart to His Word, may He pour over you His abundant blessings!

Pastor Mike & Terri
Calvary Chapel Corona

The Genealogy Of Jesus Christ

"So all the generations from Abraham to David are fourteen generations, from David until the captivity in Babylon are fourteen generations, and from the captivity in Babylon until the Christ are fourteen generations."
Matthew 1:17

Read Matthew Chapter 1:1-17

*T*raveling through the Old Testament demonstrates the love God has for mankind and their desperate need for a redeemer, the One who can cleanse man from sin. In the New Testament, we will see the beauty of Jesus Christ our Savior, and God's plan for redemption unfold before our eyes.

There were forty-two generations that had passed from the time of Abraham until the time of the Messiah. God would be faithful to fulfill His promise in sending a Savior to the people. His love would extend beyond Israel to the uttermost parts of the world.

The gift of salvation is such a precious and priceless gift. It becomes even more precious when we realize the price that was paid for this gift. As we understand how God, through so many different circumstances gave us Jesus (John 3:16), we will truly understand the wealth of this "priceless gift."

Prayer: Father, please bless our journey through the New Testament, as we know You will.

_____
_____
_____
_____
_____
_____
_____
_____
_____
_____
_____

Messiah

*"And she will bring forth a Son, and you shall call His name Jesus,
for He will save His people from their sins."*
Matthew 1:21

Read Matthew Chapter 1:18-25

What a predicament Joseph was in! He thought that Mary was with child by another man. What heartbreak he must have felt. He was no doubt confused by the circumstances that surrounded him, but God in His sovereignty, knew exactly what He was doing! He chose a man of integrity, a man who would be obedient to the high calling of God to be a father to the Savior.

After Joseph's encounter with the angel of the Lord, he began to have a greater understanding of what was happening. There is no doubt that Joseph was familiar with the Word of God. Suddenly things were making sense to him. Remembering Scripture helped him to see the truth, like Scripture from Isaiah which prophesied, ***"Therefore the Lord Himself will give you a sign. Behold, the virgin shall conceive and bear a Son, and shall call His name Immanuel." (Is. 7:14)*** God always confirms Himself, and He makes no mistakes. He carefully designs all the steps of His plan. We are so thankful that God sent a Savior and that both Mary and Joseph believed God for the impossible.

Prayer: Jesus, thank You for the special gift of salvation.

_____

_____

_____

_____

_____

_____

_____

_____

_____

Follow His Star

"For we have seen His star in the East and have come to worship Him."
Matthew 2:2b

Read Matthew Chapter 2

The Lord provided the wise men a star that would guide them to the newborn king of the Jews. It is believed that the star was a supernatural star that only the wise men could see. God in His divine sovereignty, took care of every detail to lead the wise men to Jesus.

Behind the scenes, Herod was scheming to destroy the newborn babe Jesus. Herod told the wise men to find the young child so that he could come and worship Him. When the wise men finally found Jesus with His mother Mary, they fell down and worshipped Him, presenting gifts of gold, frankincense, and myrrh and rejoiced in seeing the newborn King.

Once again, God in His divine sovereignty thwarts the plans of Herod (and Satan), and warns the wise men in a dream not to return to Herod. Our God is a God of details. He takes care of each and every detail, large or small. He always provides a way of escape for His children. If you're in doubt of His guidance, ask Him to help you to follow His "Star" Jesus.

Prayer: Thank You for Your divine sovereignty.

Power From On High

"I indeed baptize you with water unto repentance, but He who is coming after me is mightier than I, whose sandals I am not worthy to carry. He will baptize you with the Holy Spirit and fire."
Matthew 3:11

Read Matthew Chapter 3:1-12

John the Baptist baptized people unto repentance, but there is so much more for the believer in Jesus Christ. The power of the Holy Spirit, in the life of the believer, is that special touch God gives to empower us to live the Christian life. The power of the Holy Spirit also helps us to bear witness of Him.

I remember when my husband Mike and I had an opportunity to go to China, to smuggle Bibles with our Pastor at the time and a team of youth. There was such a language barrier between our team and the Chinese believers we met. Despite this obstacle, the thing that united us as believers was Jesus Christ and the power of His Holy Spirit. Even though we had difficulty communicating, our common bond in Jesus was clearly understood. This is the power that John the Baptist knew would come with Jesus.

Prayer: Father, thank You for the power of Your Spirit in our lives.

_____
_____
_____
_____
_____
_____
_____
_____
_____
_____

Beloved Son

"This is My beloved Son, in whom I am well pleased."
Matthew 3:17

Read Matthew Chapter 3:13-17

The Spirit of God had just descended upon Jesus after His baptism. Now, His heavenly Father God, had validated His Son as the Savior. This is a beautiful picture of the Trinity: the Father, the Son, and the Holy Spirit. Each one was present and had a part in this beautiful baptism.

As a parent, we take joy in seeing our children grow and succeed. Our heavenly Father was pleased with His Son too. Imagine for a moment that you knew your child was born to die for the sins of others. This is what God was so aware of. He was pleased with His Son Jesus, who would make a way of salvation for a people who otherwise would be lost forever.

As the years go by, we are even more humbled by the grace of God in our lives and the gift of salvation through Jesus. It grips our hearts as we think about the price that Jesus paid for us--sinners. This is our beloved Savior in whom we are well pleased.

Prayer: Father, thank You for Jesus.

_____
_____
_____
_____
_____
_____
_____
_____
_____
_____

Fishers Of Men

"Follow Me, and I will make you fishers of men."
Matthew 4:19

Read Matthew Chapter 4

Jesus begins His public ministry by calling out fishermen to follow Him, and He would make them "fishers of men." Can you imagine how these men might have felt? Here they are, struggling to catch fish to make a living and provide for their families, when suddenly their day is interrupted by Jesus, who invites them to follow Him. In a moment, they dropped what they were doing to follow Jesus, into a life that would forever change them.

The Holy Spirit was moving in the lives of those fishermen, and He moves in our lives today. That's how conversion is. It's sudden and it requires a change of direction. Do you remember when you first believed and received God's love? Somehow, you just knew that life was going to be different. Without anyone disclosing to you that things had to change, you just did. With new direction, Jesus brings a certain longing in our hearts to want more and more of what He has to offer. He makes us "fishers of men" too! Like these first disciples, we drop what was part of our old lives and pick up and follow Jesus.

Prayer: Thank You Jesus, for Your gift of salvation and for changing lives.

Heaven's Reward

"Blessed are you when they revile and persecute you, and say all kinds of evil against you falsely for My namesake. Rejoice and be exceedingly glad, for great is your reward in heaven, for so they persecuted the prophets who were before you."
Matthew 5:11,12

Read Matthew Chapter 5:1-12

Most of us would rather enjoy the blessings of being a child of God, rather than suffer the buffetings. Jesus makes it clear that we will suffer persecution for His namesake. How appropriate these words were for the disciples that were present during His sermon. For many of them would suffer unto death for believing in Jesus.

Do we rejoice when we are persecuted? Are we exceedingly glad when evil is spoken of us? Our first reaction to pain and persecution is revenge and defensiveness. Yet Jesus exhorts us to rejoice and be glad, for in heaven we will enjoy the rewards of our faith. Oh that we would have His heart and His mind as we suffer light affliction for His namesake.

Prayer: Thank You Lord that we can have Your joy in the midst of suffering.

Salt Shakers

"You are the salt of the earth; but if the salt loses its flavor, how shall it be seasoned?"
Matthew 5:13

Read Matthew Chapter 5:13-48

On more than one occasion, we ate something that desperately needed salt. The flavor is just not the same without the salt. What a remarkable seasoning! Salt has a twofold purpose as a seasoning and a preservative. But if it loses its purity, it no longer maintains its flavor.

Jesus uses this illustration to remind us that we need to maintain a pure and right relationship with Him. We are the ingredient that is sprinkled around the world to season the lost with the flavor of Jesus Christ. How sad it is when we forget who we represent, to a lost and dying world. We never know when someone needs some salt shaken on them.

Just the other day, we witnessed a wonderful miracle as an elderly man who was in his eighties, testified of his new found faith. It was the work of the Holy Spirit living and breathing through a believer who was willing to share his faith and season the life of another.

Prayer: Lord, thank You for letting us flavor the lives of others with the beauty of Christ.

_____
_____
_____
_____
_____
_____
_____
_____
_____

Take A Vacation From Worrying

*"Therefore I say to you, do not worry about your life, what you will
eat or what you will drink; nor about your body, what you will put on.
Is not life more than food and the body more than clothing?"*
Matthew 6:25

Read Matthew Chapter 6

If we added up the hours we have spent worrying instead of trusting, there would be enough to take a nice long vacation. It's incredible how much time we waste on worrying! We worry about the past, we worry about the future, and we worry about things that are completely out of our control. Jesus points out the example of the birds of the air, and how He uniquely provides for them. How much more will He provide for our needs!

We have been asking God to help us with needless worrying. In asking Him to help us, He has reminded us that when we are tempted to worry, we should use that time in prayer. It's amazing that when we do, we find a sense of peace that floods our hearts. We are reminded again of God's precious Word, encouraged by Scripture to, ***"Set your mind on things above, not on things on the earth." (Col. 3:2)***

Because we have our flesh to deal with, we will be tempted to worry and fret, and so we must fight the battle in the Spirit and with the Word of God. What are you worried about today? Write it down and give it to God. Find a Scripture and memorize it, and you too will find that peace that surpasses all human understanding. (Phil. 4:6,7)

Prayer: Lord, thank You for always being there to lift us up.

_____

_____

_____

_____

_____

_____

_____

A Critical Spirit

"Judge not, that you be not judged. For with what judgment you judge,
you will be judged; and with the measure you use, it will be measured back to you."
Matthew 7:1,2

Read Matthew Chapter 7:1-14

*J*esus spoke of the dangers of having a critical spirit, and the effects it would have on our own life if we do. One of the things that we have observed in our lives, is how subtle a critical spirit can be. It may begin with a constructive critique, such as pointing out a proper way to do something, and before long, we have taken it too far. When we judge others, they usually are not present. We would never have the nerve to say what we say behind their backs, to their faces. This is a sad commentary for a Christian, because while the person we are judging may not be present, the Holy Spirit is, and it grieves Him. Therefore, this warning should be heeded. Before we judge another, we should examine our own hearts to see if we possess a critical spirit.

There are times, however, when we may have to address a situation with a brother or sister, and this should not be confused with a critical spirit. We should be careful to be prayerful and speak the truth in love. *"Let no corrupt word proceed out of your mouth, but what is good for necessary edification, that it may impart grace to the hearers." (Eph. 4:29)*

Prayer: Father, help us to know that You are watching, and help our words to be uplifting.

_____

_____

_____

_____

_____

_____

_____

_____

Fruit Detectors

*"Beware of false prophets, who come to you in sheep's clothing, but
inwardly they are ravenous wolves. You will know them by their fruits."*
Matthew 7:15,16a

Read Matthew Chapter 7:15-20

Years ago when we were young believers, we would hear people quote this verse and think, "How is it that someone who says they are a believer, really be a deceiver?" Our young and optimistic outlook on life and people, blinded us to the truth in this verse. After personal schooling from the Holy Spirit and seeing this happen a few times before our eyes, we soon became aware that there sits among us in the congregation those who are wolves. They can start out by being so kind, saying all the right words, and seeming to be superior in their spiritual knowledge. In time, their shady sheep's clothing wears thin as they try to sow discord among the brethren. This can be alarming and hurtful, and this is why we are admonished in Scripture to be watchful. *"Be sober, be vigilant; because your adversary the devil walks about like a roaring lion, seeking whom he may devour." (1 Peter 5:8)*

We need not fear! We need to be alert and in prayer, praying for the gift of discernment. We can put our full confidence in Jesus Christ who is greater than any counterfeit out there. *"Because He who is in you is greater than he who is in the world." (1 John 4:4)*

Prayer: Father, thank You so much for being the truth, and help us to expose those who are liars.

_____

_____

_____

_____

_____

_____

_____

_____

What Will He Say To You?

"Not everyone who says to Me, 'Lord, Lord,' shall enter the kingdom of heaven, but he who does the will of My Father in heaven."
Matthew 7:21

Read Matthew Chapter 7:21-29

Recent statistics reveal that at least 80% of Americans believe in God or a higher power. If this was true, then why do so many live as though they don't know God? Most folks, if asked if they believe in God, would answer "yes." But how many really know Him? This is what Jesus was talking about! So many false teachers are doing their thing in the name of Jesus, while missing the mark and doing it for personal gain. How sad that day will be when Jesus says those dreaded words, *"I never knew you; depart from Me you who practice lawlessness!"* *(Matt. 7:23)*

But what about the miracles, prophesies, and gifts that were manifested? Don't those count for anything? Not if in doing them, God's will and Word were compromised. God's Word is superior to any miracle or prophecy. Knowing Him is more important to Him than promoting the idea of Him. This should challenge us all to be on bended knee and to seek Him while He may be found. Then He will say to us those most blessed words, *"Well done, good and faithful servant; you have been faithful over a few things, I will make you ruler over many things. Enter into the joy of Your Lord."* *(Matt. 25:23)*

Prayer: Father, keep our hearts pure before You.

_____
_____
_____
_____
_____
_____
_____
_____

Fear Paralyzes Faith

"Why are you fearful, O you of little faith?"
Matthew 8:26

Read Matthew Chapter 8

After witnessing miracle after miracle, the disciples were challenged with a trial. Their Lord was resting while the boat was rocking. Fear gripped their hearts and they came running to Jesus. "Lord, save us! We are perishing!" Those were their words to Jesus. Jesus responds to them by asking a question, "Why are you fearful?" He then makes them aware of their "little faith" by getting up and rebuking the winds and the sea, and making all calm.

We can lose sight of our Savior in the midst of the storms of life, but in His sovereignty He allows us to experience times of testing, so that we can witness the One who calms the storms. The disciples were building their faith in Jesus, and He allowed them to experience it. The important lesson is that when the trial came, they called upon the Lord, and He did answer.

Prayer: Father, at times our flesh is fearful. Help us to have faith in You.

Signs Or A Savior

"See that no one knows it."
Matthew 9:30a

Read Matthew Chapter 9

After a series of physical and spiritual healings, Jesus again heals two blind men. *"Then He touched their eyes, saying, 'According to your faith let it be to you.' And their eyes were opened. And Jesus sternly warned them, saying, 'See that no one knows it.'" (Matt. 9:29, 30)* Why would Jesus make a statement like, "See that no one knows it!"? You would think that the news of the healings would be something He would have wanted to share amongst the people. Then again, Jesus, knowing the heart of man, knew that many would come for wrong reasons; for signs or physical healing, when there lives needed so much more.

As a people, we can be lured into chasing signs and wonders, and no doubt God is able to perform such things. Our motives should be checked! Are we coming to Him for spiritual healing or for the signs and miracles He can perform? The greatest miracle ever is the gift of salvation. For truly, conversion of the soul demonstrates that He is God. Conversion is not something we can see, like a physical healing, but it bears the marks of the cross. We now live because He died. Perhaps that is why Jesus said, "See that no one knows it." In fact, later in Matthew, the scribes and Pharisees asked Jesus for a sign. Jesus answered them by saying, *"An evil and adulterous generation seeks after a sign." (Matt. 12:39)* We should examine our own hearts. Do we seek a sign or are we seeking Him as Savior?

Prayer: Thank You for salvation, the greatest gift of all.

_____

_____

_____

_____

_____

His Eye Is On The Sparrow

*"Are not two sparrows sold for a copper coin? And not one of them falls to
the ground apart from your Father's will. But the very hairs of your head
are all numbered. Do not fear therefore; you are of more value than many sparrows."*
Matthew 10:29-31

Read Matthew Chapter 10

We falter in the area of fear, and Jesus knew it. After warning the
disciples that they would be persecuted for their faith, He takes it a step
further to encourage them to fear God and not man. Jesus uses the
illustration of the sparrow and demonstrates how God carefully designs
and cares for them. He cares for the sparrows, which depend on God.
How much more will He care for us?

We do struggle in the area of fear, and it is manifested in many different
ways. Sometimes it comes as fear of the future, not knowing what's ahead.
The fear of failure is a popular one with the enemy; he loves to use this
one on us, to keep us in a holding pattern. There is the fear of success;
how will we cope if we are successful? And then there is the fear that the
disciples experienced, the fear of persecution. We love the fact that Jesus
disclosed to us this truth. They call the master to give an account and
they will call those of his household. (Matt. 10:25) Yes! Being part of the
family of Christ has its costs, but the benefits far outweigh the costs.
Knowing that He has our very hairs numbered, gives us peace and
reassurance that He will equip us when we face persecution.

Prayer: Lord, give us the trust that a sparrow has. Help us to depend
on You.

_____

_____

_____

_____

_____

_____

_____

Rest For Your Soul

*"Come to Me, all you who labor and are heavy laden, and I will give you rest.
Take My yoke upon you and learn from Me, for I am gentle and lowly in heart,
and you will find rest for your souls. For My yoke is easy and My burden is light."*
Matthew 11:28-30

Read Matthew Chapter 11

There is bondage in a lot of religious rules and regulations. The Jews were suffering under the burden of trying to fulfill all the "do's and dont's" of the law. They were bogged down with a yoke which became a heavy burden. Jesus, with His comforting words, offers an invitation to come unto Him and find rest for their souls. We, who love, serve, and walk with Jesus, also need to guard our hearts from self-righteous works, for truly it is a yoke that we are not called to bear.

For some, it seems easier if you give them a list of rules; some love living under the law of legalism. They love the lists that tell them, "you can't do this" and "you can't do that." They feel justified by the rules that seem to seal their faith. The truth is, there is none good but God. *"No one is good but One, that is, God." (Matt. 19:17)* Rules aren't completely bad in themselves, in fact, they are a guide for us to follow. It's when we begin to serve the rules and not the Savior that our hearts begin to grow dull to the Spirit, and we gradually come under bondage to the laws of legalism. This is something that places a heavy yoke on us and others too.

Prayer: Fill us with Your Spirit, that we might find rest for our souls.

_____
_____
_____
_____
_____
_____
_____
_____

Dull Hearts

"For the hearts of this people have grown dull. Their ears are hard of hearing, and their eyes they have closed, lest they should see with their eyes and hear with their ears, lest they should understand with their hearts and turn, so that I should heal them."

Matthew 13:15

Read Matthew Chapters 12 & 13

*H*ave you ever tried to use a dull pencil? It is so frustrating, because it lacks the sharpness it once had. The only way to be content in using the pencil is to sharpen it. Then, its fresh sharp tip encourages us to write with a little more ease and enthusiasm. Our heart is the place where God dwells, and yet we are warned in this verse of the dullness that can affect our heart. When our heart grows cold towards the things of the Lord, we are in danger of opening ourselves up to the flesh. Some of the things that can slip in our lives are a critical spirit, ears that can't hear from God, and eyes that cannot see. All these things lead to apathy.

At times, we have seen this in our own lives, and it can be traced back to an apathetic heart. It's when we fail in our personal devotion to God that we fall away from His truth, and our hearts becomes indifferent. What is the remedy for a dull and apathetic heart? It is finding the way back to the arms of our Savior and once again, asking Him to soften our crusty heart, and give us ears to hear, and eyes to see.

Prayer: Father, Your Word is convicting. Help us to feel the nudging of Your Holy Spirit and obey.

Walking On The Water

"O you of little faith, why did you doubt?"
Matthew 14:31b

Read Matthew Chapter 14

After a busy afternoon of miracles and ministering, it was time to break away from the crowds to come away and pray. This was a regular pattern of our Lord. He always took the time to renew His spirit by spending time with His Father. When evening had come, the disciples were still on the boat being tossed about by a sudden rush of wind and waves, that put the boat and the disciples at risk. Jesus uses this as an opportunity to both save and teach the disciples a spiritual lesson. He walks on water! They see Him and perceive that He is a ghost, but then He speaks those blessed words of assurance, *"Be of good cheer! It is I; do not be afraid." (Matt. 14:27)*

Peter, being his typical self, questions the Lord and asks Him to let him join Him on the water if He indeed is the Lord. Jesus, in His wisdom, invites Peter to *"Come." (Matt. 14:29)* At first there were a few faithful steps, and then Peter took his eyes off the Lord and put them on his circumstances, the wind and storms. Soon he was sinking. We too are much like Peter. Time after time we witness the miracles and the ministering of our Lord Jesus, but we take our eyes off of Him for only a moment to find that we are sinking. Jesus is faithful to help us up. He stretches out His arms and rescues us. We, like the disciples, once again have a renewed faith until the next time we have a storm at sea. Then in His faithfulness, Jesus will once again say those blessed words, *"Be of good cheer! It is I; do not be afraid."*

Prayer: Thank You for saving us, and for renewing our faith even when we falter.

Hypocrites And Unholy Hearts

"Not what goes into the mouth defiles a man;
but what comes out of the mouth, this defiles a man."
Matthew 15:11

Read Matthew Chapter 15

The scribes and Pharisees were always trying to catch Jesus and His disciples off guard with questions regarding the law. Jesus, knowing their hypocritical hearts, exposes the motives to their questions, and turns the attention to their own sinful actions. The scribes and Pharisees were concerned about the disciples having dirty hands. Jesus poses His concerns about their dirty hearts.

We too must guard our hearts from falling into the trap of judging others. It is so easy and wrong to make assumptions about people based on their outward appearance. Like Jesus, we need to look a little deeper into the heart, beginning first with our own hearts. The cutting and sharp words from the scribes and Pharisees revealed their defiled hearts. Jesus called them "hypocrites" in verse 7. We need to nurture our hearts with holy things, and pray that they will be reflected in our lives.

Prayer: Father, create in us pure hearts.

Deny Yourself

*"If anyone desires to come after Me, let him deny himself,
and take up his cross, and follow Me."*
Matthew 16:24

Read Matthew Chapter 16

Following Jesus seems so easy, until it comes time to pick up the cross. Many lose sight of their faith when the cross feels heavy and burdensome. These profound words of Jesus make so much sense. He knew that He would be taking up the cross on behalf of a lost world. He also disclosed to us the truth. Following Him would cost. The cost is a life willing to deny itself for His sake.

Jesus goes on to say more profound words, ***"For whoever desires to save his life will lose it, but whoever loses his life for My sake will find it. For what profit is it to a man if he gains the whole world, and loses his own soul? (Matt. 16:25,26)***

We have found these words to be so true. Following Jesus and bearing the burden of our cross, does have its expense, but the return is so worth it. God is in debt to no man. He gives us a fruit-filled life and the promise of salvation. While the world offers its goods, it hardly seems worth it to compromise our souls for the things of this world.

Prayer: Lord, thank You for taking up the cross for us. Help us to deny ourselves for You.

Lost Sheep, Loving Shepherd

"Take heed that you do not despise one of these little ones, for I say to you that in heaven their angels always see the face of My Father who is in heaven. For the Son of Man has come to save that which was lost."
Matthew 18:10,11

Read Matthew Chapters 17 & 18:1-14

Anyone who has children knows the magnitude of pain and fear that one feels when a child has been lost for even a moment. We have all had the experience in a store or a park, when our child has slipped out of our sight. Suddenly our world comes to a halt, and the only focus we have is finding that child. This should help us understand the heart of God. He too has the interest of His lost sheep in mind.

Sometimes, we who are walking with the Lord, get judgmental towards those who have lost their way. Instead of going into prayer for these lost sheep, we complain and sometimes even write them off. Jesus, in His wisdom, takes us to the heart of God concerning lost sheep. *"Even so it is not the will of your Father who is in heaven that one of these little ones should perish." (Matt. 18:14)*

Like the parents who find a world of relief when their child is found, so our loving Shepherd rejoices over a sheep that was lost but now found. God's passion for souls should give us a passion to pray for those who are lost or prodigals who have chosen to stray.

Prayer: Father, thank You for loving the lost.

Restoring A Brother

"Moreover if your brother sins against you, go and tell him his fault between you and him alone. If he hears you, you have gained your brother. But if he will not hear, take with you one or two more, that 'by the mouth of two or three witnesses every word may be established.'"
Matthew 18:15,16

Read Matthew Chapter 18:15-35

*H*ow many times have we followed this prescription? More often, we tend to fail in the area of loving confrontation. We squirm at the thought of having to confront another with his or her particular sin. We also sometimes talk too much about the issue with others rather than going directly to that person. Why is this so hard? Because the enemy convinces us that we will ruffle some feathers if we do.

To our surprise, we have found when we have followed the steps that Jesus outlined for us in these verses, we rarely have to go to the next step of taking another with us to confront. It's amazing how easy it is when we prayerfully ask God to anoint our words and season them with His agape love. Many times, the erring brother or sister is just waiting for the much needed help. We have even experienced times when there was no error on the other's part, it was simply a misunderstanding. Godly communication is something we can all strive to do a little better; it leads to restored lives and peace in our own hearts.

Prayer: Father, thank You for the instruction You give us in Your Word.

Harden Not Your Heart

"He said to them, 'Moses, because of the hardness of your hearts, permitted you to divorce your wives, but from the beginning it was not so. And I say to you, whoever divorces his wife, except for sexual immorality, and marries another, commits adultery; and whoever marries her who is divorced commits adultery.'"
Matthew 19:8,9

Read Matthew Chapter 19

Having a hardened heart seems to be a continual problem. Today, it appears that people walk away from marriage, even before the marriage has a chance to bloom. "He's not meeting my needs," or "She is not what I thought she would be." What is so difficult is to see how far couples can get from truth. The truth is, no other person can meet all our needs, and we cannot meet all of theirs. But God, He is the very foundation upon which we should build our marriages. If we are not establishing our marriages on God's holy foundation, then may we ask, what is our foundation? *"For every house is built by someone, but He who built all things is God." (Heb. 3:4)*

The results of a broken marriage are broken lives. Most young people struggle with their identity when their parents divorce. They generally feel responsible for the divorce, and carry insecurities with them their whole life. If your marriage is suffering, there is hope. The very Creator of marriage is here to come along side of you and your mate, to empower you to live for Him. He is the missing link and the glue that keeps the marriage together. Keep your heart soft towards the Lord, and this will prevent it from growing hard towards your mate.

Prayer: Father, we pray for all the marriages that need a special touch from You.

An Invitation To All

"So the last will be first, and the first last. For many are called, but few chosen."
Matthew 20:16

Read Matthew Chapter 20

Our Father in heaven offers us salvation. The gift is a free gift, given and distributed generously to those who would believe and receive it. Some may accept the gift later than others, but this does not change the fact that the wages that have been paid are the same. Jesus Christ, God's only Son, picked up the full tab for our salvation. Man cannot put a price tag on it.

Today's verse also implies that just because others might have committed their lives to the Lord before us, this does not give them a special place of honor. Some folks feel they should receive greater favor from the Lord because they have known Him longer, while others never really respond to His call. However, we can be confident that God is fair. God is good, for no one is good except God alone.

When we are finally with Him in heaven, all the foolishness of man's thinking will not matter. We will be focused upon Jesus. *"Looking unto Jesus, the author and finisher of our faith," (Heb. 12:2a)*

Prayer: Father, thank You for making room for all who would believe.

_____
_____
_____
_____
_____
_____
_____
_____
_____
_____

Let The Children Come

*"And Jesus said to them, 'Yes. Have you never read, Out of the mouth
of babes and nursing infants You have perfected praise'?"
Matthew 21:16*

Read Matthew Chapter 21

In spite of the Pharisees and their indignant attitudes, Jesus refers to Psalm 8:2 which speaks of infants praising the Lord in the face of enemies. Jesus and the gospel are so simple that even a child understands it. These arrogant Pharisees were envious and critical of the children praising Jesus, but even a child could recognize that Jesus was the Son of God.

As adults, we need to remember not to let our hearts become clouded with what I call *"Adult Onset Heart Disease."* You may be wondering what are the symptoms of this disease? The beginning stages start with a critical spirit, and soon one's heart becomes so cynical and crusty that it can no longer appreciate and glean from the simplicity of the gospel. Yes, even as believers we can lose sight of our Lord. We can become so knowledgeable in the Word that we become stale to its meaning. This is why Jesus loved the children and their innocent faith. *"But Jesus said, 'Let the little children come to Me, and do not forbid them; for of such is the kingdom of heaven.'"* **(Matt. 19:14)** We can take a lesson from the little ones, and by doing this we can prevent *"Adult Onset Heart Disease."*

Prayer: Father, help us to see You through the heart of a child.

Wedding Invitation

"For many are called, but few are chosen."
Matthew 22:14

Read Matthew Chapter 22

Attending a wedding is a special event. A lot of thought and planning goes into celebrating the couple's special day. Most people, if they know wedding etiquette, will come to a wedding fully prepared. Proper etiquette includes: putting on our best clothing, bringing a gift, arriving on time, and being willing to stay for the reception that generally costs the couple's families a lot of money. Normal etiquette requires that we have a personal relationship with the bride, the groom, or their families.

In the parable of the wedding feast, all were invited but few responded to the call to come. Many made light of Christ's invitation. Why? Many refused to have a personal relationship with Jesus Christ. They were unwilling to put on the wedding garments that are required to attend the occasion. Some folks believe that this is not fair, and that Christ only chooses certain people. Nothing could be further from the truth. Another way to look at this parable is, many were invited, but few responded to the invitation. Remember the proper etiquette! You have been invited to a special event, to come and celebrate the marriage supper of the Lamb. You must respond, you must RSVP. You must come believing in Him who has invited you. You must have a personal relationship with Him. You must be willing to put on the wedding garments.

Prayer: Father, thank You that You invite all to come. We pray that more would respond.

_____

_____

_____

_____

_____

_____

A Warning To Hypocrites

"Woe to you, scribes and Pharisees, hypocrites! For you pay tithe of mint and anise and cummin, and have neglected the weightier matters of the law: justice and mercy and faith."
Matthew 23:23

Read Matthew Chapter 23

The Greek word for "hypocrite" means actor. Webster's Dictionary describes the word "hypocrite" as one who pretends to be something he is not. Another way to describe a hypocrite is one who does not practice what he preaches. Jesus devoted almost this entire chapter to warning the scribes and Pharisees of the danger of being hypocrites. Not only did He warn them, but He called them hypocrites. Jesus reminded them over and over again that their outward appearance meant nothing, because they lacked truth on the inside. We are reminded of this in Scripture, **"For the Lord does not see as man sees; for man looks at the outward appearance, but the Lord looks at the heart." (1 Sam. 16:7b)**

We need to take a lesson from these warnings. Because we are sinners, we can fall into hypocrisy. We need to examine our lives to see if there lives in us any dead man's bones. It can be painful to look closely into our souls, but so profitable if we do. Jesus is God's gift to us for salvation, so thankfully we have somewhere to take our sin.

Prayer: Father, help us to be real and transparent before You and others.

_____

_____

_____

_____

_____

_____

_____

_____

_____

_____

Be Ready

"Therefore you also be ready,
for the Son of Man is coming at an hour you do not expect."
Matthew 24:44

Read Matthew Chapter 24

During a private session, in a more relaxed and intimate environment, the disciples asked Jesus about the end times and His return. Jesus gave a long and detailed answer to their question. Jesus made it clear to the disciples that even He did not know the exact time of His return. ***"But of that day and hour no one knows, not even the angels of heaven, but My Father only." (vs. 36)***

Jesus explains the importance of being prepared and knowing the signs of His coming. Anyone who watches the nightly news is aware that we are living in the "last days." It's amazing how often the highlights from the evening news line up with this chapter, and even more amazing at the fact that Jesus warned us to be ready and prepared. We should be living our lives with the expectancy of His return. Let us be aware of the times that we live in, and be ready to share our faith. ***"But sanctify the Lord God in your hearts, and always be ready to give a defense to everyone who asks you a reason for the hope that is in you, with meekness and fear." (1 Pet. 3:15)***

Prayer: Father, help us to live our lives as though You were returning today.

Communion

*"For this is My blood of the new covenant,
which is shed for many for the remission of sins."
Matthew 26:28*

Read Matthew Chapters 25 & 26

*O*nce a month, we are blessed with the opportunity of having communion at church. So much goes into the preparation of it. The ushers prepare many plates, the choir prepares many songs, and the pastor prepares us to receive it. But do we prepare our hearts? We are told in Scripture to take communion as a remembrance of what Jesus has done for us. When we reflect on what He has done for us, we are reminded of how far we once were from Him. We were desperate, lost, and lonely until Jesus came into our lives, promising us a new covenant. We will be forever grateful for how He dramatically changed the course of our lives.

Recently we heard a personal testimony from a woman who had been ill. For many months she was unable to receive communion with the congregation. This is what she missed, and when she was well enough to partake again, she better understood the deeper meaning of communion. We should open our hearts to the Lord during this special time. We should do this in remembrance of Him.

Prayer: Father, help us to appreciate what You have done for us.

Blood Money

"Then he threw down the pieces of silver in the temple and departed,
and went and hanged himself."
Matthew 27:5

Read Matthew Chapter 27

*I*magine for a moment the anguish Judas must have felt. He had made a bad decision in betraying Jesus. His remorse led him to change his mind and return the money. However, rather than seeking Jesus' forgiveness, he chose the road to suicide. How lost his soul was. Had he only believed in Jesus, He would have been granted the same grace that Peter was given when he denied the Lord.

There was a problem with the money that Judas left at the temple. The money was blood money that paid for the betrayal and subsequent death of Jesus. The hypocritical chief priests were not allowed to put the blood money into the temple treasury, so they did what they considered a good work. They used it for a burial site for strangers and the poor who died in Jerusalem. We can take a lesson from Judas and his sin against Jesus. We need to seek the Lord with a pure heart and mind. We should not be sorry that we have been caught in sin, but rather be like Peter, and be sorry for our sin.

Prayer: Father, forgive us for our sins, and help us to have true repentance when we fail You.

He Is Risen

"He is not here; for He is risen,"
Matthew 28:6a

Read Matthew Chapter 28

He is risen! We do not believe there are any greater words than these. Because Jesus has risen, we who believe in Him also have risen. We have risen above the pain of sin and death, because our Lord Jesus took the pain of the cross for us. We now have the ability to live above the difficult circumstances of sin. The powerful words, "He is risen," bring with them God's ability to do the impossible. The miracle of the resurrection should be enough to remind us, *"Is anything too hard for the Lord?" (Gen. 18:14a)*

"He is risen" means that everything in His Word is true. He is able to lift us out of a hopeless and helpless life, and bring us into a living and powerful relationship with Him. What kind of trouble do you face today? What are the burdens in your life that you need God's strength to overcome? Spend some time in worship and praise, and make your requests known to Him. He is able, because He has risen. *"Arise, shine; for your light has come! And the glory of the Lord is risen upon you." (Is. 60:1)*

Prayer: Thank You Lord for taking up the cross for our sins, and then for rising again.

_____
_____
_____
_____
_____
_____
_____
_____
_____
_____
_____

Preparing The Way

*"Behold, I send My messenger before Your face,
Who will prepare Your way before You."*
Mark 1:1

Read Mark Chapter 1

John the Baptist had the awesome privilege of being a "crier." In the Old Testament, a "crier" was sent out to clear the paths for the king's travels. Part of his responsibilities were to yell with a loud voice, "Prepare the way, clear the paths, for the king is coming." This is why John said, *"I am the voice of one crying in the wilderness: 'Make straight the way of the Lord.'" (John 1:23)*

In a sense, we have some of the same opportunities to serve the Lord. We, like the "crier," can go out before the people to prepare them for the Lord's coming. It's important that folks have the opportunity to seek the Lord, allowing Him to clear out the sin in their lives and make straight their paths.

Prayer: Father, thank You for giving us opportunities to share and help prepare the way for Your coming.

_____

_____

_____

_____

_____

_____

_____

_____

_____

_____

_____

_____

Forgiven & Healed

"When Jesus saw their faith, He said to the paralytic,
'Son, your sins are forgiven you.'"
Mark 2:5

Read Mark Chapter 2

The Pharisees and scribes were always ready to criticize and find fault with Jesus. They were "reasoning in their hearts," and belittling Jesus for His declaration that He had forgiven the paralytic. *"Why does this Man speak blasphemies like this? Who can forgive sins but God alone." (vs. 7)* Jesus knowing that they were speaking against Him said, *"Why do you reason about these things in your hearts?" (vs. 8b)* The response that Jesus gave was profound. He said, *"Which is easier, to say to the paralytic, 'Your sins are forgiven you,' or to say, 'Arise, take up your bed and walk'?" (vs. 9)* Jesus made a great point in these verses. He identified that forgiveness of sin is more important than physical healing. While He being Lord can do both, we should recognize the fact that Jesus is God, and that He came to set man free from the bondage of sin.

Jesus then healed the paralytic and said to him, *"I say to you, arise, take up your bed, and go to your house." (vs. 11)* We now see that Jesus demonstrates His power to both forgive and heal. You can imagine that this left the scribes in a quandary, trying to rationalize how He could do this. We too can often behave like the scribes. We wonder how Christ can change our circumstances. "This problem is just too big," we say. However, the bigger the problem, the bigger our God!

Prayer: Father, thank You for Your forgiveness and healing.

Family Matters

"For whoever does the will of God is My brother and My sister and mother."
Mark 3:35

Read Mark Chapter 3

Jesus was in full swing with His public ministry and was drawing quite a crowd. Many were there just to see a miracle. Others were there out of curiosity, and no doubt many were there with sincere hearts ready to receive Jesus. His family also showed up, and their presence was made known to Jesus. *"And a multitude was sitting around Him; and they said to Him, 'Look, Your mother and Your brothers are outside seeking You.'" (Mark 3:32)*

We don't know why the family showed up, and we can only imagine. Perhaps they were concerned with all the publicity He was receiving. Whatever the case, we can be assured that they were there because they loved Him. Jesus takes an opportunity to point out that obedience to God is more important than obedience to one's family. Our spiritual relationship with God goes beyond our human relationships. Being a member of the body of Christ unites us to Him in a unique way. Although Jesus is concerned with our earthly families, He is more concerned with our spiritual family matters.

Prayer: Father, help us to keep a balance between loving You and our family.

Spiritual Mysteries

"And He said to them, 'To you it has been given to know the mystery of the kingdom of God; but to those who are outside, all things come in parables,'"

Mark 4:11

Read Mark Chapter 4

Jesus often spoke in parables, and He revealed the mysteries of the parables to His disciples. Parables, earthly stories with a heavenly meaning, can keep a listener's attention and have a spiritual truth hidden within. Jesus pointed out that not all understand the mysteries of the parables. It takes real spiritual discernment to understand. The unbeliever has difficulty perceiving the secrets of heaven, because he has not had spiritual revival in his own heart. *"But the natural man does not receive the things of the Spirit of God, for they are foolishness to him; nor can he know them, because they are spiritually discerned." (1 Cor. 2:14)*

When we consider that the God of all creation opens up His truth to us, we are amazed and humbled. As disciples of Jesus, we not only benefit from the awesome gift of salvation, but we also receive the keys to His kingdom and the keys to His heart. Wow! How good is that?

Prayer: Lord, thank You for opening up our hearts to Your heart, and revealing Your truth.

Who Touched Me?

"And He said to her, 'Daughter, your faith has made you well.
Go in peace, and be healed of your affliction.'"
Mark 5:34

Read Mark Chapter 5

 *L*iving with affliction can be difficult; living with affliction for twelve years can be unbearable. Imagine that you were this woman, who had an issue of blood for that length of time. All of your finances were spent on doctor bills, and people were tired of hearing you complain. There were just no answers to your dilemma. Suddenly, you hear of a man named Jesus who is healing the sick and performing miracles. All you can think about is Jesus. If only you could just touch His garment, perhaps you have a chance of being made whole.

 The crowd is growing and multitudes are flocking around your Lord. Your chances of any personal contact appear to be slim, yet there is something inside of you crying out and impelling you to seek your opportunity. You're tired, weary, and weak, but you reach out with what little strength you have and you touch His garment. A sudden flow of peace and a feeling of being whole again fills your entire being.

 At times, we may find ourselves afflicted, discouraged, and completely spent. There is nothing in or of ourselves that can help our desperate lives. It's those times that we need to reach out for His garment in faith.

 Prayer: Jesus, thank You for Your touch.

Come Away

"And He said to them, 'Come aside by yourselves to a deserted place and rest a while.'"
Mark 6:31

Read Mark Chapter 6

*L*ife in the twentieth century is so fast paced. Daily we are constantly bombarded with phone calls, answering machines, cell phones, and electronic mail. So many things are vying for our attention and our affections.

Life for the disciples was similar but in a different way. They did not have the modern conveniences we have. They walked everywhere and had to catch fish to provide for their families. They did not have a Starbucks on every other corner to give them their "stress relief." They did however, have the same need that we do today. They needed to come away from all the stresses that beset them, to spend time with Jesus. Oh how we need the rest that Jesus gives! There is nothing in this life that can satisfy the emptiness in our souls more than Jesus. We should listen to His wise words, *"Come away."* Are you feeling tired, weary or weak? *"Come away." "Come to Me, all you who labor and are heavy laden, and I will give you rest." (Matt. 11:28)*

Prayer: Thank You that we can come to You for rest.

A Gained Soul

"For what will it profit a man if he gains the whole world, and loses his own soul?"
Mark 8:36

Read Mark Chapters 7 & 8

The enemy is a deceiver; he has blinded the eyes of so many who seek after the things of this world. People really believe if they have the material things of this world, they have arrived. Many are convinced that this life will last forever. This is so untrue! Life and death live in the same neighborhood, and at any moment our lives can be over. Just the other day, Mike did a memorial service for a man who went to work on a Friday and suffered a brain hemorrhage on Saturday. In less than a week, he went home to be with the Lord. This man knew where his gain was; it was with the Lord. The riches in this man's life were a legacy of love and devotion for his family and friends.

Jesus gives us some hard words to swallow here, and He challenges us to know where we should invest our lives. The incredible thing about living for Jesus is that we have the benefit of having a saved soul and a fruitful life. When our priorities are straight, He allows us to enjoy the things that He has provided.

Prayer: Thank You Jesus for saving our souls.

_____
_____
_____
_____
_____
_____
_____
_____
_____
_____

The Way Up Is Down

"If anyone desires to be first, he shall be last of all and servant of all."
Mark 9:35b

Read Mark Chapter 9

We live in a world that feeds us lies. It tells us that we should be looking out for number one, ourselves. We are constantly bombarded with advertisements telling us how important it is to be all and everything we can be. We are told that we should have servants and that being humble is having poor self-esteem. Oh, how we wage war with our flesh and the world that we live in. In God's economy, the way up is down; down on our knees, esteeming others higher than ourselves.

We love the words of Jesus; they are sharp and cut to the heart. Those desiring to be first need to go to the back of the line. Jesus could say these words with authority; after all, He is God and He became a servant for us. *"But He made himself of no reputation, taking the form of a bondservant, and coming in the likeness of men. And being found in appearance as a man, He humbled Himself and became obedient to the point of death, even the death of the cross." (Phil. 2:7,8)*

Prayer: Lord, keep our hearts humble, esteeming others higher than ourselves.

God Hates Divorce

"Therefore what God has joined together, let not man separate."
Mark 10:9

Read Mark Chapter 10

God designed marriage from the beginning. His intent is that a couple should stay together for a lifetime. We live in times where the word "divorce" is used casually. Marriage is about as important as buying a car or a house. When people get tired of their mates, they just trade them in for a new one. However, the results are devastating when families are torn asunder, and lives are destroyed and ripped apart because of calloused hearts.

What hurts most is when you see a couple divorce who once trusted the Lord for their lives and marriage. It's a poor testimony for the Lord and they soon become another statistic. We need to take the words of our Lord seriously, and ask Him to give us integrity and commitment in our marriages and for our mates. We have talked with people who have taken the road of divorce, only to regret it down the road when it is too late. God only gives one allowance for divorce and that is adultery. Even then, if the couple trusts the Lord, they can make the marriage work with the Lord's help. *"For the Lord God of Israel says that He hates divorce,"* (Mal. 2:16a)

Prayer: For all those who are considering divorce, Lord, help them to choose You.

_____

_____

_____

_____

_____

_____

_____

_____

Forgive And Be Free

"And whenever you stand praying, if you have anything against anyone, forgive him, that your Father in heaven may also forgive you your trespasses."
Mark 11:25

Read Mark Chapter 11

$\mathcal{E}$ver wonder why prayer is sometimes not answered? We can hinder our prayer life by having unforgiveness and malice in our hearts towards others. Jesus challenges us to examine our hearts before we enter into the privilege of intimate prayer with God. *"If I regard iniquity in my heart, the Lord will not hear." (Ps. 66:18)* When we see the sin in our own life and the amazing forgiveness available to us through Jesus Christ, it makes all the sense in the world to clear out any clutter in our hearts that would keep us from intimate fellowship with God.

We have found that whenever we have struggled with unforgiveness, it has hindered the type of communion with God that we usually enjoy. It can be painful to allow the Holy Spirit to shine His magnifying glass on our hearts, but it is fruitful when we do. Besides, when we choose to forgive, we are free from the bondage that sin has on our lives.

Prayer: Father, thank You for forgiveness.

All Is Everything

"So He called the disciples to Himself and said to them, 'Assuredly, I say to you that this poor widow has put in more than all those who have given to the treasury; for they all put in out of their abundance, but she out of her poverty put in all that she had, her whole livelihood.'"

Mark 12:43,44

Read Mark Chapter 12

Most of us are familiar with this story, the widow and her two mites. The widow obviously did not hold tightly to the material possessions she had and offered willingly out of her own poverty. Jesus gives us insight into how God looks at things. It really doesn't impress God how much we give; it's in the attitude that we give it. The rich folks gave to the treasury out of their abundance, so it really did not hurt them to give. The widow gave out of her poverty, all that she had. Both aspects of giving are important, because no matter where we fall in our economic status, we should give our firstfruits to the Lord.

Our giving should be sacrificial and with a right heart, knowing that as we honor the Lord with all we have, He will take care of us. It is often easier to give when we have little, and the more we have, the more we are challenged with our giving. We start to adopt a mentality that our wealth is ours, and that only a portion belongs to God. The widow impressed God; she believed that all she had belonged to Him, then gave everything.

Prayer: Father, help us to have the widow's heart.

_____

_____

_____

_____

_____

_____

_____

_____

_____

_____

Watch And Pray

*"Simon, are you sleeping? Could you not watch one hour? Watch and pray,
lest you enter into temptation. The spirit indeed is willing, but the flesh is weak."
Mark 14:37b,38*

Read Mark Chapters 13 & 14

The night before His death, Jesus asks the disciples to stay awake with Him and pray. We are sure they all had every intention to do just that. We often wonder what the nights were like for the disciples after His death. We know that we would have had a lot of regrets. "We should have seized every opportunity to stay awake with our Savior." Oh the regret and remorse they must have felt, especially Peter. Peter was the disciple that seemed to be wreckless and impulsive. He was always taking matters into his own hands.

Peter's faults are highlighted in the Scriptures. His weaknesses are easy to detect, unlike most of us who can hide our faults. Peter understood the blessing in forgiveness. He knew too well the pain and the desperation one feels when convicted by sin. *"'Before the rooster crows twice, you will deny Me three times.' And when he thought about it, he wept." (Mark 14:72b)* Perhaps this is why Peter had special mention after the Lord had risen from the dead. *"But go, tell His disciples—and Peter—that He is going before you into Galilee;" (Mark 16:7)* There is no doubt that Peter spent the rest of his life watching and praying.

Prayer: Father, thank You that in our weakness, You are made strong.

_____

_____

_____

_____

_____

_____

_____

_____

_____

Light In The Midst Of Darkness

*"'Eloi, Eloi, lama sabachthani?' which is translated,
'My God, My God, why have You forsaken Me?'"*
Mark 15:34b

Read Mark Chapter 15

It was a dark afternoon; it had to be, because the Son of God was bearing the punishment for our sins. Jesus had to be separated from His Father during that time He was taking the fall for us. The pain was great and the darkness greater. Imagine what it must have been like for Him. He was the God of all creation, and now all the sin of mankind was placed on Him. God, for that time, had to look away while Jesus was "wounded for our transgressions, and bruised for our iniquities." Why did He do this? Why would He, even for one moment, be separated from His perfect Father? We always ask this question when we receive His grace.

We are reminded through His forgiveness and through Scripture that Jesus could do this only because He saw us free from sin. He saw you free from sin. This was why He did it. On that dark afternoon, He saw a light that no one else could see. He saw freedom. *"He humbled Himself and became obedient to the point of death, even the death of the cross." (Phil. 2:8)* Yes, Jesus loves me, the Bible tells me so.

Prayer: Lord, for what it's worth, we want to thank You again for seeing us when You endured the pain of the cross.

The Great Commission

*"And He said to them,
'Go into all the world and preach the gospel to every creature.'"
Mark 16:15*

Read Mark Chapter 16

Webster's Dictionary describes the word "commission" as, committing something that has been entrusted to be done, or a group of people who have been authorized to deal with specific matters. That is exactly what the great commission is. Jesus commands His disciples to go into all the world with the gospel message of Jesus Christ. Who are His disciples? Anyone who believes in Him. We need to take these words to heart. The word "commission" is where we get the word "mission."

Last night I received a call from a Vietnamese woman; her name is Tracy and she on occasion has given me a manicure. In fact, I find myself going to her shop more to visit her than having my nails done. For some reason we are both drawn to one another. There is a chemistry of friendship that is being built. She seems to open her heart to me and even confess faults. I will see her today because she wants to give me "spring rolls." I am amazed that she even called; I hope that today I am able to share Jesus in a clear and meaningful way. So often, we think we have to go to another country to share Christ, when He provides opportunities in our own little world. So maybe on a personal level, we should go into our "own little world" and share Jesus.

Prayer: Lord, please help me to be obedient to share Jesus with Tracy today.

Take Notes

"In as much as many have taken in hand to set in order a narrative of those things which have been fulfilled among us, just as those who from the beginning were eyewitnesses and ministers of the word delivered them to us, it seemed good to me also, having had perfect understanding of all things from the very first, to write to you an orderly account, most excellent Theophilus, that you may know the certainty of those things in which you were instructed."
Luke 1:1-3

Read Luke Chapter 1:1-38

Luke was a doctor, and no doubt he had excellent training. Like most people who work in the medical profession, they learn early to document everything in the order that things happen. Luke is writing to Theophilus to document, in order of events, the work that Christ did while here on earth and to assure him that He is still living and powerful today.

He reminds Theophilus, a new believer in Christ, that there is certainty in those things that he first learned and believed. Luke takes the time to refresh and encourage a new believer in Christ. We too should remember to exhort those who are learning about their faith, taking the time to invest in them the things of the kingdom. As we travel through Luke's gospel, let's emulate his habit of taking notes. You will be surprised at how God will help you to recount the things you learn.

Prayer: Father, thank You for the way You use different people and personalities to inspire and exhort others.

_____

_____

_____

_____

_____

_____

_____

_____

_____

Her Son, Her Savior

"My soul magnifies the Lord, and my spirit has rejoiced in God my Savior."
Luke 1:46,47

Read Luke Chapter 1:39-80

"Mary Had a Little Lamb" is a nursery rhyme we used to sing. Have you ever thought about the "little lamb" that Mary, the mother of Jesus, had? We tend to forget that Mary had this little Son, who would one day be her Savior. She raised Him as we moms do; she loved and nurtured Him with a mother's love. Mary was called to do some incredible things as a young woman, but the most incredible was to be present at the cross. *"Now there stood by the cross of Jesus His mother," (John 19:25a)*

> *Mary had a little lamb, her Son, her Savior He would be;*
> *Mary's little lamb would wash her sins away,*
> *And everywhere that Mary went, Jesus came to be*
> *Everything that Mary needed to be forgiven and set free*
>
> *Now Mary's little lamb is our Savior and our Lord;*
> *And everywhere that we go, Jesus is to be,*
> *All we ever need to be set free*
> *Forgiven from a life of darkness, new life He gives*
> *To everyone who believes that Jesus is their Lord.*
>
> *TLR*

Prayer: Father, thank You for sending Jesus as a sacrifice for our sins.

No Room In The Inn

"And she brought forth her firstborn Son, and wrapped Him in swaddling cloths, and laid Him in a manger, because there was no room for them in the inn."
Luke 2:7

Read Luke Chapter 2:1-14

There was no room in the public inn for Mary to deliver her Son Jesus, so He was born in a stable, which more than likely was a shelter for animals. The lowly birth of our Lord is just another example of the humility He willingly endured, even at birth. Today, what we find to be so heartbreaking is that in the hearts of people, there still isn't room for Jesus.

Folks find room in their lives for everything, but Jesus. They are caught up in their own lives and careers, and try to build financial empires. Even sadder yet, is to see the apathy in the church today. As believers in Jesus Christ, we too need to guard our hearts from becoming crowded with the things of this life. We need to open our hearts, making ample room for Jesus, trusting Him to abundantly meet any need we might have.

Prayer: Father, help us to give You first place on the throne of our hearts.

_____

_____

_____

_____

_____

_____

_____

_____

_____

_____

Matters Of The Heart

"But Mary kept all these things and pondered them in her heart."
Luke 2:19

Read Luke Chapter 2:15-52

The word "ponder" means to weigh heavily, to attentively meditate on a matter. The young Mary had a lot to think about. You wonder how such a young girl, called to such a great task, could endure the pressure and excitement that permeated her world. Yet she could be confident in this one thing, that she was called by God to carry out the specific task of being an earthly mother to the Son of God.

We would imagine that Mary, like all of us who dwell in this flesh, had moments where she did not quite understand what was happening in her life. Perhaps she even thought that she was imagining all the events that led up to the birth of her Son. But even so, God no doubt met her where no one else could. *"I sought the Lord, and He heard me, and delivered me from all my fears." (Ps. 34:4)* He reminded Mary that all was in His mighty hand. What things might you be pondering in your heart today? Offer them up to the Lord and commit them to Him, trusting that He has everything in control.

Prayer: Father, in the midst of all of life's demands, help us to take time to ponder Your ways and Your truths.

Prepare The Way Of The Lord

*"The voice of one crying in the wilderness:
'Prepare the way of the Lord; make His paths straight.'"*
Luke 3:4

Read Luke Chapter 3:1-20

Luke's gospel moves right from the birth of Christ to the beginning stages of His public ministry. We find John the Baptist preparing the way for Jesus and His public ministry. John describes himself to be like the Crier in the Old Testament. The job of a Crier was to go before the king and declare to the people that the king was coming. They were to clear away any obstacles on the roads, making a clear and straight path so there would be no hindrances to his coming. Isaiah refers to this very thing in the Old Testament. *"The voice of one crying in the wilderness: 'Prepare the way of the Lord.'" (Is. 40:3)* How profound these words were.

Are there obstacles in your life that might be hindering the King from having a clear passage to your heart? Clear away! Make His paths straight, and make room for Him. He has already offered you the free gift of salvation; now is the time. He is here to avail Himself to you as your personal Savior and King.

Prayer: Father, there are many things that clutter the road to our hearts, help us to prepare the way for You.

_____
_____
_____
_____
_____
_____
_____
_____

Jesus, The Example

"When all the people were baptized, it came to pass that Jesus also was baptized; and while He prayed, the heaven was opened. And the Holy Spirit descended in bodily form like a dove upon Him, and a voice came from heaven which said, You are My beloved Son; in You I am well pleased.'"
Luke 3:21,22

Read Luke Chapter 3:21-38

No wonder it pleased the Father to see His Son Jesus as the example. This confirmation from heaven and the voice of God's approval anoints Jesus as He begins His public ministry. This kind of applause from heaven is so characteristic of the Father cheering on His Son. "Good job" is what God was saying. God saw the example and knew what challenges faced our Lord. Like the father who cheers for his son in Little League, God was there with Jesus, shouting, "I am with You and I am pleased." The only difference is that God knew the outcome. He knew that His Son Jesus would endure much suffering for a people who would hardly notice nor understand His sacrifice.

We all face challenges and even some severe suffering. But are you aware that the God of heaven is cheering you on? The finish line is not that far off especially when we know that God is applauding and helping us to finish. This, of course, would never be possible without the example that Jesus gave by dying for us.

Prayer: Thank You Lord, for Your example.

It Is Written

"It is written, 'Man shall not live by bread alone, but by every word of God.'"
Luke 4:4

Read Luke Chapter 4:1-15

*I*n an effort to tempt Jesus, Satan strikes out! The powerful response from Jesus was, "It is written." Jesus used the power that is in God's Word to strike back at Satan. And of course, we know that it worked. But do we really understand the importance that lies in being equipped with God's Word? Too often we falter because we don't know His Word. We simply cannot stand on what we do not know. But, we can stand on what we do know, and we should all know this: *"For the word of God is living and powerful, and sharper than any two-edged sword, piercing even to the division of soul and spirit, and of joints and marrow, and is a discerner of the thoughts and intents of the heart."* (Heb. 4:12)

We never have to defend God's Word; we can be confident in it. We love the quick response of Jesus, "It is written." Are you allowing God to write His Word upon your heart? Are you equipped when asked about it? Can you stand on its promises in the face of Satan's attacks? Is it hidden in your heart? Does it keep you from sin? *"Your word I have hidden in my heart, that I might not sin against You." (Ps. 119:11)* If not, start today to purpose in your heart to find time to meditate and devote yourself to it.

Prayer: Father, thank You for the gift of Your Word.

_____

_____

_____

_____

_____

_____

_____

Jesus, Lord Of Jubilee

"The Spirit of the Lord is upon Me, because He has anointed Me
to preach the gospel to the poor; He has sent Me to heal the brokenhearted,
to proclaim liberty to the captives and recovery of sight to the blind, to set at
liberty those who are oppressed; to proclaim the acceptable year of the Lord."
Luke 4:18,19

Read Luke Chapter 4:16-44

*J*esus' ministry is now out in the open. He proclaims that He is Lord! He quotes Isaiah 61 to reveal that He is indeed anointed by God. ***"The Spirit of the Lord God is upon Me, because the Lord has anointed Me." (Is. 61:1)***

Like the year of Jubilee, Jesus provides a fresh new start for those who are poor, brokenhearted, blind, and oppressed. Jesus offers new hope, as it is evident that man cannot live under the bondage of the law. The world needs a Savior, and Jesus, the Son of God, was anointed for the task. The Jubilee that Jesus brings to our lives is freedom, freedom from the sting of sin. What might you be up against today? Are you feeling the need for a fresh, new start? Yield your heart to the Lord of Jubilee.

Prayer: God, thank You for the freedom we have in Jesus.

Be Not Wise In Your Own Eyes

*"But when Jesus perceived their thoughts, He answered and said to them,
Why are you reasoning in your hearts?"'*
Luke 5:22

Read Luke Chapter 5:1-26

Scripture tells us that the Word of God discerns the thoughts and intents of man's heart. *(Heb. 4:12)* We know that Jesus was and is the Word. The recent forgiveness that Jesus extended to the paralytic caused the scribes and Pharisees to predictably do what they were famous for, reason with their minds. Before they could even speak their minds, Jesus revealed that He knew their thoughts.

We could learn a lesson from the mistakes of the scribes and Pharisees. Our limited human understanding can often cloud the things that are revealed to our spirits. Because the Lord knows all our thoughts and intentions, we need to be open to His Word and His truth, leaving room for correction in our lives. The truth is, we can be wrong. Whenever we think we are right about something, we should go to the Scriptures and check it out. At times, this can be painful because of what is revealed. We are admonished by Scriptures like…*"Do not be wise in your own eyes; fear the Lord and depart from evil." (Prov. 3:7)* There is a peace in knowing that God will keep us in check as we yield our hearts and minds to Him.

Prayer: Father, in a world that often fails to understand You, please help us to seek Your wisdom.

Do You Need A Doctor?

"Jesus answered and said to them, 'Those who are well have no need of a physician, but those who are sick. I have not come to call the righteous, but sinners, to repentance.'"
Luke 5:31,32

Read Luke Chapter 5:27-32

In our society, there are all kinds of diseases to be concerned about; heart disease and cancer are the leading causes of death. People are very concerned about their health and will go to great lengths to extend their lives. I too suffer with a physical infirmity; it's called thyroid disease. For the rest of my human life I will be taking medication to aid me in living a healthy and productive life. It took a while for my disease to be diagnosed, but a good physician was able to determine what was wrong.

The disease of sin has also been diagnosed, and statistics show that one out of every person, suffers from this disease. If the disease goes untreated, there is a 100% certainty that it will affect where one spends eternity. Thankfully, there is a prescription for the disease of sin, and it is Jesus Christ. He laid down His life so that we would have the treatment we needed for the deadly disease of sin. We just need to respond by repenting and receiving Christ as our Savior and Physician. The incredible thing is, He even makes house calls!

Prayer: We will be forever grateful for Your "treatment" for the disease of sin.

_____
_____
_____
_____
_____
_____
_____
_____
_____

Jesus, A Practical Example

"And He said to them, 'Can you make the friends of the bridegroom fast while the bridegroom is with them? But the days will come when the bridegroom will be taken away from them; then they will fast in those days.'"

Luke 5:34,35

Read Luke Chapter 5:33-39

After being questioned regarding why He and His disciples did not seem to take fasting as seriously as the scribes and Pharisees, and even John and his disciples, Jesus responds by saying that His time here on earth was much like that of a wedding celebration. Jewish weddings were a time to celebrate by eating and being merry. There is a time and a place for fasting and it has its purpose. The indication is that Jesus, knowing His time with the disciples would be short, used it much like the time that the groomsmen spent with the bridegroom before a marriage.

The words of Jesus are so real and practical. We should use the occasions that God gives us to celebrate with Him. The fact that Jesus sat and ate and fellowshipped with the disciples is so awesome! It shows God's desire to have a loving, intimate relationship with His people.

Prayer: Thank You for being a practical example.

_____

_____

_____

_____

_____

_____

_____

_____

_____

_____

_____

The Lord Of The Sabbath

"And He said to them, 'The Son of Man is also Lord of the Sabbath.'"
Luke 6:5

Read Luke Chapter 6:1-23

*J*esus once again gets questioned about His etiquette concerning the law and the Sabbath. In a wise response to the scribes and Pharisees, Jesus quotes Scripture from the Old Testament. He recalls the time when David ate the showbread from the house of God and even gave some to the men who were with him. God did not punish David for this act. *(1 Sam. 21:1-7)* You get the feeling from the words of Jesus that the law was never intended to bring people under bondage. The scribes and Pharisees seemed to have a desire to find fault with Jesus.

We need to be careful not to get what we call "the virus of the Pharisees." It's a sickness that not only affects the carrier but hurts others too. It starts with a little self-righteousness and then it turns into a critical spirit, and finally you are no longer able to detect the love of God. Using God's Word to bring others into bondage is not its intended purpose. The Word of God should free us from the bondage of sin. We can learn a lesson from the words of Jesus. Love the Lord of the Sabbath and not the law of the Sabbath.

Prayer: Father, help us to represent Your heart when representing Your Word.

Love Your Enemies

"But I say to you who hear: Love your enemies, do good to those who hate you,"
Luke 6:27

Read Luke Chapter 6:24-49

The body of Christ has been under persecution from day one of Christ's public ministry. The words of Jesus remind the church that the persecution they suffer is because of their faith in Him. God calls us to live above the circumstances of persecution, and be obedient to His call to extraordinary love. It is not possible to have this kind of love apart from God. It's hard to continually be the one turning your cheek, but this is the sacrificial cost of living a life that pleases God.

King David suffered affliction from his enemies, and yet we see how he chose to allow the Lord to be His strength in the midst of suffering. *"You prepare a table before me in the presence of my enemies."* *(Ps. 23:5)* If we will be obedient to God's call to love, even when wronged, God will step in and give us His supernatural peace. *"When a man's ways please the Lord, He makes even his enemies to be at peace with him." (Prov. 16:7)*

What are some of the enemies that you face today? Will you pause for a moment and remember that you are a child of God. There is nothing in our lives that God does not see or have His hand upon. Yes, even the enemies we face.

Prayer: Help us to have the kind of faith we need, to trust You with the giants that come against us.

_____

_____

_____

_____

_____

_____

_____

All For Jesus

"There was a certain creditor who had two debtors. One owed five hundred denarii, and the other fifty. And when they had nothing with which to repay, he freely forgave them both. Tell Me, therefore, which of them will love him more?"
Luke 7:41,42

Read Luke Chapter 7

*J*esus reveals His heart for sinners in these passages. He reminds us that we are all sinners, and the one who has been forgiven much has a deeper respect for the beautiful gift of grace. We can take a lesson from these words of Jesus. Too often we think we are more righteous than another, perhaps because we haven't fallen as far as them, or we haven't sinned as much. The truth is, sin is sin, and all sinners need a Savior. The woman in this story knew her wrongs, and knew what she had been forgiven. She was willing to lay down her life and give the very best she had to her Savior. It makes us stop and think, "Are we giving our all for Jesus?"

We all need to be careful not to become like the scribes and Pharisees who had an outward appearance of being good, yet inwardly were *"full of dead men's bones and all uncleanness." (Matt. 23:27)* It's what is in the heart that really matters. To keep us humble, we need to remember the grace we have received in our own lives. Where would we be without the grace God has extended to us? *"For by grace you have been saved through faith, and that not of yourselves; it is the gift of God, not of works, lest anyone should boast." (Eph. 2:8,9)*

Prayer: Father, help us to remember how much we have been forgiven.

_____
_____
_____
_____
_____
_____
_____

By The Wayside

"Those by the wayside are the ones who hear; then the devil comes and takes away the word out of their hearts, lest they should believe and be saved."
Luke 8:12

Read Luke Chapter 8:1-15

When I was converted to Christianity back in 1976, it was the desire of my heart to see all my family and friends saved. I would boldly witness to anyone who would listen. I was certain that my new found faith in Christ was the answer to the hopelessness that permeated my little world. Time after time, I would take friends and family members to outreaches where I knew they would hear a clear gospel message. Many responded to the invitation to receive Christ, but that's as far as it went.

They heard the Word, but the enemy was quick to steal away the seed that was planted in their hearts. This was such a frustration to me. How could they receive Christ and do nothing with it? Then I remembered back to the time in my early teens, when someone witnessed to me and asked me if I wanted to receive Christ. I responded by saying "yes." Not much happened after that. My true conversion came later. I don't know why some fall by the wayside while others are firmly planted in the faith. I do know this however--that we should never lose hope. Keep praying and believing that He can bring someone back, if only they choose to believe.

Prayer: Father, thank You for salvation and the conversion of souls.

_____
_____
_____
_____
_____
_____
_____
_____
_____

Light Reveals Truth

"For nothing is secret that will not be revealed,
nor anything hidden that will not be known and come to light."
Luke 8:17

Read Luke Chapter 8:16-56

My sister and I were talking this week about a "magnifying mirror" that she purchased. It is called a Magnum Mirror. The purpose of the mirror is to expose those things that one cannot see in a smaller mirror. She said she was shocked to see things on her face that she could not believe were there. The Magnum Mirror reveals every little wrinkle, blotch, and blemish and brings to light the stark reality that one is aging.

God's Word is much like the Magnum Mirror--the closer one gets to it, the more in touch they are with the truth. The writer of Hebrews shares with us how God's Word exposes truth and brings to light all things that are hidden. *"And there is no creature hidden from His sight, but all things are naked and open to the eyes of Him to whom we must give an account." (Heb. 4:13)* I am both convicted and convinced by this truth. Convicted, because it reveals that my sin cannot be covered up, and when I err, I need to repent. Convinced, because it confirms that nothing surprises God. It also encourages me because God loves me, even though my nature is to sin. I am also admonished to allow the magnifying mirror of the Holy Spirit to expose anything in my life that might separate me from the truth.

Prayer: Father, thank You for Your Word and what it reveals to me.

The Cost Of The Cross

"Then He said to them all, 'If anyone desires to come after Me,
let him deny himself, and take up his cross daily, and follow Me.'"
Luke 9:23

Read Luke Chapter 9:1-36

Salvation is a free gift from God and no one can earn it; however, following Jesus has a cost. We tend to cheapen the work Jesus did on the cross when we talk only about the grace of God. Grace is a beautiful thing, and we are glad that God has extended it to us. We know we don't deserve it. When we ponder verses such as this one, we have to be realistic. There is a cost to following Jesus. The cost is described by Jesus in His own words, **"Let him deny himself and take up his cross, and follow Me." (Matt. 16:24)**

Jesus warns that there is suffering involved in serving Him and death to self. We know that most of the apostles were martyred for their faith. The early church suffered great persecution and horrible deaths for their commitment to Jesus. Even today, many are dying for their Christian faith. We need to take off our rose-colored glasses and realize the cost of following Jesus. For some of us, it might be a light affliction, like being misunderstood by family or friends. Or perhaps, it might be dying to oneself and sacrificing things that appeal to the flesh. We truly believe that Jesus meets us and gives us supernatural strength when we are willing to deny ourselves daily for Him. What might there be in your life today that Jesus may be asking you to deny? Trust Him and follow Him. You won't be sorry.

Prayer: Father, thank You for sacrificing Jesus for our sins.

If You Want To Be Great

*"Whoever receives this little child in My name receives Me; and whoever receives
Me receives Him who sent Me. For he who is least among you all will be great."*
Luke 9:48

Read Luke Chapter 9:37-62

These are powerful words from Jesus, particularly in a society that
focuses so much on being great and being first. Even the disciples struggled
with the fleshly desire to be noticed. If we were all honest, we too would
admit that the idea of being great is appealing.

We love the words of Jesus, because there is an invitation for all to
come and be great in His kingdom. It starts by realizing that *"apart
from Him we can do nothing." (John 15:5b)* When we first got
saved, we used to sing a song, "If you want to be great in God's kingdom,
learn to be the servant of all." This is what Jesus meant when He spoke
about greatness in His kingdom; it means laying down one's own fleshy
desire for recognition and to instead serve others, lifting them up. We see
that true greatness can be achieved; it just depends on whose eyes you
want to be great in.

Prayer: Father, thank You for sending Your great Son Jesus to die for
us. Help us to die for Him.

A Harvest Field At Starbucks?

"Then He said to them, 'The harvest truly is great, but the laborers are few; therefore pray the Lord of the harvest to send out laborers into His harvest.'"
Luke 10:2

Read Luke Chapter 10:1-20

Just yesterday, my friend Denise and I had an incredible and unexpected opportunity to share Jesus with a young man at Starbucks. As we sat down to enjoy a frappuccino, there were two young men sitting next to us, attempting to sell us a membership at a fitness center. We had to decline because we were already members, but the conversation kept going, and we took the opportunity to slip some thoughts in about the Lord. The one young man said, "I am a believer, but he is not," pointing to his co-worker. To our surprise, the UNbelieving young man wanted to explain to us what he did believe. He said, "I believe in energy and keeping one's body in shape." After listening to him share his vision about life, we began to share with him the simple gospel message of Jesus Christ. He explained to us that he had never heard the gospel shared with him that way and would have to "really think" about what he had learned.

We saw the excitement in his Christian co-worker, and we too were filled with joy. We know that we were there to water seeds that had already been planted. "Yes," there is a harvest field, even at Starbucks. We as ambassadors for Christ, need to remember that we carry light, hope, and salvation to a dying world. Pray that God would make you aware when you are out in the marketplace, that there are souls that need to hear the Good News.

Prayer: Thank You for the opportunity to work in the harvest field. Help me not to miss them.

_____
_____
_____
_____
_____
_____

Martha, Martha

"And Jesus answered and said to her, 'Martha, Martha, you are worried and troubled about many things. But one thing is needed, and Mary has chosen that good part, which will not be taken away from her.'"

Luke 10:41,42

Read Luke Chapter 10:21-42

Martha was clearly caught up in the work of serving others. She finds herself agitated at her sister Mary who appears to be relaxing at the feet of Jesus, while she was burdened with single-handedly carrying the weight of serving. Most women I know, do have what is known as the "Martha Syndrome." We have a lot to do and things must get done. Jesus' response to Martha was not a harsh rebuke, but more of an admonishment to step back from the cares of this life and spend time with Him.

The work will get done is what Jesus was saying, and it will always be there, more work and more serving. Jesus highlights the importance of choosing Him first, making Him a priority, and trusting that all will fall into place after we have spent quality time with Him. Can you imagine what would have happened if Martha would have just stopped what she was doing and sat at the feet of Jesus? No doubt she would have been blessed and when others needed to eat, they just might have stepped up to help. I am a Martha by nature. I love to serve others and keep busy. I have learned over the years, if I put Jesus first, my time increases and miraculously it all gets done!

Prayer: Father, help me to be still before You.

_____

_____

_____

_____

_____

_____

_____

_____

What Is Your Spiritual Temperature?

"He who is not with Me is against me,
and he who does not gather with Me scatters."
Luke 11:23

Read Luke Chapter 11:1-23

*T*hese are powerful words! Jesus makes a clear statement about one's commitment to Him. We are either for Him or against Him; there is no in-between. When we waver, this should raise a red flag within our hearts, and cause us to do a heart check on where we are with Jesus. Think about it for a moment. Would you want someone to be on your team who is neutral in their commitment? When someone is undecided, they compromise their beliefs.

Jesus said it best, *"So then, because you are lukewarm, and neither cold nor hot, I will vomit you out of My mouth." (Rev. 3:16)* Being lukewarm brings no value to the kingdom of God. In fact, it scatters and distorts God's purposes as Jesus stated in our verse today. When you look at it through the eyes of Jesus, you get a better understanding. He is, after all, the bridegroom and we are the bride. Any bridegroom, or bride for that matter, wants to know that they have the full affection of their beloved. If your heart has grown cold towards the things of God, repent and ask God to fill you with a fire and a passion for Him, and draw close to Him. This will get your spiritual temperature to where it needs to be.

Prayer: Father, help our spiritual temperature to be hot, not luke-warm.

Spiritual Eyeglasses

"The lamp of the body is the eye. Therefore, when your eye is good, your whole body also is full of light. But when your eye is bad, your body also is full of darkness."
Luke 11:34

Read Luke Chapter 11:24-36

When we were young believers, we would always hear people say, "garbage in, garbage out." The gist of that saying goes along with the words of Jesus. We need to be careful about what we allow our eyes to see. We wage a war with our flesh and our spirit, and this is why we need to guard our minds from evil. *"Watch and pray, lest you enter into temptation. The spirit indeed is willing, but the flesh is weak."* *(Matt. 26:41)*

The advertisement industry spends millions of dollars each year to persuade us that we are not good enough without their products. They use only the best and most beautiful models to sell their ideas. They try to lure us with visual images, and if we are not careful, we will succumb, desiring their product. So we have to keep a balance, and our balance is found in God's Word. *"Turn away my eyes from looking at worthless things, and revive me in Your way." (Ps. 119:37)* Jesus is not saying that we can't have anything that appeals to our eyes, but rather if there is evil involved, we need to do a heart and mind check. We need to carry spiritual eyeglasses, and that is the Word of God.

Prayer: Father, help us to keep our eyes from evil.

From Prison To Praise

*"Woe to you lawyers! For you have taken away the key of knowledge.
You did not enter in yourselves, and those who were entering in you hindered."*
Luke 11:52

Read Luke Chapter 11:37-54

Jesus gives a sharp rebuke to the lawyers; they had put such a yoke of bondage on the people and prevented them from drawing near to God. They had the keys to enter in, but did not use them; instead, they locked men's souls up. Rather than letting the words of Jesus penetrate their hearts, they sought to catch Him in something that they might accuse Him of.

The truth hurts and it can be painful. There are two roads we can travel down when we are confronted by the truth of God. We can resist like the lawyers did, or we can relinquish our rights to be right, and humble ourselves and repent. Choosing the narrow road may seem hard, but it is always right. Is your soul imprisoned by the bondage of lies? Jesus is our public defender and has given us the keys to freedom. *"Bring my soul out of prison, that I might praise Your name;" (Ps. 142:7a)* If only the lawyers would have used their knowledge to seek truth, then they would have been praising Him too.

Prayer: Father, thank You for the freedom we have in Your Son, Jesus.

_____
_____
_____
_____
_____
_____
_____
_____
_____
_____

Confession & Conviction

"Also I say to you, whoever confesses Me before men,
him the Son of Man also will confess before the angels of God."
Luke 12:8

Read Luke Chapter 12:1-34

Have you ever had to defend someone who had been accused of a crime they did not commit? It's amazing how convincing the prosecutors can be; their aim is to evoke a guilty verdict. In the world's courtroom, Jesus is the innocent party, and we are and will be called to defend and give testimony for Him. People will make their judgments about Him based on the facts that we present. This should motivate us to be well-prepared to rightly represent Him before men. We should stand on the Words of Jesus and be proud to testify for Him.

The world may ridicule us and wreck havoc around us, but heaven rejoices at our testimony in Jesus. What a joy it is to know that Jesus will give testimony of our faithfulness to Him. *"But let all those rejoice who put their trust in You; let them ever shout for joy, because You defend them; let those also who love Your name be joyful in You." (Ps. 5:11)*

Prayer: Help us to stand strong in our convictions for You.

_____
_____
_____
_____
_____
_____
_____
_____
_____
_____
_____

Is There Evidence Of Your Faith In Christ?

"But he who denies Me before men will be denied before the angels of God."
Luke 12:9

Read Luke Chapter 12:35-59

This is an alarming statement that requires self-examination. Do we deny Jesus? This is what we will be asked when we stand before the Lord. For most believers, the reaction to this would be, "Of course we don't deny Jesus." But do we? Do we deny Him in our personal witness? Do we deny Him when we hide our faith so as not to ruffle feathers? Ouch, these words hurt!

The gist of this statement is that we are to be bold in our convictions about Jesus. When we were young believers, there was a bumper sticker that said something like this, "If you were on trial for your faith, would there be enough evidence in your life to convict you?" Ouch, that hurts even more! The wonderful thing about our Lord is that He gives us His Word to exhort us to action. These words of Jesus should motivate us to start gathering facts about our faith and allow them to sink deep into our hearts, so that we will naturally confess Him in all that we do. Remember, we can't stand on what we don't know.

Prayer: Father, help us to be bold in our faith and in our confession of You.

The Narrow Gate

"Strive to enter through the narrow gate, for many, I say to you,
will seek to enter and will not be able."
Luke 13:24

Read Luke Chapter 13:1-30

There is a misconception among people today; many say they are confident they will go to heaven simply because they are "good people." There is only one way to heaven, and that is through Jesus Christ, God's Son. *"I am the way, the truth, and the life. No one comes to the Father except through Me." (John 14:6)* The gift of salvation is a free gift, so why do so many reject it? Maybe because they think they have everything under control and that their problems are manageable.

Entering in by the narrow gate requires losing your life to Jesus. It means that you have chosen to go His way, because you know there is no other way. Unbelievers have taken the broad road, which eventually leads to eternal destruction. If people could be sinless on their own, they would not need a Savior. Without Him, there is no road that will lead you to heaven.

Prayer: Father, for those who are lost, and traveling on the broad road, help them to see and choose the narrow one.

_____
_____
_____
_____
_____
_____
_____
_____
_____
_____
_____

Jerusalem, Jerusalem

"O Jerusalem, Jerusalem, the one who kills the prophets and stones those who are sent to her! How often I wanted to gather your children together, as a hen gathers her brood under her wings, but you were not willing!"
Luke 13:34

Read Luke Chapter 13:31-34

Jesus was grieved in His heart over Jerusalem and the rejection of the prophets sent by God. Like a parent who wants to take his children and protect them from the evil of this world, Jesus felt their pain and would have nurtured and guided them, if only they were willing. Like the stubborn ones of Jerusalem, we too can be unyielding on issues, cross our arms, and be unwilling to let Jesus come in and dwell with us the way He desires.

Jerusalem killed the prophets and Jesus, thus rejecting the very God they believed they served. How was that possible? By stubbornness! We need to be careful, for our stubbornness and rebellion kill the spirit. Remember Saul in the Old Testament? He thought he was right and believed he could be his own king. Consequently, his stubbornness cost him his crown. *"For rebellion is as the sin of witchcraft, and stubbornness is as iniquity and idolatry. Because you have rejected the word of the Lord, He also has rejected you from being king." (1 Sam. 15: 23)* Don't be like Jerusalem and Saul, they missed out on the blessings of God because they chose rather to live under the burden of sin.

Prayer: Father, help us to see truth and open our blind eyes.

_____
_____
_____
_____
_____
_____
_____
_____

Notoriety Or Humility

"But when you are invited, go and sit down in the lowest place, so that when he who invited you comes he may say to you, 'Friend, go up higher.'"
Luke 14:10

Read Luke Chapter 14

*J*esus is making a point about humility here. He is saying "don't seek the best, but rather be lifted up." In ancient times, the best seat in the house was the one closest to the host. We live in a self-seeking world that promotes notoriety; it's not what you know, but who you know that counts. In the spiritual world, it's no different. Knowing Jesus is everything! He sees the heart of the matter, and blesses those with a contrite heart.

Not long ago, after the Couple's Retreat, we had the rare opportunity to go on our first cruise. The entire trip was anointed by the Lord. Miraculously, we were able to go for only $172.50 per person!! We were with our friends Corky and Vicky who serve in the marriage ministry; all of us were very exhausted from the time and energy that we put into the recent Retreat. We boarded the ship, and that evening at dinner the four of us received an invitation to dine at the captain's table the following evening. Mike and I really did not think it was a big deal, but Corky and Vicky informed us that they had been on at least seven other cruises and had never been invited to dinner with the captain. Wow!! This was really something; out of 1,300 people on the ship, He allows us to be invited to dinner with the captain. This verse came alive and brought a whole new meaning to letting the Lord lift you up.

Prayer: Father, thank You that we don't have to lift ourselves up.

A Party At Home & In Heaven

"I will arise and go to my father, and will say to him, Father, I have sinned against heaven and before you, and I am no longer worthy to be called your son. Make me like one of your hired servants.'"
Luke 15:18,19

Read Luke Chapter 15:1-24

Falling away from the Loving Father's arms can be detrimental to one's soul. Waking up after the fall can be even more eye opening. The prodigal son who comes to his senses begins to realize that his circumstances were due to the lifestyle he chose for himself. He then realized, after further self-examination, that even his father's servants were in better hands than he. The depth of sorrow that he felt, led him to repentance and humility. Willing to work as a servant for his Father, he picked up his tired and weary soul and went home.

Surprised by his father's response, he finds that not only does his father receive him back as a son, but he throws a party for him. This is what Jesus meant when He said, *"Likewise, I say to you, there is joy in the presence of the angels of God over one sinner who repents." (Luke 15:10)* For those of you who have prodigals in your life, don't lose heart. Keep praying, and in time they will appreciate just how much they had in Christ and in you.

Prayer: Thank You for the gift of being able to come home.

_____
_____
_____
_____
_____
_____
_____
_____
_____

Be Careful of Spiritual Jealousy

"And he said to him, 'Son, you are always with me, and all that I have is yours.'"
Luke 15:31

Read Luke Chapter 15:25-32

Sometimes we don't rejoice with others, we weep at their success. In this case, the brother of the prodigal son is rather perturbed at the hoopla going on over his brother's return. He did not understand the consequences of sin and the joy of repentance and forgiveness. He did not see how low his brother had gone and the depth of darkness he had experienced. He only saw what appeared to be a reward for wrong living.

We remember when our daughter Corrie was in high school. At times, she was challenged by the difficulty of taking the narrow road. One day, she came home and said to us, "You will never know how hard it is to be a Christian in high school." We replied, *"Corrie, you're right; we will never know how hard it is to be a Christian in high school, and you will never know how hard it is to not be a Christian in high school."* If only we had known the Lord during our high school years! Yes, at times it seems like those of us who are walking the narrow road aren't getting the same attention as those who aren't. Thank God we can have a healthy relationship with Him without compromising.

Prayer: Father, thank You for Your staying power, and help us to have a passion for the lost.

Serve One Master

"No servant can serve two masters; for either he will hate the one
and love the other, or else he will be loyal to the one and despise the other.
You cannot serve God and mammon."
Luke 16:13

Read Luke Chapter 16:1-13

I remember a time when I was younger, that I juggled three different jobs at the same time. There was confusion in my life, and I did not know what I really wanted to do. I remember seeking the Lord about it and this very Scripture came to mind. I needed to get my priorities in order and trust God with my circumstances. I soon narrowed my job down to one, and soon after to none. Things fell into place, and I was right where God wanted me.

When we try to serve two masters or three in my case, we can become double-minded. Double-mindedness leads to instability, and instability causes us to waver in our faith in God. I think James said it best, *"For let not that man suppose that he will receive anything from the Lord; he is a double-minded man, unstable in all his ways."* (James 1:7,8) If you are struggling with trying to serve two masters, narrow it down to the One who will bring you true freedom, Jesus.

Prayer: Father, forgive me for the times I wavered in my faith.

_____

_____

_____

_____

_____

_____

_____

_____

_____

_____

God Knows Your Heart

*"And He said to them, You are those who justify yourselves before men,
but God knows your hearts. For what is highly esteemed among men
is an abomination in the sight of God.'"*

Luke 16:15

Read Luke Chapter 16:14-18

Over the years I have heard others (and probably myself too) say, in a defensive tone, "God knows my heart." Yes He does, and that should alarm us. In the case of the Pharisees, they sought to seek approval among men, and this did not impress God. In fact, He called it an abomination.

The idea that God knows my heart can be both comforting and convicting. Lately, it seems like He has been impressing upon my heart, the desire to do things for Him that no one else can see or will ever know about. This is kind of exciting, because He truly does reward those things that are done for Him in secret. I must confess though that the flesh can be weak; there is the temptation to want recognition and perhaps even some appreciation. Ouch! Being honest can be painful. Truly there is greater joy in serving our Lord out of a genuine love for Him, rather than the praise of man. Knowing that God knows my heart, and that He sees, hears, and knows everything concerning me, helps me to keep His heavenly perspective. *"But you, when you pray, go into your room, and when you have shut the door, pray to your Father who is in the secret place; and your Father who sees in secret will reward you openly." (Matt. 6:6)*

Prayer: Father, thank You for knowing my heart and loving me anyway.

_____

_____

_____

_____

_____

_____

_____

Without Christ

*"But Abraham said, 'Son, remember that in your lifetime you received your good things,
and likewise Lazarus evil things; but now he is comforted and you are tormented."*
Luke 16:25

Read Luke Chapter 16:19-31

Jesus' teaching on the young man Lazarus, brings to light the reality of living a life apart from His salvation. He presents a clear picture of the consequences of living a life for one's own self. He speaks of Hades, that place of eternal separation from God. It's evident that upon death there is no chance to go back and make right what we have wronged. This should admonish us in two areas. First, we need be sure that we are walking with God. Second, we need ask God to give us a passion for souls.

We are having difficulty seeing beyond this verse right now. We shudder to think of the many we know, who stand to live in eternal torment if they don't respond to salvation through Jesus Christ. On the other hand, we are truly humbled by the grace we have been given through Jesus Christ.

Prayer: Lord, tears flow and our hearts seek You for a greater passion and compassion for souls.

_____
_____
_____
_____
_____
_____
_____
_____
_____
_____
_____

No Excuse

"Then he said, 'I beg you therefore, father, that you would send him to my father's house, for I have five brothers, that he may testify to them, lest they also come to this place of torment.'"
Luke 16:27

Read Luke Chapter 16:19-31

In this parable of the rich man and Lazarus, we see the side of hell that we don't often want to consider; it's the side of torment. After realizing that there is no second chance upon death, the rich man pleads for Father Abraham to go and warn his brothers who are still alive. The rich man believes that if Father Abraham will go to his brothers, they will certainly repent and believe. *"But he said to him, 'If they do not hear Moses and the prophets, neither will they be persuaded though one rise from the dead.'" (Luke 16:31)*

While we have breath, each one of us is given an opportunity to believe in God. The chances of someone believing in God because a spirit from the afterlife testifies of torment, are slim. Many people think God is not fair, and that perhaps they never had a chance to hear the gospel message. *"For since the creation of the world His invisible attributes are clearly seen, being understood by the things that are made, even His eternal power and Godhead, so that they are without excuse." (Rom. 1:20)* There is a saying that goes, "If you can't live for Jesus now, how will you die for Him later?"

Prayer: Father, help us to share Christ now, while there is still time.

_____

_____

_____

_____

_____

_____

_____

_____

_____

_____

Speak The Truth

*"Take heed to yourselves. If your brother sins against you,
rebuke him; and if he repents, forgive him."*
Luke 17:3

Read Luke Chapter 17

So often we encounter situations where we are called to confront and then to forgive. One of the most difficult things that the family of Christ struggles with concerns this matter. When we don't follow the advice Jesus gives in this verse, we can be at odds with others for years. Going to the person who sins against us is often the last thing we do. We allow bitterness to build in our hearts, and we may even go to others before confronting the one who sinned against us.

When our words were seasoned with love, we have been amazed at the outcome of instances when we had to confront a brother or sister in Christ. Usually it's taken care of right away and we move on. We need to remember that if we are walking in the Spirit, we should not fear confrontation or reproof. We should both give it and receive it, as from the Lord. Our adversary, the devil, is thrilled beyond measure when we are not at peace with others. Choose to follow God's plan and we are free from the bondage of UNforgiveness.

Prayer: Father, help us to forgive and represent You well.

The Problem With "I"

"The Pharisee stood and prayed thus with himself, 'God, I thank You that I am not like other men--extortioners, unjust, adulterers, or even as this tax collector. I fast twice a week; I give tithes of all that I possess.'"
Luke 18:11,12

Read Luke Chapter 18:1-17

There is a saying that goes like this, "Don't let your own lips kiss you." Basically, this is what the Pharisee was doing, portraying a holier than thou attitude. God is not impressed with even our best works. ***"But we are all like an unclean thing, and all our righteousnesses are like filthy rags;" (Is. 64:6)***

The problem with the Pharisee is that he used too may "I's." I am convicted by this, because it reminds me how often I say "I." Lately, the Lord has been impressing upon me to be quiet, to listen more than I speak. This is challenging, yet revealing, as I listen and learn more about others. The words that the Pharisee used were a window into his heart. He thought highly of himself and put down others to make himself look good. Perhaps we should all take time to examine our own hearts and see if we are speaking too highly of ourselves.

Prayer: Lord, please help me to clear the selfish clutter in my life.

Surprised By God

"But He said, 'The things which are impossible with men are possible with God.'"
Luke 18:27

Read Luke Chapter 18:18-43

After Jesus declared how hard it is for a rich man to enter the kingdom of heaven, He clarifies that this is only possible with God. We are often discouraged by those who seem oblivious to God's truth. It often seems as though they will never experience that beautiful grace we know. However, we need to reflect back to the times when we ourselves did not know God. We must have seemed like impossibilities and "lost causes" to those believers who surrounded our lives.

Not long after I was saved, I came across a girl at a Christian concert, that I went to high school with. She was shocked that I had come to know the Lord. I remember her saying, ***"You're the last person in the world that I thought would get saved."*** "Wow," I thought. "Was I that bad?" Compared to this gal, I probably was. She seemed to have it all together, and back then I looked like I was falling apart. I was surprised and blessed by the God of possibilities when He touched my tattered life and saved me. Yes! Anything is possible with God.

Prayer: Father, thank You that You mend tattered and torn lives.

_____
_____
_____
_____
_____
_____
_____
_____
_____
_____

Jesus, Friend To Sinners

"Today salvation has come to this house, because he also is a son of Abraham;
for the Son of Man has come to seek and to save that which was lost."
Luke 19:9

Read Luke Chapter 19:1-10

During the time of Jesus, probably the most despised of men were tax collectors. They could do no right in the eyes of the people. Zacchaeus, a tax collector, took the time to climb up into a tree to see Jesus coming his way. You get the idea that Zacchaeus had a heart to know Jesus. When the mobs began to mutter and complain about Zacchaeus and his shady career, he owned up to his wrong and immediately responded to Jesus; he promised to pay back anyone he had cheated.

We seem to forget that Christ came for the lost, and His main mission was to save sinners. So difficult to understand, yet so profound to know that He takes broken souls and restores them to a place where they can't help but praise Him for His goodness. What tree must you climb so that you too may see Jesus? He is coming your way and would like to have intimate fellowship with you in your home. The little effort Zacchaeus made, not only afforded him friendship with God, but eternal security.

Prayer: Lord, help us to see sinners as potential friends in Christ.

Faithful In The Small Things

"And he said to him, 'Well done, good servant;
because you were faithful in a very little, have authority over ten cities.'"
Luke 19:17

Read Luke Chapter 19:11-48

What profound words these are! Recently, someone called the church office because they had driven by the property of our new church which is under construction. The gentleman was impressed by the building, and like so many others have said, "I can't wait until it's completed so I can start attending. And by the way, do you have any positions open for hire?" The response given to him was, "Don't wait until we are finished building to come and enjoy what God has been doing these past nine years. Oh, and by the way, we have several people who have been faithful for years that we would love to hire should the Lord open the doors."

Promotion comes from the Lord and He rewards those who are faithful in the small things. When folks advance themselves into bigger things without learning the importance of being obedient and faithful in the small things, they often lack the staying power and the humility it takes to stay committed.

Prayer: Father, help us not to despise the small things.

_____
_____
_____
_____
_____
_____
_____
_____
_____
_____
_____

The Rejected Stone Is The Right Stone

*"Then He looked at them and said, 'What then is this that is written:
The stone which the builders rejected has become the chief cornerstone?'"*
Luke 20:17

Read Luke Chapter 20:1-19

Often the things that seem to be the most insignificant are the most important. We see this portrayed all throughout the Gospel. "The last will be first," "the humble will be exalted," "those who lose their lives gain them... " It is so clear that God's ways are not man's ways. *"For My thoughts are not your thoughts, nor are your ways My ways,' says the Lord." (Is. 55:8)*

Nothing or no one can stop the work of God. Though Christ was rejected by many, He became exalted by the mighty hand of God. Are you being rejected because of your faith in Christ? Realize that you are a child of God, and nothing or no one can take His love away from you. God is working through the most unlikely vessels to accomplish His mighty and incredible purposes.

Prayer: Father, thank You for the precious Chief Cornerstone, Jesus.

_____
_____
_____
_____
_____
_____
_____
_____
_____
_____
_____

Jesus And His Wise Response

*"And He said to them, 'Render therefore to Caesar the things that are
Caesar's, and to God the things that are God's.'"*
Luke 20:25

Read Luke Chapter 20:20-47

In another attempt to try and catch Jesus at fault, the Pharisees
asked Jesus if it was lawful for a Jew to pay taxes to Rome. Jesus, who
knew their crafty and wicked hearts, outwits them with His response in
this verse. Unfortunately for the Pharisees, Jesus used His words to twist
their attempt to condemn and seize Him.

Above all, we are to honor God, but we are also to obey the laws of the
land. God is the one who has ordained governments and authorities. As
believers, we have an obligation to comply with the laws of our land,
however, we have an even greater obligation to comply with God's
commands. It's amazing how Jesus used His one-liner to halt the
Pharisees' plot to seize Him. His hour had not yet come, and even the
hour of His death was in His Father's hands.

Prayer: Help us to honor You, and pray for and honor our country.

Be Ready

"But take heed to yourselves, lest your hearts be weighed down with carousing, drunkenness, and cares of this life, and that Day come on you unexpectedly."
Luke 21:34

Read Luke Chapter 21

*J*esus takes some time to focus on the end times. He speaks about the many signs that will take place before His second coming. In our verse today, the focus is to be ready. This verse reminds us of what our friend, Uncle John, always says to people when he witnesses to them. *"If you were to die tonight, would you be ready to meet your Maker?"* While these words seem imposing, they really are powerful.

Imagine for a moment that you knew you had only a short time before your death. How would you want to spend that time? Hopefully you would live your last days for Christ and see to it that your house was in order. And, you would probably want to make sure that your loved ones had a clear cut understanding of the simple gospel message of Jesus Christ. There is urgency in the word "ready;" it means "now," "let's go," "were almost late." These words aren't to scare us, but rather prepare us. We all remember the story of Noah--how for 120 years, he preached and warned of impending doom, even while being ridiculed and mocked. Noah testified of God's judgment up until the time the first raindrops fell, and it was too late to get aboard the ark.

Prayer: Father, help us to see the urgency of redeeming souls.

In Remembrance

"This is My body which is given for you; do this in remembrance of Me."
Luke 22:19b

Read Luke Chapter 22:1-30

The communion experience is always a blessing. We have the opportunity to do this in church and in our homes, at Bible studies and alone. When we reflect on what communion really means, it can be extremely humbling. The God of all creation gave up such a precious part of Himself to die for a people who would hardly appreciate or notice His sacrifice. Tears flow from my eyes. So often I forget or take for granted all that He did just for me.

To Remember
I need to remember not to forget
The sacrifice You made for my sins
Your blood and Your body You so willingly gave
So that I would not die, but that I might live.

Sweet sacrifice is what I believe
In giving your life for me.

Help me to remember not to forget
Each drop of blood that You shed
For every wrong I would ever do
Was covered so well by You.

Communion so precious, a privilege
We need to remember sweet Jesus of Calvary.
TLR

Prayer: Father, thank You for the reminder not to forget.

_____
_____
_____
_____
_____
_____

Denying The Lord

"Then He said, 'I tell you, Peter, the rooster shall not crow this day before you will deny three times that you know Me.'"
Luke 22:34

Read Luke Chapter 22:31-71

How many times have we faltered in our faith? Too many to count! The Lord allows His disciples' failures to be recorded in His Word. We get to have a close-up look at their faults. We may even, on occasion, judge their mistakes. "I would not have denied My Lord," we might say or think. Are we any different? Absolutely not! Others just don't have the privilege of seeing us falter in our faith, like we see Peter.

If we look closely at our lives, we might be able to see how we deny Jesus. We deny Him when we don't honor Him with our belongings. We deny Him when we are numb to the needs of others. We deny Him when we don't spend time with Him. We deny Him when we allow the cares of this life to crowd Him out. We deny Him when we... fill in the blank. All the while He wants to restore us, as He did Peter. He willingly receives us back into His arms as He did Peter. Hopefully like Peter, we will repent from our denials of Christ. *"So Peter went out and wept bitterly." (Luke 22:62)*

Prayer: Father, forgive us when we falter in our faith.

_____

_____

_____

_____

_____

_____

_____

_____

_____

_____

_____

King Of The Jews

"Then Pilate asked Him, saying, 'Are You the King of the Jews?'
He answered him and said, 'It is as you say.'"
Luke 23:3

Read Luke Chapter 23:1-25

The accusers of Jesus lied about Him as they twisted the truth. The only truth they got right was that He is the King of the Jews. The sad thing is that they did not recognize it. They saw Him as a lunatic and a liar, and failed to see Him as Lord.

Even Pilate could not find fault with Jesus, nor could Herod. It was the demand of the people to crucify Him that swayed their decisions. Yet the truth is, God allowed this because it was His will that Jesus came to suffer for the sins of man. Jesus was on God's timetable and not man's. His hour was about to come. This King of the Jews not only provided the road to salvation for them, but made it available to the gentiles. Yes, He is a King, the one and only true King who is seated on the throne of our hearts.

Prayer: Lord, for all the rejection you suffered, our hearts are sorrowful, but thankful for salvation.

While We Still Breathe

"Assuredly, I say to you, today you will be with Me in Paradise."
Luke 23:43

Read Luke Chapter 23:25-43

Salvation is at the very doorstep of our hearts, while we still breathe; the thief on the cross realized something that the people did not. Death was knocking at his door, yet he saw Jesus as the road to salvation and asked Jesus to remember him. There have been many times when we have had opportunities to share Jesus with folks who were on their deathbeds. Many responded saying, "I can't receive Him now, because I have lived my life apart from His truth." The thief on the cross causes people to examine their lives and their lack of faith. The thief did not have an opportunity to do many works for the Lord, but what he did offer was faith, belief in Jesus.

While we still breathe, there is hope and opportunity to receive Him. The thief on the cross next to Jesus did not look at the obstacle he faced in death, he looked at the one opportunity he had and that was to believe. His faith won him a trip to Paradise where he would live eternally with his beloved Savior Jesus. The amazing thing about this little story is that even in His death, Jesus was offering salvation to any who would believe. It is never too late, while we still breathe.

Prayer: Father, thank You for examples in Your Word, like the thief on the cross.

Into Your Hands

"And when Jesus had cried out with a loud voice, He said, 'Father, into Your hands I commit My spirit.' Having said this, He breathed His last."
Luke 23:46

Read Luke Chapter 23:44-56

Have you ever wondered what it must be like to breathe your very last breath? The picture of Jesus on the cross is painful enough, but then there are those final words, *"Into your hands I commit My spirit."* As believers in Christ we have this confidence, that when we breathe our last breath, we too will find ourselves safe in the hands of our loving God. Sometimes we have difficulty committing ourselves to the Lord; we often take matters into our own hands. We mess up and finally relinquish our cares to Him who is able to use His hands to work things out to His glory. We know that in the case of Jesus, He would soon rise again changing the course of history, making all things possible.

What is there in your life that you hold too tightly in your hands? Let it go! Into His hands commit your life. Consider the words of King David. After many trials and troubles, he knew only one thing, *"But as for me, I trust in You, O Lord; I say, 'You are my God.' My times are in Your hand." (Ps. 31:14,15)*

Prayer: Father, thank You for being our all and everything.

But He Is Risen

"He is not here, but is risen!
Remember how He spoke to you when He was still in Galilee."
Luke 24:6

Read Luke Chapter 24

"But He is risen!" These few words changed the course of history. For in them we see the promise fulfilled that He would rise again on the third day. *(Luke 24:7)* There is no doubt that the human mind had difficulty believing this after Christ was crucified. How could He rise again? The fact that Christ rose again gives us a living hope. We are reminded of the Apostle Paul's words when we think of this living hope. *"Now hope does not disappoint, because the love of God has been poured out in our hearts by the Holy Spirit who was given to us. For when we were still without strength, in due time Christ died for the ungodly." (Rom. 5:5,6)*

His death for us seems to be enough, but His resurrection gives us the knowledge that He is ever before us. Christ lives in us and through us and gives us the power to live for Him. Think about how He resurrects our lives from the death that sin brings to us. Yes the words "But He is risen," are few yet very powerful and profound.

Prayer: Thank You God, for doing all that You did by giving Your Son Jesus to die and rise again.

_____
_____
_____
_____
_____
_____
_____
_____
_____
_____

He Is

"In the beginning was the Word, and the Word was with God, and the Word was God."
John 1:1

Read John Chapter 1:1-28

Our limited, finite minds cannot comprehend the creative and concise God we serve. So, He beautifully illustrates it for us in John 1:1. He is and always has been with God, and His Word is and always has been. His Son is and always has been God. So often in life we battle the "ifs" and the "whys." We question and we challenge the things that are beyond our comprehension. However, the thing that is required to truly understand is faith. Simple faith, just believing that He is and was, is enough. God lives in the eternal and we only know in part. Paul eloquently described this in his letter to the church at Corinth. *"For now we see in a mirror, dimly, but then face to face. Now I know in part, but then I shall know just as I also am known." (1 Cor. 13:12)*

Prayer: Father, in our limited understanding, help our faith to grow.

_____

_____

_____

_____

_____

_____

_____

_____

_____

_____

_____

_____

_____

Come And See

"He said to them, 'Come and see.' They came and saw where He was
staying, and remained with Him that day (now it was about the tenth hour)."
John 1:39

Read John Chapter 1:29-51

*C*uriosity about where the Lord was staying, was the topic that eventually led to Peter's salvation. Jesus and His words, ***"Come and see,"*** are very intriguing and inviting. As ambassadors of Christ, it's important that we follow His example and invite others to join us. "Come see what God has done," should be our initial response to the curiosity others have about our Lord.

Just this week we were at a pastors' conference, and in the midst of it we were called out to visit a member of our congregation who was ill at a nearby hospital. As we ministered to her and anointed her with oil, we began to hear loud sobbing coming from the bed next to us. The sobbing increased, as did our curiosity. We walked around the curtain and asked the women sobbing, "Are you alright?" She said, "No! I am not. I just want to go home!" We asked her name and she said, "It's Jennifer." We assured her that we would be in prayer for her. We said our good-byes to the woman from our church and as we were leaving, the Holy Spirit prompted us to ask Jennifer if we could pray for her. She reached out her hand to us and said, "Yes." We prayed for God's comfort and peace to come upon her life. The point of this little story is that the name of Jesus is so powerful, and carries with it the continual message to ***"Come and see."*** We later learned that not long after we prayed for Jennifer, she was released from the hospital.

Prayer: Father, thank You for the opportunities to "come and see." We also want to lift up Jennifer and pray for her salvation.

_____
_____
_____
_____
_____
_____

The Water & The Wine

"Jesus said to them, 'Fill the waterpots with water.'"
John 2:7a

Read John Chapter 2:1-12

This little story about water turning to wine may seem a bit surprising, but not really. Jesus was doing what was natural to Him and that was taking care of needs. It would have been a great embarrassment to the host of the wedding had Jesus not performed this miracle. Jewish weddings were a time of celebration, and great emphasis was given to hospitality. The interesting thing about Jesus and His provisions is that not only the recipient's faith is encouraged, but so are those who witness it. No doubt this was a huge faith builder for the disciples. *"And His disciples believed in Him." (John 2:11b)*

What provisions are needed in your life today? Realize this; He sees, hears, and knows how to change the circumstances in your life that at this moment seem so bleak. Take some time and sit at His feet; pour out your heart to Him. In God's economy, turning water into wine is a small thing. He can make something out of nothing. Be reminded today that He has an unlimited supply of all things. *"And my God shall supply all your need according to His riches in glory by Christ Jesus." (Phil. 4:19)*

Prayer: Thank You that You are the God of provision.

_____

_____

_____

_____

_____

_____

_____

_____

_____

_____

Simple Truth

"Jesus answered and said to them, 'Destroy this temple,
and in three days I will raise it up.'"
John 2:19

Read John Chapter 2:13-25

After cleansing the temple, the Jews began ordering Jesus to show them signs to confirm He was indeed the Messiah. Notice the cool response of our Lord. He throws them off by answering them with the above verse. They were floored by His response. It took forty-six years to build the temple and this Jesus was going to rebuild it in three days? They were convinced He must be a lunatic. They, the supposed masters of the Scriptures and the law, were themselves so near but so far away from spiritual truth.

We too, need to be careful that we don't get so lost in legalism that we miss the simple message of the gospel. It is possible to get what's called a "brain cramp," when we try in our own human understanding to figure out why or how God is going to do this or that. We need to remain faithful in our simple faith of just believing, trusting, and obeying His word. The sovereignty of our God will help everything to fall into place. After all, He did die for our sins and rise again on the third day, just as He said He would.

Prayer: Father, thank You for the simplicity of the gospel.

_____
_____
_____
_____
_____
_____
_____
_____
_____
_____

New Life

"Most assuredly, I say to you, unless one is born again, he cannot see the kingdom of God."
John 3:3

Read John Chapter 3:1-3

Before I was saved, I would hear Christians say, *"You must be born again."* That truly sounded odd to a young woman of eighteen. "How is that possible?" I would think. Because I was not born anew, I could not understand what this meant. Nicodemus posed the same questions of Jesus. However, until one actually experiences the precious new life that Christ gives, it only sounds like an implausible idea.

Each year as I celebrate another spiritual birthday, I am truly grateful for the gift of being born again. The blinders came off my eyes when I first believed, and my new life unveiled the new discovery that God is loving and merciful and desires to have an intimate friendship with me. It has been a journey of unending blessings and even the burdens have taught me that He never asks me to carry them alone. New life is the promise that comes from simply believing and receiving Jesus as one's personal Savior. New life is a conversion of the soul; it is something you can't see, but others can tell you have experienced it. The invitation to have new life is the heart of the gospel message and given freely to all who would believe.

Prayer: Lord, thank You for the precious gift of new life.

_____
_____
_____
_____
_____
_____
_____
_____

Why Christ Died

"For God so loved the world that He gave His only begotten Son,
that whoever believes in Him should not perish but have everlasting life."
John 3:16

Read John Chapter 3:4-36

It is the strongest love that ever was; that's why Christ died. God in His complete devotion and passion for man and their souls, provided all He could give so that we might have the opportunity to live again. This kind of love is hard to humanly understand. Most of us would have trouble sacrificing one of our own children for another's sins. To give us eternal life is the reason why Christ died for us. God lives in the eternal, and with Him there is no end.

The older we get, the more aware we are of how precious the blood of Jesus really is. Forgiveness of sins is priceless. There is so much talk, and even arguing among God's people regarding salvation and predestination. To simplify things, we need to return to the simple gospel message of Jesus Christ. In His invitation to come and believe, God leaves no one out, it's inclusive. All are invited to come and enter into a personal relationship with Him, and are given the promise of life everlasting; but sadly, not all RSVP.

Prayer: Father, give us Your heart and Your passion for souls.

_____

_____

_____

_____

_____

_____

_____

_____

_____

_____

Living Water

"Jesus answered and said to her, 'If you knew the gift of God, and who it is who says to you, 'Give Me a drink,' you would have asked Him, and He would have given you living water.'"
John 4:10

Read John Chapter 4:1-26

*I*n this verse Jesus speaks of Himself as being Living Water, the kind of water that overflows and promises abundant life and life everlasting. There are so many things that are vying for our attention in this world, so many things that want to quench the Spirit of the Living God. The truth is, there is nothing in this world that can satisfy our souls the way He can.

The offer of living water and everlasting life was given to the woman at the well. Jesus also revealed to her the truth about her life. He brought to light the fact that she had been living a life that would only cause her to thirst again; she needed to drink from the Living Water. In a world where many are trying to fill up on the temporary pleasures of this world, it is so important that we have the Living Water and everlasting life to offer to a thirsty world.

Prayer: Father, help us to be ready to minister to those who might be at the well.

_____

_____

_____

_____

_____

_____

_____

_____

_____

_____

Unless We See

"Unless you people see signs and wonders, you will by no means believe."
John 4:48b

Read John Chapter 4:27-54

*J*esus had done so many miracles in the midst of the multitudes to whom He ministered. Many people believed because of the miracles He performed. However, even in seeing miracles there are still skeptics among us. We are a skeptical people by nature, and we often can't comprehend how God can do something unless we see. This must grieve the heart of God. Could it be that He is grieved by our unbelief? He certainly must be blessed when we believe without seeing. Later in John chapter 20, we see the perspective that Jesus has about believing, when He addresses Thomas. *"Jesus said to him, 'Thomas, because you have seen Me, you have believed. Blessed are those who have not seen and yet have believed.'" (John 20:29)*

Because we falter in our faith, we are very much like babies who must learn to trust and believe. Time after time, God proves Himself to us and we finally start to "get it" and believe without seeing. Thank God He is patient with us!

Prayer: Lord, thank You for tolerating our unbelief.

And Jesus Came Along

"He said to him, 'Do you want to be made well?'"
John 5:6b

Read John Chapter 5:1-15

The man had been handicapped for thirty-eight years, and Jesus comes along and asks, *"Do you want to be made well?"* Without a doubt, the man wanted to be made well. However, he probably never thought it would happen the way it did. Jesus tells the man, *"Rise, take up your bed and walk." (vs. 8)* We too sometimes wait to be made well, and all the while the Lord is right before us, extending His hand and offering us His divine help. We can't see His resources because we only see what's before us. The man had been ill for thirty-eight years, and sat by that pool hoping someone would have the decency and compassion to put him in when the waters stirred. Then Jesus came along, and in a matter of moments He changed this man's life and fulfilled prophecy while doing it. *"Then the eyes of the blind shall be opened, and the ears of the deaf shall be unstopped. Then the lame shall leap like a deer." (Is. 35:5,6)*

What trouble are you facing today? In what way do you need Jesus to come along side you? Could it be that the only thing you can see is the pool? Take some time and turn your eyes upon Jesus, and say, "Yes Lord, I want to be made well."

Prayer: Lord, help us to see that You can, when we can't.

_____

_____

_____

_____

_____

_____

_____

What Do You Believe?

"For if you believed Moses, you would believe Me;
for he wrote about Me."
John 5:46

Read John Chapter 5:16-47

In a recent poll, 80% of the American population claim to have faith in God. Yet, the fruit we see is far less. It's not enough to say you believe, you must know why you believe. The Jewish people claimed to believe in the God of the Old Testament, but did they really know Him? If they had known the Word of God, they would have gladly received Christ as their Messiah. We know from the Old Testament, there were over three hundred prophecies about Christ and His coming. Yet, the very people who claimed God to be their Lord, rejected the Savior, His Son, because of their ignorance and lack of knowledge regarding God's Word.

We can't stand on what we don't know, so it is vital as believers in Christ that we become familiar with His Word, so that our faith can grow in Him, and we can rightly divide His Word. *"But they have not all obeyed the gospel. For Isaiah says, 'Lord, who has believed our report?' So then faith comes by hearing, and hearing by the word of God." (Rom. 10:16,17)*

Prayer: Father, help our unbelief.

_____
_____
_____
_____
_____
_____
_____
_____
_____
_____

Do Not Be Afraid

"But He said to them, 'It is I; do not be afraid.'"
John 6:20

Read John Chapter 6:1-21

*H*ow beautiful are the words from Jesus, ***"Do not be afraid."***
Fear is an enemy to our faith. Fear clouds our vision and robs us of joy
and hope. When we see through the eyes of fear, we only see the giants
that are before us. When we turn our eyes upon Jesus, we begin to see
through His eyes, and our fears fade away. The disciples, even though
they spent time with the Lord, had their share of moments when fear
gripped their hearts.

Do Not Be Afraid

Do not be afraid, it's Me
I will calm the storms and set you free
Fear seems to grip your heart
Look to Me for a new start
The giants aren't that big at all
When your eyes are on Me , you will not fall
Do not be afraid, it's Me
I will walk on water to help you see
That all is well, well with Me
Don't worry, doubt or fret
Into My arms is where you find rest
Do not be afraid, it's Me
I am all you need to see

TLR

Prayer: Father, thank You for turning fear into faith.

Are You Hungry?

"And Jesus said to them, 'I am the bread of life. He who comes to Me shall never hunger, and he who believes in Me shall never thirst.'"
John 6:35

Read John Chapter 6:22-71

Our bodies have an appetite that never seems to end. No matter how full we get, we still find ourselves hungering and thirsting again and again. In this verse, the words of Jesus are so powerful because they are so true. Before Christ, our lives were hopeless and nothing seemed to satisfy, leaving us with feelings of total despair and emptiness.

When Jesus touched our lives, we had a new kind of hunger; it was a hunger for Him. The difference is that He does satisfy. When we hunger and thirst after Him, we can be confident that He will meet us in a way that will bring the kind of satisfaction which makes life worth living. He gives us purpose and promise and power to live above the circumstances that used to be so hopeless. If you're hungry, take some time to fill up on the bread of life.

Prayer: Lord, thank You for the feast of fellowship that we have with You.

There Is Something About His Name

"The world cannot hate you, but it hates Me because
I testify of it that its works are evil."
John 7:7

Read John Chapter 7:1-9

Just the mention of the name Jesus evokes animosity in the world. Have you ever noticed how ruffled people get when His name is mentioned? They get defensive, critical, and cruel. Before Christ, we too were defensive. There is power in His name. Jesus explained to His brothers that it was He who was hated by the world, not them.

The mere fact that we are associated with Christ brings about hatred. In His name, there is light and it exposes the darkness of this world. The Apostle Peter writes about the suffering that the saints endure because of His name. *"If you are reproached for the name of Christ, blessed are you, for the Spirit of glory and of God rests upon you. On their part He is blasphemed, but on your part He is glorified."* *(1 Peter 4:14)* There is just something about His name; to some it means life, and to others it means death.

Prayer: Father, thank You for Your Son Jesus and the power that is in His name.

_____
_____
_____
_____
_____
_____
_____
_____
_____
_____

Judge Righteously

"Do not judge according to appearance,
but judge with righteous judgment."
John 7:24

Read John Chapter 7:10-52

*W*hat we see on the outside is not always the truth. We make judgments based on outward appearances. Jesus said we should make our judgments righteously. So how do we do that? We pray for discernment and pray for God to show us in His Word. No one really knows the heart the way God does. *"Do not look at his appearance or at his physical stature, because I have refused him. For the Lord does not see as man sees; for man looks at the outward appearance, but the Lord looks at the heart." (1 Sam. 16:7)* People so often say, "God knows my heart!" This is so true, and what He sees is truth.

The condition of the heart is what makes or breaks a person. Jesus was being judged for making a man well on the Sabbath. The Jews circumcised on the Sabbath, yet they could not see straight when it came to Jesus and His decision to heal on the Sabbath. Our vision can become clouded when we only see what appears to be right on the outside.

Prayer: Father, help us to see through Your eyes and Your heart.

_____
_____
_____
_____
_____
_____
_____
_____
_____
_____

He Who Is Without Sin

"So when they continued asking Him, He raised Himself up and said to them,
'He who is without sin among you, let him throw a stone at her first.'"
John 8:7

Read John Chapter 8:1-20

How piercing these words must have been. Imagine that you were the accuser, and you heard these words. How would you react? We know that they were *"convicted by their conscience." (vs. 9b)* One by one they shamefully left the presence of Jesus. We too hold up stones, ready to cast them at those who are sinners. We forget that God's Word says, *"for all have sinned and fall short of the glory of God." (Rom. 3:23)* If it weren't for God's grace, we would all be like the Pharisees and scribes, lost in a religion that tries to live by rules and regulations.

Jesus did not give the woman permission to continue in sin. He simply told her to go and sin no more, forgiving her, but not condoning her behavior. It is so much better when Jesus is left to judge a matter, because when He does, it's always righteous judgment. He provides a way for the sinner to get right with Him and move on in their relationship with Him. On the other hand, Satan loves to take people down, making no provisions for their future.

Prayer: Father, thank You for righteous judgment.

Pleasing God

"The Father has not left Me alone,
for I always do those things that please Him."
John 8:29b

Read John Chapter 8:21-59

Jesus had an ultimate goal and purpose, and that was total obedience to His Father God. He pleased God through sacrifice and humility. It's hard to comprehend why He did it or how He did it. We know that Jesus was God in the form of a man, suffering the agony of being in the flesh, knowing that He would lay down His life for a people who would hardly notice. Why? Because He always did those things that pleased the Father. The word "please" means to be agreeable, to give pleasure, and to satisfy. This was His aim.

Jesus not only pleased the Father, but the Father was pleased to use Him as a vessel for the eventual salvation of man. *"Yet it pleased the Lord to bruise Him; He has put Him to grief." (Is. 53:10)* To think that God our Father was satisfied by the death of His Son Jesus, brings tears to our eyes. It motivates us to want to please Him with our lives. It seems a small thing to live a life that pleases Him.

Prayer: Father, may our lives bring You some pleasure.

Who Was Really Blind?

*"Jesus answered, 'Neither this man nor his parents sinned,
but that the works of God should be revealed in him.'"*

John 9:3

Read John Chapter 9:1-12

The world is always trying to put a spin on why God allows certain things to happen to some people. Why are some people born blind, or deaf, and why are some born deformed? Is it because of sin? These are questions we all have asked from time to time. Again, our limited finite minds can't comprehend how God could bring glory out of such tragedy.

In our own family, we have an aunt who was born with a muscular deficiency and told that she would never walk. For years we watched her and witnessed God working and moving in her life. She not only walks, but she swims, she drives a car, is happily married, and has a son. She is probably one of the most committed children's ministry workers in the world. God has been glorified in her life over and over again. We also have a nephew who is autistic, and he is one of the greatest blessings anyone could ever have. For whoever can't see the glory of God revealed in His people, they are the ones who are blind. Who then should we feel sorry for? Those who can't see the glory of God, for they are truly blind. *(2 Cor. 4:3,4)*

Prayer: Father, thank You for being glorified in Your creation.

_____

_____

_____

_____

_____

_____

_____

_____

I Was Blind, Now I See

"He answered and said, "Whether He is a sinner or not I do not know.
One thing I do know: that though I was blind, now I see."'
John 9:25

Read John Chapter 9:13-41

After being interrogated by the Jews, the once blind man comes back with a quick response. *"I was blind, but now I see."* The Jews were so caught up in finding fault with Jesus, that they failed to notice the miracle. The man had been blind from birth and was healed by Jesus, and instead of celebrating with him, he was put on trial.

When our eyes are opened by Jesus, we suddenly see through His eyes. We are converted in a moment, and the world cannot comprehend our new found sight. Jesus clarifies this at the close of this chapter. *"And Jesus said, 'For judgment I have come into this world, that those who do not see may see, and that those who see may be made blind.'" (John 9:39)*

It is really amazing that those who could see, lost sight when the blind man was given his sight. This holds true to this day, for so many are blinded by the truth.

Prayer: Father, thank You for helping us to see.

Open Door

*"I am the door. If anyone enters by Me, he will be saved,
and will go in and out and find pasture."*
John 10:9

Read John Chapter 10:1-10

Every home has an entrance; there is a way to come in. The same holds true for those who enter the kingdom of heaven. There is only one way, one door by which we can come in and that is through Jesus. There are many doors that appear to be a way to the Father, but all these doors really lead to dungeons. A dungeon is a place that is dark and cold and gives no light, no hope. It's a place of separation. The doorway to Jesus leads us to pastures that are green and have beautiful light and perpetuate growth and life.

Open Door

I saw an open door
Afraid to enter, I chose others
They all led me to darkness
I was so lost
I decided to go through one more
To my surprise I saw the light
This door exposed all other doors to be a lie
Truth is what I now see
Green pastures, life, now I am free
I thank You and praise You, from the bottom of my heart
There is no way other than Jesus, in Him I will abide.
TLR

Prayer: Father, thank You for opening the door to life.

Lay It Down

"No one takes it from Me, but I lay it down of Myself."
John 10:18a

Read John Chapter 10:11-42

Jesus willingly laid His life down; no one could take it from Him unless He offered it. This makes His sacrifice for us even more precious. When we review our own lives and see the sin, we are even more humbled.

As we think about the things we need to lay down in our own lives, we are challenged; what can we lay down for Him? How about *pride, arrogance, anger, resentment, laziness...?* The list goes on. No matter how far we have come in our relationship with Christ, there is still the need for us to die to the flesh and lay it down daily. Jesus said it best, *"If anyone desires to come after Me, let him deny himself, and take up his cross daily, and follow Me." (Luke 9:23)*

What is it in your life today that Jesus is calling you to lay down for Him? Look at His sacrifice upon the cross and His life that He laid down for you. This should help you to die to the flesh, and lay it down for Him.

Prayer: Father, we thank You for setting the example, for showing us how to die daily.

_____

_____

_____

_____

_____

_____

_____

_____

_____

_____

_____

_____

Seeing His Glory

"Jesus said to her, 'Did I not say to you that if you would believe you would see the glory of God?'"
John 11:40

Read John Chapter 11:1-44

How many times do we miss the glory of God, because we are too busy doubting that He can come through? Everything looks like a mountain before us; we only see the obstacles and not the opportunities. We grab hold of something and believe that it is the one thing that God can't fix. How limited our finite minds are!

Lazarus was dead, but God wasn't. He would be glorified by bringing Lazarus back from the dead. We should not be surprised by this, because God is the giver of life. He can give and take it away. Perhaps there is something in your life today that feels hopeless, dark, and dead. Realize that God can be glorified through our lives as we trust Him with the most difficult and impossible of situations. It's been our experience with God that the greater the impossibility, the greater His power, the greater He can be glorified. *"But Jesus looked at them and said, "With men it is impossible, but not with God; for with God all things are possible." (Mark 10:27)*

Prayer: Father, thank You for making <u>all</u> things possible.

_____

_____

_____

_____

_____

_____

_____

_____

_____

_____

Lazarus, Come Forth!

"Now when He had said these things,
He cried with a loud voice, 'Lazarus, come forth!'"
John 11:43

Read John Chapter 11:38-57

*J*esus cried with a loud voice, ***"Lazarus come forth!"*** There is speculation as to why Jesus cried with such a loud voice. Some think that it was because He was so filled with emotion because of His love for the family; others think it was so the crowd could hear Him. It was probably a little of both. The important thing is that He spoke with boldness, and Lazarus who was once dead, now was alive.

Jesus is in the business of bringing life to those who were once dead. Thinking back over our lives, it's hard to remember life without Jesus. However, there was a time when we were dead, spiritually dead! But one day, Jesus spoke those beautiful words to us too. "Mike and Terri, come forth!" We responded and have been living and breathing for the Lord ever since. This is what separates Jesus from any of the false messiahs. No one else has ever raised anyone from the dead, no one else has ever died for another's sins, and no one else can bring life to a dead soul. No wonder He has the name above all names. ***"Therefore God also has highly exalted Him and given Him the name which is above every name." (Phil. 2:9)***

Prayer: Father, thank You for giving us a reason to live.

115

Sparing No Expense

"But Jesus said, 'Let her alone; she has kept this for the day of My burial. For the poor you have with you always, but Me you do not have always.'"
John 12:7,8

Read John Chapter 12:1-19

Judas was always concerned about money; perhaps that was his downfall. Mary had anointed Jesus with costly oil, and Judas questioned why the fragrant oil had not instead been sold and the money given to the poor. These were his words, but the truth is Judas could not see the importance or the significance of using the costly oil on Jesus. True love will spend money, time, and talent, for the one they love. True love spares no expense.

At this moment, Mary did not worry about the cost or the needs of the poor. She was focused on one thing, her love for Jesus. Mary proved her love with action; she was always at the feet of Jesus, showing her heartfelt respect and love for Him. How timely was her act of love, for it was as Jesus said, He was being prepared for burial. It was a common thing in those days to use the fragrant oil for embalming. Whether Mary or the others understood this is not clear, but it is clear that Jesus understood. He would soon give His life as a ransom for our sins. He spared no expense, pouring out His life to bring fragrance to ours.

Prayer: Father, thank You for Mary's loving example. Help us to spare no expense in loving You.

_____
_____
_____
_____
_____
_____
_____
_____
_____

My Hour Has Come

"The hour has come that the Son of Man should be glorified."
John 12:23b

Read John Chapter 12:20-50

All through the gospels, Jesus is quoted saying, **"My hour has not come."** But now, the hour had arrived for Him to die, and we can only imagine what went through His heart and mind. He must have had some mixed emotions. He would be leaving the disciples whom He loved, and giving up His life in a most excruciating way, for a world that would hardly notice it at the time. Yet excitement probably filled His heart too. Finally, there would be a settlement for man's sins, an avenue whereby man could be saved from the tyranny of sin.

What about the hour in our life? There is that hour in each of our lives when we too will be faced with death. What kind of testimony do we want to leave? Do we want to be known for all we did for the Lord or for all He has done for us? If we knew how much time we had left, we would no doubt be spending every opportunity living life fully for Him. We too should live as though our hour had come.

Prayer: Thank You Lord, for never giving up; for truly, Your hour was the most heroic and profound act of love ever bestowed upon mankind.

_____
_____
_____
_____
_____
_____
_____
_____
_____
_____

Spiritual Bath

*"Jesus answered him,
'If I do not wash you, you have no part with Me.'"
John 13:8b*

Read John Chapter 13:1-17

$\mathscr{P}$eter is known for his aggressive and impulsive temperament, and he displays it very honestly in this scene. Washing feet was a job for servants; there was no way that Peter was going to allow Jesus to wash his feet. *"You shall never wash my feet!" (John 13:8)* This was Peter's response to Jesus. That was until Jesus clarified that if He did not wash his feet, then he would not receive the spiritual bath that makes it possible to have personal fellowship with Him. In a matter of moments, Peter's heart changed. He realized that there was no way he was going to give up intimate communion with Jesus.

Think of the missed opportunities, if we did not have the spiritual bath that He gives. It is that special time when He cleanses us and washes us with His Word. Those are the times that we are renewed, corrected, and close to our Lord's heart. Is the Lord calling you to come a little closer? Respond like Peter, after He heard the Lord's voice. *"Lord, not my feet only, but also my hands and my head." (John 13:9b)*

Prayer: Lord, thank You for washing our feet and our lives.

Foolish Things

"Simon Peter said to Him, 'Lord, where are You going?' Jesus answered him,
'Where I am going you cannot follow Me now, but you shall follow Me afterward.'"
John 13:36

Read John Chapter 13:18-38

Peter was a man who spoke what was on his mind. He was not an educated man, so he asked a lot of questions. Somehow, in his questions to Jesus, he often missed the point. Jesus, being patient with Peter, answered the questions knowing that someday Peter would understand clearly what He meant. We love the men that Jesus chose as His personal disciples. Peter's mistakes remind us that God is in control and is working His purposes in our lives. *"But God has chosen the foolish things of the world to put to shame the wise, and God has chosen the weak things of the world to put to shame the things which are mighty." (1 Cor. 1:27)*

Just when we think we get it, we too are humbled and reminded that we are fools for Christ. We will never fully get it, not in this life. We are continually being refined and transformed into His image. It can be alarming when we see how we miss the mark, yet it can be comforting to know that He will perfect His work in us. Despite our weaknesses, He is still working in us!

Prayer: Father, thank You for Your grace.

_____
_____
_____
_____
_____
_____
_____
_____
_____
_____

They Are One

"Believe Me that I am in the Father and the Father in Me,
or else believe Me for the sake of the works themselves."
John 14:11

Read John Chapter 14:1-11

When we were young Christians, we did not struggle at all with Jesus being God, and the Holy Spirit being the third Person of the Godhead. Somehow we just divinely knew and accepted it to be true. Probably this is because of the immediate, radical conversion we had in our own lives. We knew that if God could transform a heart, the way He did ours, it was not really a big deal for Him to come in the form of a man and bring salvation to those who would believe. When we were introduced to the Holy Spirit, that too made sense, because our loving Father would not leave us here alone without the help of His Spirit. No problem for us. The Father, the Son and the Holy Spirit are One.

As we grew in the Lord, we remember someone using an orange to explain the Trinity. There were three significant parts to the orange, the peel, the heart, and the seed. This was simple enough for us to understand. We complicate things far too much when we try to understand God's ways with our finite minds. We live by faith and that's what separates Christianity from all other religions. We live for and believe in the God of all creation.

Prayer: Father, thank You for the three different, yet important and integral parts of You.

_____

_____

_____

_____

_____

_____

_____

_____

Another Helper

*"And I will pray the Father, and He will give you another Helper,
that He may abide with you forever..."*
John 14:16

Read John Chapter 14:12-31

We often have misunderstandings about the work of the Holy Spirit in our lives. Some think He is an emotional experience that only works when we are manifesting the gifts of the Spirit. Others discount the work of the Holy Spirit and don't believe that certain gifts of the Spirit are for today. We find truth in the Scriptures and that is the ultimate guide by which we should measure our opinions and convictions. We love how Jesus so simply states in this passage that He won't leave us alone, but He will pray to the Father and He will give us another Helper, the Holy Spirit.

Another Helper! Who wouldn't want that? We need all the help we can get, and God gives it to us through His Spirit. He will abide in us forever. Wow! Now who can argue with that? When we see the Spirit for who He is, we generally welcome Him into our lives. Without the help of the Holy Spirit we would be pretty much like the Pharisees and scribes, trying to live this life in the power of our flesh. No thanks; we welcome all the help that God wants to give us to live this life fully for Him, now and forevermore.

Prayer: Father, thank You for the Holy Spirit.

Abiding In Christ

*"Abide in Me, and I in you. As the branch cannot bear fruit of itself,
unless it abides in the vine, neither can you, unless you abide in Me."*
John 15:4

Read John Chapter 15:1-8

No doubt this is one of our most favorite chapters in the Bible. We love the word "abide," and we love what it means in the life of a believer. It means to be at home with, to remain in, to stay with. This is what abiding means. It is the place where we receive our nourishment and our growth. It is what some call the abundant life. When we abide in Christ, we are encouraged and we grow. We begin to bear fruit, and the fruit bears more fruit. Abiding in Christ brings promise and purpose.

So many things in this life try to pull us away from the vine, and at times we feel like we are barely hanging on. However, we can be assured that Jesus is still with us and will even allow us to be cut back like roses so that we might bear more fruit. Sometimes we experience seasons in our lives that feel as though nothing is there, but we have confidence that if we remain in Him, we will bring forth fruit in due season. Abiding in Christ is that place where we no longer are just believers, but receivers of the abundant life God desires to give us on a daily basis.

Prayer: Lord, thank You for the gift of abiding.

_____
_____
_____
_____
_____
_____
_____
_____
_____
_____

What A Friend We Have In Jesus

"No longer do I call you servants, for a servant does not know what his master is doing; but I have called you friends, for all things that I heard from My Father I have made known to you."

John 15:15

Read John Chapter 15:9-27

Have you ever had a friend who knew something you didn't? When you find out that they had the "inside scoop" on something and did not reveal it to you, it can be aggravating. In this verse, Jesus gets up close and personal with His disciples and us. He is vulnerable and shares His deep emotions about the friendship He shares with us. He reveals that He does not see us as servants who never really know the master's business. Instead, He shares how <u>ALL</u> the Father has revealed to Him, He reveals to us. He holds nothing back from us; the resources of God's kingdom are passed down to us. We are full recipients of a heavenly inheritance that has an unlimited trust fund of never-ending riches, all given at His expense. This kind of friendship deserves respect and honor.

We have a friend in Jesus, and this motivates us to respond to Him by seeking Him and spending adequate time with Him. We will never know the depth of this friendship if we act as though we are just acquaintances.

Prayer: Lord, thank You for Your friendship.

_____
_____
_____
_____
_____
_____
_____
_____
_____
_____

Spirit Of Truth

"I still have many things to say to you, but you cannot bear them now. However, when He, the Spirit of truth, has come, He will guide you into all truth; for He will not speak on His own authority, but whatever He hears He will speak; and He will tell you things to come."
John 16:12,13

Read John Chapter 16:1-15

The work of the Holy Spirit is a beautiful and awesome power in our lives. Without it, we could never comprehend God. Years ago, when Mike was on staff at Calvary Chapel Moreno Valley, we had an opportunity to travel with our Senior Pastor John Milhouse and a team of high school students into mainland China to smuggle Bibles. It was no doubt the roughest trip, physically, that we had ever been on. However, spiritually it was the most rewarding. The Holy Spirit was revealed in the most incredible ways. It was so amazing to see how He helped us bear witness to God's truth with the Chinese brethren. We could not speak the same language, but we completely understood that we were spiritually connected to one another by the Holy Spirit. All through the trip, He led us, He guided us, and He spoke the truth in love to us. If we had known beforehand how physically difficult the trip was, perhaps we would not have gone. But after the trip, we knew that we would have no trouble going again, should God call us. The Lord does not always reveal to us everything at once, because He knows we can't handle it. He, through His Holy Spirit and in His perfect timing, shows us things to come.

Prayer: Father, thank You for the Holy Spirit.

His Peace

"These things I have spoken to you, that in Me you may have peace. In the world you will have tribulation; but be of good cheer, I have overcome the world."
John 16:33

Read John Chapter 16:16-33

How appropriate this verse is for the times we are living in. There is much tribulation in our world today. We are in the midst of war with Iraq and so many things are hanging in the balance. We are not sure what is more disturbing, the fact that we are at war, or the apathy that seems to permeate our world. We find ourselves moving from one emotion to the next. How our heart grieves for the lost and yet, we know the Lord grieves even more. Yes, we need His peace. Take comfort in the knowledge that He is already victorious. He has already overcome the world. *"For He Himself is our peace." (Eph. 2:14a)*

His Peace

As I look around the world
Panic fills my heart, I need peace
Concerned for those who don't know
His love, His joy, His peace
What will it take for them to see?
All that He is, is all that we need

Wanting to solve it, all I know
To Him in prayer is where I'll go
His peace, His peace, is what I need
For in it, there is victory.
TLR

Prayer: Father, thank You for Your peace that passes all human understanding.

Finishing Well

"I have glorified You on the earth.
I have finished the work which You have given Me to do."
John 17:4

Read John Chapter 17:1-19

*W*e don't always think of Jesus as once being in that glorified state with His Father God. This text confirms that Jesus had been with the Father from the beginning. *"And now, O Father, glorify Me together with Yourself, with the glory which I had with You before the world was." (John 17:5)* Now it was time to return to the Father. What emotions our Lord must have faced as He pondered the path He would soon take. It was a path that would lead Him to death and lead us to life. He had finished His work, but His work would continue forever, and countless lives would be affected by His sacrifice.

What about our lives? Are we who we want to be? What kind of legacy will we leave this world? Are we going to leave a spiritual inheritance for our loved ones? These are important questions we need to ask ourselves. One day, we too will be glorified with our Father. We want to hear those precious words, *"Well done, good and faithful servant." (Matt. 25:21)*

Prayer: Lord, help us to finish well.

_____
_____
_____
_____
_____
_____
_____
_____
_____
_____

Jesus & His Prayer For All Believers

"Father, I desire that they also whom You gave Me may be with Me where I am, that they may behold My glory which You have given Me; for You loved Me before the foundation of the world."
John 17:24

Read John Chapter 17:20-26

The love that Jesus had for mankind speaks loudly in this verse. Jesus prays for all believers, that they would behold the glory He knew through His father. His prayer was not only for the believers then, but for those who believe now and in the future. The burden for souls lies heavily upon Jesus. He prayed for them while He was here, sparing no expense, giving His own life for them. He continues to have a passion for souls. ***"Therefore He is also able to save to the uttermost those who come to God through Him, since He always lives to make intercession for them." (Heb. 7:25)***

What love and compassion He has for us! He keeps giving and giving to us; He is blessed by our faith in Him. We can please Him even more if we would just have a greater passion for souls, and realize that this world indeed is not our home. One day, we too will be glorified with Him.

Prayer: Lord, we need to have a passion for the lost.

Whom Are You Seeking?

*"Jesus therefore, knowing all things that would come upon Him,
went forward and said to them, 'Whom are you seeking?'"
John 18:4*

Read John Chapter 18:1-24

They came with lanterns, torches, weapons, and a detachment of troops to arrest our Lord. This was overkill, seeing how Jesus knew all things, and knew that He was about to change the course of history by willingly laying down His life.

Knowing they had come to seek Him, Jesus still posed the question, ***"Whom are you seeking?"*** You get the feeling that there must have been intense conviction among the crowd at the mention of His name. ***"Then the detachment of troops and the captain and the officers of the Jews arrested Jesus and bound Him." (John 18:12)*** This is what we call a lot of drama! There was no need for such a scene to take place, yet all things were just as God ordained them to be. Even though Jesus was arrested, you could not chain the gospel message that He brought and came to fulfill. Paul later wrote of this in his letter to Timothy, ***"Remember that Jesus Christ, of the seed of David, was raised from the dead according to my gospel, for which I suffer trouble as an evildoer, even to the point of chains; but the word of God is not chained." (2 Tim. 2:8,9)*** In their efforts to try and quench the work of God, they were unleashing its power to free and to save.

Prayer: Lord, thank You for Your obedience.

Everyone Who Is Of The Truth Hears My Voice

"You say rightly that I am a king. For this cause I was born, and for this cause I have come into the world, that I should bear witness to the truth. Everyone who is of the truth hears My voice."
John 18:37b

Read John Chapter 18:25-40

Yes it's true! We must have open ears and an open heart to bear witness to His truth. Although Pilate found no fault with Jesus, he failed to bear witness to the truth. It's not enough to just believe in the "idea" of Jesus; we must carefully consider the truth behind His coming. We know from previous chapters that Jesus said, *"I am the way, the truth, and the life. No one comes to the Father except through Me." (John 14: 6)* We don't come to the Father by just saying we believe, we must go a step further and bear witness of His truth.

The other day, we met a young man that was born to a family that practices Buddhism. In asking him about his beliefs, he really did not have a whole lot of passion or purpose in them. It was just a philosophy, something to say that he was, because that's all he knew. We had an opportunity to share the gospel message about Jesus, and at the end of our conversation he said, "I believe in reincarnation and if I live a good life, I will come back and live another." We shared with him about eternal life. He asked, "What is eternal life?" The door was open for us to proclaim the truth. In time, we pray that he will know and bear witness to the truth.

Prayer: Father, please give us even more boldness to share the truth.

God Is In Control

"Jesus answered, You could have no power at all against Me unless it had been given you from above. Therefore the one who delivered Me to you has the greater sin.'"

John 19:11

Read John Chapter 19:1-16

In an effort to avoid responsibility for Jesus, Caiaphas passes the buck to Pilate. Pilate finds no fault in Jesus, but hopes to see Him do a miracle. A miracle is what He was about to do--that is, lay His life down willingly. God is in control! No man has control over the destiny of the Son of God. This is inspiring and comforting to us, because it is a reminder that our lives are under God's control and no one elses. Living for the Lord means understanding that <u>all</u> things rest in His hands. Our eternal security, our days, and times are all in His sovereign care.

Jesus could have called upon a troop of angels to deliver Him from the shame and affliction of the cross. Nevertheless, He was completely in control, despite the unusual circumstances that surrounded Him. He knew the hour had come and that all things were working for the purpose of His coming. What type of Pilates are there in your life today? Do you realize that as a child of God, you can have confidence that He orders your steps and even uses difficult people to accomplish His purposes? The sovereignty of God over man's ways is beyond our human comprehension.

Prayer: Father, thank You that You control all things in our lives.

His Final Hour

"So when Jesus had received the sour wine, He said, 'It is finished!'
And bowing His head, He gave up His spirit."
John 19:30

Read John Chapter 19:17-42

The hour of His completion had come. Jesus did everything that Scripture testified He would do. In His death, He fulfilled every prophecy and every promise ever made about Him. The incredible thing is that He did it willingly. In one moment, on a dark afternoon before Passover, the gospel message of Jesus Christ, the Savior of the world, was completed. There would no longer be a need for the sacrifice of animals for the remission of sin. Jesus paid the price in full with His precious blood.

He would soon be glorified with His Father God. Jesus would be restored to that place He had known from the beginning. The word "freedom" took on a new meaning that afternoon. For as we will see in the coming chapters, through His death and in His resurrection, He brought a new found freedom. This freedom would deliver man from the burden of guilt and sin. *"For God so loved the world that He gave His only begotten Son, that whoever believes in Him should not perish but have everlasting life." (John 3:16)*

Prayer: Father, thank You for providing all we need through Jesus, Your Son.

The Empty Tomb

"Now the first day of the week Mary Magdalene went to the tomb early,
while it was still dark, and saw that the stone had been taken away from the tomb."
John 20:1

Read John Chapter 20:1-10

Mary Magdalene had a passion for Jesus! He had delivered her from demons and took her broken and tattered life and gave it new meaning. She was the last one at the cross when Jesus was crucified and the first one at His tomb. The problem was that the tomb was empty. The linen burial cloths were still on the ground as though someone had stolen His body. This appeared to be a problem, but it really had a powerful purpose. He had risen from the grave, just as He said He would.

The empty tomb means that we can be confident that He is who He says He is, and because of that, He continues to live. The empty tomb confirmed to Mary and His disciples the words that Jesus spoke about His death and His resurrection. Jesus, while He was on earth, delivered people from the bondage of sin. And in His resurrection He still delivers sinners from the bondage of sin.

Prayer: Thank You Father, for the empty tomb.

His Voice

"Jesus said to her, 'Mary!'
She turned and said to Him, 'Rabboni!' (which is to say, Teacher)."
John 20:16

Read John Chapter 20:11-31

*I*magine how incredible this moment must have been. Mary finds herself bereaved and broken because she had just been at the tomb, and Jesus was not there. She had been weeping, because for a few moments melancholy and discouragement overtook her. Then she heard His voice! In that one moment when He spoke, all hope was restored to Mary's heart. She began to cling to Him as if never wanting to let Him go.

What a comfort the voice of the Lord is! For in it, all is well with our souls. His voice is with us today; He still speaks to His people. His voice is heard through His Word. His voice is heard through our pastors and teachers. His voice is heard through the body of Christ. Yes, He is risen and risen indeed. Are you hearing His voice today? If not, spend some time alone with Him, confess your faults and your need to hear Him. He wont' let you down.

Prayer: Thank You, Lord, for the reminder and reassuring presence of Your voice.

He Showed Himself

"After these things Jesus showed Himself again to the disciples at the Sea of Tiberias, and in this way He showed Himself:"
John 21:1

Read John Chapter 21:1-14

After His resurrection, Jesus took the opportunity to show Himself to His disciples. Not only did He show Himself to them, but He even provided breakfast. What a moment this must have been! This is one of my most favorite stories in the New Testament. Years ago, at a Women's Retreat, I gave a message on this text. Little did I know just how powerful this message would be in my own life, even to this day.

In my preparations for the message, my daughter Corrie who was 14 at the time, shared with me her discouragement about not being asked to baby-sit for anyone. All of her friends were getting baby-sitting jobs, and why had God forgotten her? I grabbed her hand and prayed that God would provide her with a job and that He would show Himself to her. Not five minutes later, the phone rang with a request for her to baby-sit. This was a powerful faith-builder in her life and mine. What are you in need of today? Don't hesitate to call upon God, because He knows your needs and knows how to show Himself to you.

Prayer: Lord, thank You for showing Yourself.

_____

_____

_____

_____

_____

_____

_____

_____

_____

_____

He Did So Much More

"And there are also many other things that Jesus did,
which if they were written one by one, I suppose that even the world itself
could not contain the books that would be written."
John 21:25

Read John Chapter 21:15-25

At the end of the gospel according to John, the writer concludes there is so much more that Jesus did that goes unrecorded. Like the writings placed upon John's heart, Jesus is writing a testimony on each one of our hearts. He continues to move in the midst of those hearts that are set on Him, those hearts that abide in Him. We have learned so much through this gospel, and forever our hearts will be grateful.

The personal relationship that Jesus extends to believers is amazing. He extends an invitation to come and see, to come and know, to come and experience. We must RSVP, we must respond. There is urgency in His call. Don't forget; respond while you have time. Come and receive all that He is, because all that He is, is all that we need. He did so much and will do so much more, if only we will believe.

Prayer: Thank You for Your mighty works through Your Son, Jesus Christ, our Savior.

The Promise Of The Holy Spirit

"And being assembled together with them, He commanded them not to depart from Jerusalem, but to wait for the Promise of the Father, 'which,' He said, 'you have heard from Me; for John truly baptized with water, but you shall be baptized with the Holy Spirit not many days from now.'"
Acts 1:4,5

Read Acts Chapter 1:1-5

What a wonderful promise this is! The promise of the power of the Holy Spirit was given. God would not leave us as orphans but would unite us by His Spirit. The word "baptism" means to immerse or to dip. The body of Christ is put in spiritual union with one another as God immerses us with power from the Holy Spirit. There is far too much confusion today over the Holy Spirit. The confusion comes when we don't rely on the promises of Scripture.

It is completely impossible to live a fruitful and abundant life without the power of the Holy Spirit. Oh, how we need it! The promise of this power brings a confident hope that Jesus will equip us for all and everything we need to be witnesses for Him.

Prayer: Thank You for this awesome and precious promise.

_____
_____
_____
_____
_____
_____
_____
_____
_____
_____
_____
_____

Witness For Jesus

*"But you shall receive power when the Holy Spirit has come upon you;
and you shall be witnesses to Me in Jerusalem, and in all Judea and
Samaria, and to the end of the earth."*
Acts 1:8

Read Acts Chapter 1:6-26

The disciples were concerned about when Christ would return again; however, it was really the gospel they needed to be concerned about. They would receive power from the Holy Spirit to be witnesses for Him. To this very day, we glean from the testimony of the early disciples of Jesus Christ. They were obedient in sharing the gospel because the Holy Spirit had empowered them to do it, even in the face of extreme opposition. Most of the apostles gave up their lives for their faith in Jesus Christ so that we today would have the gospel message. Their obedience spread the gospel to the ends of the earth.

What kind of a witness are you for Christ today? Do you lack the power to share your faith? Take some time and ask God to empower you with His Spirit to be a witness for Him, a living testimony of Jesus Christ.

Prayer: Thank You for the power of the Holy Spirit.

Filled With The Holy Spirit

"And they were all filled with the Holy Spirit and began to speak with other tongues, as the Spirit gave them utterance."
Acts 2:4

Read Acts Chapter 2:1-13

What an afternoon this must have been! People from all over the known world were in Jerusalem. Many witnessed the evidence of God's Spirit moving upon the believers. Each person heard tongues in their own language. This was an act from heaven. They were speaking praises to God. This was an incredible thing; some were perplexed saying how can this be? Others were mocking, thinking they were filled with new wine. Whatever the case, this was a monumental moment. The church was filled with supernatural power from the Holy Spirit.

Without power from the Holy Spirit, there would be no thriving church. It was the indwelling of the Holy Spirit that gave the early Christians the power to live a productive and fruitful life. This is still the case today. If we did not have the indwelling of the Holy Spirit within us, we would lack the spiritual fortitude to live the Christian life. How thankful we are for the work of the Holy Spirit in our lives. We should not fear the Holy Spirit, but embrace Him. We need all God's resources to represent Him.

Prayer: Thank You for the gift of Your Holy Spirit.

_____
_____
_____
_____
_____
_____
_____
_____
_____

Peter's Sermon

"Then those who gladly received his word were baptized;
and that day about three thousand souls were added to them."
Acts 2:41

Read Acts Chapter 2:14-39

On that day, the anointing of the Holy Spirit was so powerful that Peter gave his first sermon. This man who had failed Jesus and always seemed to say the wrong things, at the wrong time, gave the most awesome message. The result of his message was about three thousand saved souls. What an altar call that must have been! The amazing thing about the Holy Spirit and Peter's message is that it continues to this day. Salvation is available to all who will believe.

The church was established through the death of Jesus Christ and grows daily as people respond to the simple but powerful message of the gospel. What an awesome thing it is to be included in the number who believe!

Prayer: Thank You Lord for salvation and for the anointing You put on preachers to preach.

A Church Is Born

*"And they continued steadfastly in the apostles' doctrine and fellowship,
in the breaking of bread, and in prayers."*
Acts 2:42

Read Acts Chapter 2:40-47

The result of Peter's sermon brought the establishment of the early church. The Lord was orchestrating the fellowship of believers. What a beautiful time it must have been. All of these new found believers sought to be together in fellowship. They would travel to one another's homes, where they would fellowship around the Lord Jesus Christ. They would break bread (probably communion) as well as feast together, a practice that has remained to this day in the church.

Recently we heard a woman say, "I wonder what the Lord would think of the church today?" Hopefully He would be pleased with the ones who have remained true to their calling. It's a shame to say that so many churches have departed from the truth. They have capitulated and sought to be seeker-friendly. The church has a job, and it's not to water down the gospel or try to become seeker sensitive. The church is the result of the death and resurrection of Jesus Christ; we who believe have a responsibility to stay true to its purpose.

Prayer: Father, help us to stay true to You and to Your church, the body of Christ.

Beautiful Healing At The Gate Beautiful

"And a certain man lame from his mother's womb was carried,
whom they laid daily at the gate of the temple which is called Beautiful,
to ask alms from those who entered the temple;"
Acts 3:2

Read Acts Chapter 3:1-10

What a day this must have been for the lame man! He got up as usual and was taken to the beautiful gate at the temple, where once again he was laid in front of the gate. His disability would draw the attention of the passersby in hopes of a handout. No doubt his donations were going well, because people were going in and out of worship. His disability moved the people to either compassion or guilt, so they gave to his need.

Peter and John, who had just recently experienced baptism of the Holy Spirit, were filled with faith and fire. *"Then Peter said, 'Silver and gold I do not have, but what I do have I give you: In the name of Jesus Christ of Nazareth, rise up and walk.'" (Acts 3:6)* One can only imagine the moment. This man who was expecting a few coins, received healing, supernatural healing from the Lord Jesus Christ. For the first time, this man was able to walk into the temple; and he did, walking and leaping and praising God. What a testimony to all around and what an encouragement to Peter and John! What a beautiful healing at a beautiful gate!

Prayer: Lord, thank You for Your healing power.

Times Of Refreshing

"Repent therefore and be converted, that your sins may be blotted out,
so that times of refreshing may come from the presence of the Lord,"
Acts 3:19

Read Acts Chapter 3:11-26

After the lame man was healed, the people were amazed and came to Peter and John. Peter takes the opportunity to share Christ with them. Peter's message was filled with both reproof and love. He reminds the people that even though they were sinners, there was hope if they would repent and turn their hearts towards Jesus.

Christians today need to become more acquainted with the word "repentance." We too often get comfortable with our lives and don't heed God's Word to repent. We wonder why we feel so stressed and we become calloused in our hearts. We have found that a calloused heart leads to a critical spirit. A critical spirit will suffocate love in our lives and separate us from God. Peter's call for repentance is a call for refreshment. Instead of calloused and critical hearts, we will have compassionate and caring hearts. This is what will speak both God's love and healing to others. How refreshing that is!

Prayer: Father, keep our hearts pure and clean, continually flowing with refreshment.

Salvation Comes Through Jesus Christ Only

"Nor is there salvation in any other, for there is no other name
under heaven given among men by which we must be saved."
Acts 4:12

Read Acts Chapter 4:1-12

Salvation comes only through Jesus Christ! There is only one way to the Father and that is through Jesus Christ. The very mention of the name of Jesus causes people to feel UNcomfortable. Why? Because there is power and conviction in His name. The apostles, being filled with the Holy Spirit, could not stop speaking about salvation through Jesus Christ. What an awesome testimony we carry with us as believers.

There is no other religion or faith in the world that brings with it the message of hope that we have through Jesus Christ. No other religion or faith offers a personal one-on-one relationship with the true and living God. No other religion or faith has ever had its leader die for their sins and rise again. This is what separates the Christian faith from any other, and that is why we can say with boldness that there is no other name except Jesus, whereby man can obtain salvation.

No other name brings such hope
No other name brings such life
No other name will salvation come
But through God's Son, Jesus Christ.
TLR

Prayer: Father, thank You for the gift of salvation.

It's All About Jesus

"Now when they saw the boldness of Peter and John,
and perceived that they were uneducated and untrained men,
they marveled. And they realized that they had been with Jesus."
Acts 4:13

Read Acts Chapter 4:13-25

Peter and John were being interrogated, because God's power was being displayed and miracles were happening. The anointing on Peter and John came from the empowerment of the Holy Spirit. When the power of the Holy Spirit is upon our lives, we take on the character of Jesus. Peter and John were fisherman with no education; there was nothing notable about these men, other than they had been with Jesus. Being with Jesus and being filled by His Spirit is evidence of God's power that cannot be denied by men.

Imagine if we were arrested for our faith in Jesus, and the only evidence they had against us was that we had been with Him. Would there be enough evidence to convict us? Let's pray so. It's all about Jesus, even the mention of His name brings conviction. *"Therefore God also has highly exalted Him and given Him the name which is above every name, that at the name of Jesus every knee should bow, of those in heaven, and of those on earth, and of those under the earth." (Phil. 2:9,10)*

Prayer: Father, help us to remember that it's all about Jesus.

144

All Things In Common

"Now the multitude of those who believed were of one heart and one soul;
neither did anyone say that any of the things he possessed was his own,
but they had all things in common."
Acts 4:32

Read Acts Chapter 4:26-52

$\mathcal{T}$he early church was so filled with God's love and had a unique oneness. They were united in Christ by His Holy Spirit. Everything they owned personally was commonly shared. Imagine what a testimony this was! We are selfish by nature, and even a young child learns early to say the word "mine." It takes a supernatural touch by God to realize that all we have has been given to us by God. It's been our observation over the years that when God touches someone, they want to give back to Him.

We can take a lesson from the early church; we all could be a little more of one heart and one soul. After all, we are of one body; we are all God's children. It makes so much sense that if we have in our own possession something that another family member really needs, we should be willing to share.

Prayer: Lord, help our hearts to remain open to those who really have needs.

_____
_____
_____
_____
_____
_____
_____
_____
_____
_____
_____

145

Serving Yourself

*"And he kept back part of the proceeds, his wife also being aware of it,
and brought a certain part and laid it at the apostles' feet."*
Acts 5:2

Read Acts Chapter 5:1-21

We learned in our previous chapter that everyone had everything in common; they shared. Everyone who had land sold it and gave it to the apostles for the needs of all. Ananais and Sapphira had just sold their land and had only given a portion to the church. They kept back a portion for themselves, because of greed. Satan had filled their hearts with selfishness, and this prompted them to lie to the Holy Spirit. God was not requiring them to give all; it was always their choice. The trouble came when they decided to be deceptive in their giving. Because of their lies, both Ananais and his wife Sapphira breathed their last breath. Imagine the fear that fell upon the church. *"So great fear came upon all the church and upon all who heard these things." (Acts 5:11)*

Imagine the purification that went forth within the church. This may seem harsh, but God is holy and He was establishing the church. It was important that everyone understood His holiness. *"For God chastens us for our profit, that we may be partakers of His holiness." (Heb. 12:10)*

Prayer: Father, thank You for Your correction.

If It's Of God

"...but if it is of God, you cannot overthrow it -- lest you even be found to fight against God."
Acts 5:39

Read Acts Chapter 5:22-42

Gamaliel, a brilliant spiritual leader and a Pharisee, stands up and speaks up regarding the apostles and their preaching. He reminds the Jewish leaders that there had been many who had come with different doctrines, but they did not last. Gamaliel's words were used to spare the lives of the apostles, at least for a time. No one could stop the work of God. Gamaliel was certain that the apostles and their gospel of Jesus Christ would go the way of others. He believed that their work would soon die off and be forgotten.

The church always grows in the face of opposition and persecution. It's amazing the strength that God gives His people to endure in times of testing. There is no prison, no threat of man or leader that can stop the work of the gospel. Praise be to God who never allows man to overthrow His will. This encourages us in our personal and public lives knowing that God is in complete control. *"What then shall we say to these things? If God is for us, who can be against us?" (Rom. 8:31)*

Prayer: Father, thank You that nothing can ever stop the gospel message of Your Son, Jesus Christ.

_____

_____

_____

_____

_____

_____

_____

_____

_____

_____

Problems & Priorities

"Then the twelve summoned the multitude of the disciples and said,
'It is not desirable that we should leave the word of God and serve tables.'"
Acts 6:2

Read Acts Chapter 6:1,2

With growth comes problems! The early church had grown beyond what the apostles could handle by themselves. The widows were being neglected in the daily distribution of needs. What wisdom the apostles had. They knew they had problems that needed to be addressed, but they also had priorities. So they called a meeting to encourage leadership among the godly. This is where we get the concept of elders and deacons.

So often, the members in a church judge the pastor for not being able to meet every human need that arises. The most important calling for a shepherd is to feed the sheep. Jesus, when He appeared to the disciples on the sea, admonished Peter, **"Feed My sheep." (John 21:17b)** All pastors should have a servant's heart and be willing to minister to the practical needs of the body. They must do this without compromising their call to equip the body. If a pastor has done his work well, he will have raised up godly leadership to come alongside and help. This turns the problem into a solution.

Prayer: How thankful we are for the countless servants we have known over the years who have assisted in servicing the body of Christ.

_____
_____
_____
_____
_____
_____
_____
_____
_____

Full Of Faith

*"And the saying pleased the whole multitude. And they chose Stephen,
a man full of faith and the Holy Spirit, and Philip, Prochorus, Nicanor,
Timon, Parmenas, and Nicolas, a proselyte from Antioch."*
Acts 6:5

Read Acts Chapter 6:3-7

And so the first deacons of the church were chosen. It was necessary for these men to be full of faith and the Holy Spirit. Why? One cannot do the work of the ministry without the ingredients of faith and the Holy Spirit. The countless attacks and pressures that come against God's servants cannot be dealt with in the realm of the flesh. You must have power from on high.

It would not be long before these godly men would be persecuted for their faith. Stephen, especially in this chapter, faces opposition from the lies of the enemy. There were false witnesses brought to testify against Stephen. But Stephen, full of faith and the Holy Spirit, shined in the face of such opposition. *"And all who sat in the council, looking steadfastly at him, saw his face as the face of an angel." (Acts 6:15)* Even in opposition and persecution, Jesus shines bright in the lives of believers.

Prayer: Father, let our lives shine bright for You through Your power.

_____
_____
_____
_____
_____
_____
_____
_____
_____
_____

False Witnesses

"Then they secretly induced men to say, 'We have heard him speak blasphemous words against Moses and God.'"
Acts 6:11

Read Acts Chapter 6:8-15

The enemy is a counterfeit, always trying to take the place of first position. Stephen was not a deceiver, but the council of Jewish leaders were deceived. They were lost in a religious organization. They valued their legalistic laws above even God, to the point that they did not follow their own laws. *"You shall not bear false witness..." (Ex. 20:16)* It's amazing that the very thing they wanted to preserve, they perverted with lies.

Many will come against the work of God, but not one will succeed. Even though it appears in this chapter that the Jewish religious leaders had an overwhelming advantage, the church still continued to grow and to stand. Jesus said it best when He established the church, *"I will build My church, and the gates of Hades shall not prevail against it." (Matt. 16:18b)* Stephen was not in fear for His life. He was pleased to be an ambassador for Christ, even if he was being falsely accused. This reminds us of a saying that we often quote: *"We shine the brightest when we stoop the lowest."* Stephen's ability to shine was proof that he was stooping before His Lord with total dependency.

Prayer: Father, thank You for examples from Your Word, like Stephen.

Resisting The Holy Spirit

"You stiff-necked and uncircumcised in heart and ears!
You always resist the Holy Spirit; as your fathers did, so do you."
Acts 7:51

Read Acts Chapter 7

After Stephen's interrogation and defense of his faith, he addresses the high priest and gives him a history lesson. The lesson included countless reminders of how Israel rebelled against God and resisted His Spirit. Now they were resisting His Son, Jesus Christ. The testimony of the early church was a testimony of truth, and it wracked the minds and hearts of the Jewish leaders to the point of envy, lies, and murder.

There is danger in resisting the person and the power of the Holy Spirit. The danger is a hardened heart. As believers, we too can fall prey to a hardened heart. We need to be careful and cautious of what we allow into our lives; so many things can stifle the work of the Spirit and separate us from God. *"Today, if you will hear His voice, do not harden your hearts as in the rebellion." (Heb.3:15)* There is absolutely nothing more painful then being separated from God. He is always ready to receive His children back into His arms, but there must be a turning away from sin. The rebellion of the high priest and religious council towards God and His Spirit caused them to harden their hearts and close their ears. Their stubbornness would not allow them to receive the beauty of the testimony of Christ; to them it was a stumbling block .

Prayer: Father, forgive us for the times we have faltered in our faith.

_____
_____
_____
_____
_____
_____
_____
_____

Lost Saul--Lost Soul

"As for Saul, he made havoc of the church, entering every house,
and dragging off men and women, committing them to prison."
Acts 8:3

Read Acts Chapter 8:1-25

$\mathcal{H}$ere we see how one man with such a wretched heart sought to persecute the church of Jesus Christ. Saul persecuted the church with passion. He sent believers, both men and women, to prison for their faith in Jesus. Saul was like a wild boar; his intentions were to destroy the body of Christ. In fact, Saul ordered the death of Christians.

Saul was lost in his religion--he truly believed that what he was doing was right, so he did it with conviction. Saul was a lost soul. However, the very thing he fought so hard against was the very thing that would eventually shed light upon his dark and lost soul. So many folks are blinded to the truth because they are lost in a lie. We should pray that God lifts the blinders off their eyes and reveals to them His heart. This can happen, and we will see in coming chapters how God lifts the blinders from Saul's eyes.

Prayer: Father, please forgive us for the times when we failed You because we did not see the truth.

Simple Message, Saving Power

"And he answered and said, 'I believe that Jesus Christ is the Son of God.'"
Acts 8:37b

Read Acts Chapter 8:26-40

*I*f we knew how ready some hearts are to receive the message of the gospel, we would share our faith more. God clearly set up this divine appointment with Philip and the eunuch. God generally prepares a heart by the work of the Holy Spirit to receive Him; we just need to be obedient to the daily opportunities He brings our way.

The eunuch was ready and waiting. God had prepared his heart, and he just needed someone to come alongside to confirm and guide him in the direction he should go. Philip gives him the simple gospel message. *"He simply preached Jesus to him." (vs. 35)* The simple message of Jesus Christ has the power to save souls. As believers in Jesus, we need to ask God to give us His passion for souls. We have a trust fund that we carry with us as Christians; it's a trust fund that is supposed to be shared with others. God calls all of us to do the work of an evangelist, and we can do it in the most natural of settings. Workplace, family functions, soccer fields, grocery stores--just about every setting brings with it opportunities to preach the simple message of Jesus Christ.

Prayer: Father, as we represent You in the marketplace, help us to be "aware to share."

Questions From Jesus

"Saul, Saul, why are you persecuting Me?"
Acts 9:4b

Read Acts Chapter 9:1-19

As we saw in previous chapters, Saul continued his zealous attacks upon the body of Christ, being more fervent than ever before. But God put a stop to Saul's persecution with a bright light from Heaven. The light was so bright that he was blinded by it. Jesus then revealed to Saul that his attacks against the church were indeed attacks against God Himself! *"I am Jesus, whom you are persecuting." (vs. 5)* Saul's only response was, *"Lord, what do you want me to do?" (vs. 6)* Saul thought he was doing the right thing by suppressing the Christian movement. But, in one moment, Saul was corrected and converted.

Saul was blinded following the incident with Jesus, *"When his eyes were opened he saw no one." (vs. 8)* God allowed Saul to be blind in order that he might see. Sometimes we have to lose our worldly sight so that we might be able to see what God has for us. This reminds us of the words of Jesus. *"Whoever loses his life will preserve it."* (*Luke 17:33b*) Saul lost his life on the road to Damascus, but he gained his life with Jesus. He would be the recipient of a new heart and a new name.

Prayer: Thank You Lord for the beauty of conversion.

_____
_____
_____
_____
_____
_____
_____
_____

The Church Flourishes

"Then the churches throughout all Judea, Galilee, and Samaria had peace and were edified. And walking in the fear of the Lord and in the comfort of the Holy Spirit, they were multiplied."
Acts 9:31

Read Acts Chapter 9:20-43

Saul's conversion was not received that well in the beginning, after all, he had wreaked havoc throughout the church. The body of Christ was very fearful of him. It took the wisdom and comfort of the Holy Spirit and the elders of the church to calm their concerns. We don't always understand what God is doing, and so we question Him. The important thing is that in our questions, we are also truly seeking answers. God is always faithful to reveal His heart and when we listen, we find peace in the midst of our questions.

After the calm came peace and growth in the church. Isn't that the way it usually is! The trials come and the tribulations challenge our faith. The early church faced incredible opposition and through it they learned the art of counting it a joy to suffer for their faith in Jesus Christ. *"My brethren, count it all joy when you fall into various trials, knowing that the testing of your faith produces patience."* *(James 1:2)* So then, in their suffering they found peace.

Prayer: Father, help us to reflect joy in the midst of turbulent times.

_____

_____

_____

_____

_____

_____

_____

_____

_____

155

God's Universal Heart

"What God has cleansed you must not call common."
Acts 10:15b

Read Acts Chapter 10:1-23

*T*he love of Jesus Christ had been revealed first to the Jews, and many Jews believed and received Him as their Messiah. Now it was time for God to share the Gospel's power and wealth with the Gentiles. God's heart is a universal heart that extends to the entire world. The message of the cross was for all people, of all nations. God loves all, and desires to have a personal and intimate relationship with them.

It took a vision in which an angel spoke to Cornelius--and a vision to Peter, to bring both Jews and Gentiles together. This was an incredible occurrence, because we must be aware that from birth, Jewish people had been taught that Gentiles were unclean. God provides equal opportunity and He reveals this through His Son Jesus Christ. *"For God so loved the world that He gave His only begotten Son, that whoever believes in Him should not perish but have everlasting life." (John 3:16)* We are thankful that God has a universal heart.

Prayer: Father, thank You for Your heart for the world.

_____
_____
_____
_____
_____
_____
_____
_____
_____
_____

United By Faith

"...because the gift of the Holy Spirit had been poured out on the Gentiles also."
Acts 10:45b

Read Acts Chapter 10:24-48

The gospel message came first to the Jews, then to the Samaritans, and then to the Gentiles. They were united in their faith by the Holy Spirit. This is still the case today; believers throughout the entire world, with completely different ethnic backgrounds and languages, are united by their faith in Jesus Christ through the power of the Holy Spirit. *"Jesus Christ is the same yesterday, today, and forever." (Heb.13:8)* He extends the invitation to believe and invites all to be a part of the body of Christ.

When we have the opportunity to travel on mission's trips or even on vacations, we are always amazed to meet other believers and have immediate fellowship. Our faith in Jesus Christ is what brings us together and it's His Spirit that binds us in fellowship. The more mature we become in our relationship with Jesus, the more aware we are of the uniqueness of our position as children of God. *"There is neither Jew nor Greek, there is neither slave nor free, there is neither male nor female; for you are all one in Christ Jesus." (Gal. 3:28)*

Prayer: Thank You Lord for Your love for all mankind.

_____

_____

_____

_____

_____

_____

_____

_____

_____

_____

The Mission Field

"When they heard these things they became silent; and they glorified God,
saying, 'Then God has also granted to the Gentiles repentance to life.'"
Acts 11:18

Read Acts Chapter 11:1-18

When Jesus gave what we know as the "Great Commission," we are not sure the disciples really understood the concept of going into *"all the world." (Mark 16:15)* From birth, the Israelites were taught not to have fellowship with Samaritans or Gentiles. However, the compassion of our Lord extends to all people. The fruit of the Holy Spirit was evident in the lives of the disciples as they assessed what God was doing; they could not deny the fruit in their lives was from Him, so they acknowledged it.

The mission field was wide open and the gospel message was being sent forth with power. Do you realize that we are called to the mission field? Yes, and it can be in the most natural of settings. The supermarket, the bank, the nail shop, the doctors office--we are all called to take with us the precious gospel message. We need to ask God to give us a passion for souls and be ready to speak love to a lost and dying world.

Prayer: Father, please forgive us for the times we have been unwilling to share Your gospel.

_____

_____

_____

_____

_____

_____

_____

_____

_____

_____

_____

Brotherly Benevolence

*"Then the disciples, each according to his ability,
determined to send relief to the brethren dwelling in Judea."*
Acts 11:29

Read Acts Chapter 11:19-30

$\mathcal{I}$n the churches throughout Judea, there was a crisis, a financial need for the staples of life, and so the newly converted Gentile believers responded. This is the hallmark of the church--to respond to needs with action. One of the fruits we see in the body of Christ in our fellowship is response, looking out for the needs of others. Just yesterday, someone came into our church office and brought in an anonymous gift for a family that had been out of work for some time. What a blessing it was to see the family receive this gift! It was as if God was "snuggling" them, reminding them that He loved them.

In a world that seems to look out for its own needs, it is refreshing to know that through Jesus Christ we can show love through random acts of kindness. The language of love is understood universally through giving. Is there someone in your life today that might be blessed by a gift of some sort? Is there someone in need that you can help? Brotherly benevolence is commanded in Scripture by our Lord. *"Let brotherly love continue." (Heb. 13:1)* God always repays those who help others in need.

Prayer: Father, please help us to identify those in need that You want us to help.

_____
_____
_____
_____
_____
_____
_____
_____
_____

Herod Persecutes The Church

"Now about that time Herod the king
stretched out his hand to harass some from the church."
Acts 12:1

Read Acts Chapter 12:1-19

$\mathcal{H}$erod had an evil heart and he sought to harass the church. He was successful in killing James, the brother of John, with a sword. This was not a surprise to James for he had been told by Jesus Himself that He would drink from the cup of sacrifice. *"You will indeed drink My cup,..." (Matt. 20: 23a)* James is the only apostle whose death is recorded in the New Testament.

We need to remember that God is always watching and taking notes of those who come against His kids. *"Vengeance is Mine, and recompense; their foot shall slip in due time; for the day of their calamity is at hand, and the things to come hasten upon them." (Deut. 32:35)* We will see in coming chapters that Herod will reap the reward of his wrath. The Lord is indeed watching.

Prayer: Father, help Your children to trust You in times of testing.

_____

_____

_____

_____

_____

_____

_____

_____

_____

_____

_____

Slip Up

"Then immediately an angel of the Lord struck him, because he did not give glory to God. And he was eaten by worms and died."
Acts 12:23

Read Acts Chapter 12:20-24

A s we learned in our previous devotion, *"their foot shall slip in due time." (Deut. 32:35b)* Herod slipped up alright! So much so that for a moment, he sought to take away the glory from God. The result was death and an ugly one at that. Taking glory from God is one of the most foolish things a person can do. Our very breath comes from the hand of God--anything that we are or have is given to us by Him.

So many things have happened in this one chapter. Peter is released from prison by the hand of God, reminding us that the gospel cannot be chained. Herod persecutes and then receives back what he dished out. The book of Acts, thus far, is an adventurous one. The incredible thing that stands out is that through all of these events, the church grew! *"But the word of God grew and multiplied." (Acts 12:24)*

Prayer: Father, how we thank You that You are in complete control.

_____
_____
_____
_____
_____
_____
_____
_____
_____
_____

Everyone Who Believes

"and by Him everyone who believes is justified from all things from which you could not be justified by the law of Moses."
Acts 13:39

Read Acts Chapter 13:1-41

The word "justified" is a legal term used when one is brought to justice and proclaimed innocent of a crime. Jesus Christ, our great defender, brings justification to all those who believe in Him. We were guilty and deserved punishment for our sins. He took it upon Himself to be the full payment for our sins.

When we were new believers, we were told that the word "justified" meant *"just as if I had never sinned."* That is how God views those who believe and follow after His Son, Jesus Christ. At Antioch, Paul clearly gives an incredible message of hope. To "everyone who believes"--a simple but powerful message.

To everyone who believes
The keys of the kingdom are given
To everyone who believes in Jesus
They are given freedom
To everyone who believes
There is justification
To everyone who believes
Not guilty, but forgiven
TLR

Prayer: Lord, thank You for justification through Jesus and the opportunity to believe.

_____
_____
_____
_____
_____
_____

Sometimes, You Just Need To Move On

"But they shook off the dust from their feet against them, and came to Iconium.
And the disciples were filled with joy and with the Holy Spirit."
Acts 13:51,52

Read Acts Chapter 13:42-52

The gospel message was rejected by the Jews at Antioch. Persecution rose up against Paul and Barnabas, so they shook the dust from their feet and moved on. Sometimes we need to shake off the dust from our feet and move on too. For a number of personal reasons, folks often reject the gospel message. We need to be open to the Holy Spirit's leading as we evangelize and not take it personally when they reject Christ. Jesus addresses this issue in Luke, *"He who rejects you rejects Me, and he who rejects Me rejects Him who sent Me." (Luke 10:16b)*

It is liberating to know that as we share our faith in Christ, the gospel will go out and accomplish its purpose. We learned long ago that some will respond, while others will reject the gospel. Trying to press the issue of salvation to an unresponsive heart is very much like trying to give pearls to swine. *"Do not give what is holy to the dogs; nor cast your pearls before swine, lest they trample them under their feet, and turn and tear you in pieces." (Matt. 7:6)*

Prayer: Father, help us to have discernment when sharing our faith.

_____
_____
_____
_____
_____
_____
_____
_____
_____

To God Be The Glory

"Men, why are you doing these things?"
Acts 14:15a

Read Acts Chapter 14:1-18

*P*aul and Barnabas were grieved in their spirits because of the confusion that took place at Lystra. God had healed a lame man, and now Paul and Barnabas were mistaken for gods, to the point that the people sought to give them glory. *"The gods have come down to us in the likeness of men!" (vs.11)* Paul and Barnabas knew that all glory belonged to God and not to them.

We have always admired the Billy Graham evangelistic ministry for their integrity. Early on in the ministry, God clearly spoke to Billy Graham and his team of co-laborers. *"Keep your hands off the glory."* Their motto is "To God is the glory" and this too was the motto of Paul and Barnabas. We can take a lesson from these men. Any gifts, talents, abilities, or possessions are all made possible because of the sovereign hand of God. When we try and take credit for God's goodness, we settle for the fleeting praises of men. When we step away from the glory, God does great things.

Prayer: Lord, keep our heart humble before You.

_____
_____
_____
_____
_____
_____
_____
_____
_____
_____

Stay Awhile

"Now when they had come and gathered the church together, they reported all that God had done with them, and that He had opened the door of faith to the Gentiles. So they stayed there a long time with the disciples."
Acts 14:27,28

Read Acts Chapter 14:19-28

When you are in fellowship with God and His people, you just want to stay awhile. The fellowship is sweet and the need for exhortation is necessary. There is no doubt that Paul and Barnabas were in need of refreshment, and no doubt the church needed to be built up by their faith and experience in the Lord.

It is important as believers that we understand the necessity of fellowship. We learn later in the chapters to come, how we should not forsake fellowship. Whenever we go through a trial or tribulation, we tend to want to withdraw from people. The truth is, we need our brothers and sisters to remind us of Christ. When we are in fellowship we are always reminded why it's so important. We gain strength, wisdom, and Koinonia--intimate fellowship.

Prayer: Father, help us to draw near and not draw back in our fellowship with You and others.

Unnecessary Yokes

"Now therefore, why do you test God by putting a yoke on the neck of the disciples which neither our fathers nor we were able to bear?"
Acts 15:10

Read Acts Chapter 15:1-21

We have noticed over the years that Christians sometimes try to put unnecessary yokes on others, this may stem from their own personal convictions about matters. We too, at times, have been caught up in the moment and have fallen prey, putting others and even God in a box. In the case of the Jewish believers and the Gentiles, the yoke was a heavy one. They were trying to make it a law that Gentile believers had to be circumcised to be saved. This yoke was something that not even Jewish believers could bear.

The yoke in this matter was the law. The law was intended to convict man and show him how much he needed a Savior. When we try to put others under bondage, we quench their spirits. Paul clearly communicates this, *"For the letter kills, but the Spirit gives life." (2 Cor. 3:6b)* When we allow the Holy Spirit to do the work in others, there is freedom for both us and them.

Prayer: Father, forgive us for the times we failed You and others.

_____
_____
_____
_____
_____
_____
_____
_____
_____

Divine Differences

"Then the contention became so sharp that they parted from one another.
And so Barnabas took Mark and sailed to Cyprus;"
Acts 15:39

Read Acts Chapter 15:22-41

There are times in ministry when we don't see eye to eye with one another. There are differences in agreement, and sometimes they are divinely designed by God to bring about a new direction. These times can be painful because we don't clearly see the path that God has before us. Evidently, Paul and Barnabas had a disagreement over Mark and his departure during their first missionary journey. The lesson that stands out to us in regards to the argument, was that Paul and Barnabas kept it between each other. They did not continue in the argument; they simply parted ways and continued in the ministry where they believed God had called them.

When there are differences between ministries, we need to be careful that we are not allowing Satan to use them as an opportunity to divide the body of Christ. We should take the higher and humble road, just agree to disagree, and move on to the call God has in our life. We know from Scripture that later on in his ministry, Paul reconciled the problem in his heart and found room for Mark in the ministry. *"Only Luke is with me. Get Mark and bring him with you, for he is useful to me for ministry." (2 Tim. 4:11)*

Prayer: Father, thank You for the powerful testimonies of Your work, even through human differences.

Closed Doors, New Direction

*"After they had come to Mysia, they tried to go into Bithynia,
but the Spirit did not permit them."*
Acts 16:7

Read Acts Chapter 16:1-15

There are those times in our lives when God says "no." Paul, Silas, and Timothy were headed in a direction that they felt God was leading them, but the doors were closed. No doubt they were frustrated when they learned that they were forbidden by the Holy Spirit to minister in certain areas. However, they were mature enough in the Lord to realize that God was obviously leading them elsewhere.

Is there an "elsewhere" in your life today? Are there closed doors? Are you willing, like these servants of God, to be led in a new direction? We can't always see the "why" of our circumstances, but we do know the God of our circumstances. God sees the bigger and broader picture, while we have limited understanding of all that He is doing. In this text, the lesson that stands out to us is that these disciples were willing to be led by the Holy Spirit. They were sensitive and open to what He was doing. God was faithful to direct them in the way they should go. ***"And a vision appeared to Paul in the night. A man of Macedonia stood and pleaded with him, saying, "Come over to Macedonia and help us." (Acts 16:9)*** They had a new fervor and a new vision for what God was doing in the "elsewhere."

Prayer: Father, help us to believe You and be obedient when You want us to be elsewhere.

_____

_____

_____

_____

_____

_____

_____

Midnight Miracles

*"But at midnight Paul and Silas were praying and singing hymns to God,
and the prisoners were listening to them. Suddenly there was a great earthquake,
so that the foundations of the prison were shaken; and immediately all the
doors were opened and everyone's chains were loosed."*
Acts 16:25,26

Read Acts Chapter 16:16-40

Imagine the moment; the prison was dark, gloomy, and depressed. Then the voices of praise began to worship the Lord, and suddenly the prison became a sanctuary. The prisoners were listening and were being blessed, as was our Lord. The earthquake came and the prisoners could have vanished, but they stayed in place because they had been touched by God.

When we are in worship to our Lord, He makes even the darkest places seem bright. Sometimes we just need to praise Him and glorify His name. Do you need a miracle in your life today? If so, why not begin to offer up the sacrifice of praise. Praise will lift you out of captivity and bring freedom to your soul. That is where your miracle begins.

Prayer: Father, thank You for the reminder to praise You through these times of testings.

_____

_____

_____

_____

_____

_____

_____

_____

_____

_____

_____

Put Away The Foreign Gods

"Now while Paul waited for them at Athens, his spirit was provoked within him when he saw that the city was given over to idols."
Acts 17:16

Read Acts Chapter 17:1-21

An idol is something that we worship more than we do God. It could be a statue, an icon, a foreign god, or another person. While Paul was on his trip to Athens, he saw with his own eyes how far the people were from the living God. He was grieved at what he saw; for indeed, what he saw was a people who were dedicated to yoking themselves in fellowship with demons. Paul was grieved by the wasted potential and deception.

We might look at this text and agree with Paul's disillusionment; however, we should consider our own lives. Do we worship false gods? Is there something in our own lives that takes the place of God? How much time are we dedicating to personal pleasure as opposed to personal devotion? If we look closely at our lives, we may be surprised at how far we too can get from the living God. We need to redirect our hearts towards the one and only true God. In the Old Testament, Jacob had to do some housecleaning and heart cleaning with his own family. Rachel, Jacob's wife, lost sight of her God when she stole a foreign idol. *"And Jacob said to his household and to all who were with him, 'Put away the foreign gods that are among you, purify yourselves, and change your garments.'" (Gen. 35:2)*

Prayer: Father, help us to keep our hearts clean and pure from idol worship.

_____
_____
_____
_____
_____
_____
_____
_____

The Unknown God

"Therefore, the One in whom you worship without knowing,
Him I proclaim to you:"
Acts 17:23b

Read Acts Chapter 17:22-34

While in Athens, Paul had discovered an altar. On it was inscribed these words, "TO THE UNKNOWN GOD." How grieved Paul's heart must have been; for in seeing this, he saw just how very lost the people were. However, Paul saw this sad obstacle as an opportunity to introduce them to the KNOWN GOD. Because the people of Athens lacked biblical understanding, Paul addressed them in a fashion in which they could relate. They would now be accountable for what they learned.

This reminds us that there is a God-shaped hole in everyone's life. Whether they understand it or not, people who don't know God know that there is something more than this life offers. Folks all over the world have altars where they worship in hopes of attaining a way to find what is UNKNOWN to them. We love how Paul put feet to his faith in sharing the simple message of the gospel with the people of Athens. Even though some mocked Paul, still others believed. We need to be aware that most people do not know the living God, but He uses us to preach the gospel to make Him known to a world in which He is unknown.

Prayer: Father, thank You for the precious gift of the gospel.

Apollos & His Ministry

*"This man had been instructed in the way of the Lord; and being fervent in spirit,
he spoke and taught accurately the things of the Lord, though he knew
only the baptism of John."*
Acts 18:25

Read Acts Chapter 18

Growth is what we see in this text. We are always growing and learning, and we should not despise it. Apollos was a gifted teacher, but lacked the full knowledge of the death and resurrection of Christ and the gift of the Holy Spirit. God used a godly and wise couple, Aquila and Priscilla, to educate Apollos on the events that occurred after the baptism of John. Apollos was teachable, and this only enhanced his ministry.

Are you teachable? Or are you offended when you are corrected? When we were young, we spent many years being offended by others. This reflected a lack of growth in our own lives. We should be open to correction, especially if it concerns our ministry and the Word of God. Apollos was confident in who he loved and wanted to rightly represent Him. We too should be confident in God and His Word and realize that we don't know everything. But the Holy Spirit, our teacher, will reveal all truth to us; even if He uses another to correct us.

Prayer: Father, thank You for those times when You corrected us.

_____

_____

_____

_____

_____

_____

_____

_____

_____

_____

_____

Receive The Holy Spirit

"'Did you receive the Holy Spirit when you believed?' So they said to him,
'We have not so much as heard whether there is a Holy Spirit.'"
Acts 19:2

Read Acts Chapter 19:1-20

It is possible to believe in God and not have the gift of the Holy Spirit. As we learned in the previous chapter, even Apollos had not yet learned of the Holy Spirit. They had only heard of the baptism of John and their need to repent. It is not enough to just repent; we need power to live a victorious Christian life. This power comes from the gift of the Holy Spirit.

The Holy Spirit not only unites the body of Christ, but He is a helper and a teacher of truth. *"But the Helper, the Holy Spirit, whom the Father will send in My name, He will teach you all things."* *(John 14:26a)* Are you lacking power in your life? Do you need help? Do you need comfort? Receive the Holy Spirit, embrace Him, and He will come alongside you and empower you in the way that only He can. The Holy Spirit is the heart of God. Who wouldn't want to have all that He offers?

Prayer: Father, how we praise You for the power that comes from Your Spirit.

Hearts Of Devotion Stir Up Commotion

"So not only is this trade of ours in danger of falling into disrepute, but also the temple of the great goddess Diana may be despised and her magnificence destroyed, whom all Asia and the world worship."

Acts 19:27

Read Acts Chapter 19:21-41

    E phesus was known for their great worship of the fertility goddess Diana. Prior to hearing the gospel message of Jesus, sales of small idols of Diana had increased and there were great profits made from the worship of this false god. However, the mention of Jesus and the response to the gift of salvation were causing the idol worship market to plummet. This caused an uproar among those who made their living by making and selling these idols. The craftsmen went to the mats, so to speak, and began to persecute those who were preaching Christ.

    Today, wouldn't it be nice if we saw "idol worship" sales plummet because people were coming to Christ? Imagine what it would be like for the movie industry if people just quit buying tickets to worship the idols of Hollywood; or if secular music artists, who promote Satan worship, would see a drop in sales because people were getting saved. No doubt it would cause commotion. But think about it; all the commotion would be because people's hearts were devoted to the one and only true God.

    Prayer: Father, we thank You for salvation and how we once were blind, but now we see.

_____

_____

_____

_____

_____

_____

_____

_____

_____

None Of These Things Move Me

"And see, now I go bound in the spirit to Jerusalem, not knowing the things that will happen to me there, except that the Holy Spirit testifies in every city, saying that chains and tribulations await me. But none of these things move me; nor do I count my life dear to myself, so that I may finish my race with joy, and the ministry which I received from the Lord Jesus, to testify to the gospel of the grace of God."
Acts 20:22-24

Read Acts Chapter 20:1-24

Years ago when Terri and I took the call to come to Corona to serve the community, we were both looking for every open door and confirmation from God that affirmed He truly was directing us. A missionary friend of ours shared the above verses with us. We clung to these verses with all of our hearts. We were particularly impressed with Paul's words, ***"none of these things move me."*** Our emotions and feelings were being moved, however, we know that we walk by faith and not by feelings. There was power in these words, and comfort. As Christians, we should (like Paul) expect that trials and tribulations await us wherever we go. We should be committed to the call that He has placed on us. We should not consider our life so dear to ourselves that we never move forward in our faith.

Is God placing a call on your life today? Are you looking for Him to confirm and direct you in the way you should go? Do you want to have Paul's heart and mindset? Oh, the beauty of these verses. Ten years later, looking back on all the trials and tribulations, how thankful we are for these verses and the power they gave us to continue the ministry that God has called us to.

Prayer: Father, thank You for Your incredible Word, and its ability to move us.

_____

_____

_____

_____

_____

_____

The Blessing In Giving

"I have shown you in every way, by laboring like this, that you must support the weak. And remember the words of the Lord Jesus, that He said, 'It is more blessed to give than to receive.'"
Acts 20:35

Read Acts Chapter 20:25-38

Paul, as he was about to set sail, gives some closing thoughts to those whom he loved and served. He reminds them that his labor was a labor of love, and not to forget those who are weak. He also reminds them to remember the words of Jesus and the blessing in giving. Putting others before ourselves is not something that comes naturally. It takes the agape love of God, and Paul knew it.

We have often said, *"When we grow up, we want to be like Paul."* Those of us who have been touched by Paul's words of wisdom throughout the Scriptures might say the same thing. On the other hand, Paul would say, *"When I grow up, I want to be like Jesus."* Paul's example to the church in giving was born out of a true commitment to Jesus Christ. He could boldly exhort others to follow his example, because he followed Jesus. *"Imitate me, just as I also imitate Christ." (1 Cor. 11:1)* We need to move beyond the blessing of just receiving, so start giving. That is where the true joy comes from!

Prayer: Father, how we thank You for giving all that You had. Help us to follow Your example.

Ready To Die

"Then Paul answered, 'What do you mean by weeping and breaking my heart? For I am ready not only to be bound, but also to die at Jerusalem for the name of the Lord Jesus.'"
Acts 21:13

Read Acts Chapter 21

Paul's quick response to the challenges that laid before him, amaze us. Paul was ready! He was ready for the obstacles because he saw the opportunities. While everyone else was falling apart, Paul was in control of his emotions. In his heart, Paul was convinced of God's call on his life, and he was willing and ready to die for Jesus.

The passion Paul had for Jesus was born out of a life that was submitted to Him in absolute surrender and obedience. Are there obstacles that you face today? Are you like Paul, ready to die to your flesh and submit to Him in absolute surrender? If so, like Paul you will see your obstacles as opportunities.

Prayer: Father, light the fire of passion for You in our hearts.

Appointed By God

*"Arise and go into Damascus, and there you will be told all things
which are appointed for you to do."*
Acts 22:10b

Read Acts Chapter 22

$\mathcal{P}$aul was giving his defense. He defended his position and his faith in Christ. Paul owned up to his past by taking responsibility for the persecution he zealously put the church through. *"I persecuted this Way to the death, binding and delivering into prisons both men and women." (vs. 4)*

Paul clearly articulates his own conversion experience. He testifies of Jesus and the calling He placed on his life. Paul is commissioned by Christ to go to Damascus and await the things that He will appoint him to do. When we read this passage, we are compelled to look a little deeper at its meaning. Paul's encounter with Jesus was personal, as He dealt with Paul's sin of persecuting His church. *"Saul, Saul, why are you persecuting Me?" (vs. 7b)* Now that Jesus and Paul had settled things, it was time to move forward into a faith-filled life.

The church that Paul once persecuted would now have a new voice that would direct them into a deeper communion with Jesus. When a life is touched by Jesus, there is no end to both the potential and possibilities that God will provide. Do you ever wonder what your purpose in life is? If so, look at Paul's life and seek God, and you too can be assured that He will appoint you for service.

Prayer: Lord, for all those who need passion to serve You, please help them.

Be Of Good Cheer

"But the following night the Lord stood by him and said, 'Be of good cheer, Paul;
for as you have testified for Me in Jerusalem, so you must also bear witness at Rome.'"
Acts 23:11

Read Acts Chapter 23:1-22

*I*t must have been a dark night of the soul for Paul. He had just given his defense and now was back in the barracks waiting to see what would come of it. No doubt Paul had some concern about his future, but assuredly he looked to his Savior Jesus for comfort. Jesus showed up to minister to Paul with these powerful words, *"Be of good cheer."* How refreshing and comforting these words must have been for Paul to hear. They gave him a renewed heart and hope in the only <u>One</u> able to lift him above these difficult circumstances that permeated his world.

If you are in the midst of a dark night of the soul, first seek Jesus. Look for Him to stand by you and say those precious and powerful words, *"Be of good cheer."* It's when we are all alone and no one else sees but God, that He meets us in our black cloud of despair and turns on the lights to our souls. This is what makes Him such a unique Savior and Lord of light.

Prayer: Father, thank You for Your mighty hand and Your presence in times of great need.

No Weapon Formed Against You

"And he called for two centurions, saying, 'Prepare two hundred soldiers, seventy horsemen, and two hundred spearmen to go to Caesarea at the third hour of the night; and provide mounts to set Paul on, and bring him safely to Felix the governor.'"
Acts 23:23,24

Read Acts Chapter 23:23-35

While the Jews band together to seek the life of Paul, God was busy preparing protection for him. It was not Paul's time to die; he still had work to do, letters to write, and a journey to Rome. God made a way of escape for Paul. As children of God, we need to be aware of His sovereignty and wisdom in our lives. Paul's destination was safe in the Father's hands.

As children of God, we face all kinds of attacks and afflictions. At times, it may even appear that the enemy is gaining ground in our lives. We can be assured that nothing can happen to us that does not first pass through the throne room of God. *"No weapon formed against you shall prosper." (Is. 54:17a)*

All Around Me

All around me are things that want to harm me
All around me pain is what I see
All around me is clouded by the enemy
All around me my future looks dimly
All around me Your eyes are on me
All around me nothing shall harm me.
TLR

Prayer: Father, thank You for Your protection.

The Fellowship Of The Saints

"So he commanded the centurion to keep Paul and to let him have liberty, and told him not to forbid any of his friends to provide for or visit him."
Acts 24:23

Read Acts Chapter 24:1-23

Once again Paul is back in the barracks, only this time he has some liberties. Perhaps the greatest need, other than Jesus, that Paul had was the need for fellowship. God in His sovereignty always knows what's best. When we are down in the dumps, there are few things that are more welcome than a cup of coffee and fellowship with the saints. The mere fact that we are together in fellowship brings strength to our hearts and health to our bones.

When we are going through difficulties, there is a temptation to isolate ourselves from those who can build us up in the faith. This temptation comes from the enemy; if he can get us to isolate ourselves, he has more of an opportunity to devour us. The Lord beautifully orchestrated opportunities for fellowship in Paul's time of need. If you are going through a tough time, pick up the phone and invite someone over for fellowship. *"And let us consider one another in order to stir up love and good works, not forsaking the assembling of ourselves together, as is the manner of some, but exhorting one another, and so much the more as you see the Day approaching." (Heb. 10:24,25)*

Prayer: Lord, thank You for the wonderful gift of friendship and fellowship.

_____
_____
_____
_____
_____
_____
_____
_____

Forgotten By Man, But Known By God

*"But after two years Porcius Festus succeeded Felix;
and Felix, wanting to do the Jews a favor, left Paul bound."
Acts 24:27*

Read Acts Chapter 24:24-27

*P*aul was kept bound for a long time, and we are sure he must have wondered why? Although Paul had been forgotten by man, God was cleary orchestrating His own plan and will in Paul's life. Paul had lots of time to think, pray, and write. We still glean from Paul's writings today. Like Joseph in the Old Testament, God was working things together for the good in Paul's life.

Is there something that you are bound by today? Is something keeping you from moving forward? Be sure that all is right in your heart and soul before God. Know that even though you may feel forgotten, God is writing a testimony on your heart too. We must come to grips with the reality that pain and suffering can actually bring about good things when we yield them over to the Lord. Paul learned the deep meaning of suffering and yet through all of it, he chose the higher road. *"We are hard pressed on every side, yet not crushed; we are perplexed, but not in despair; persecuted, but not forsaken; struck down, but not destroyed." (2 Cor. 4:8,9)*

Prayer: Father, thank You for the pain. It helps us to know You more.

_____

_____

_____

_____

_____

_____

_____

_____

_____

God's Umbrella

"Let those who have authority among you go down with me
and accuse this man, to see if there is any fault in him."
Acts 25:5

Read Acts Chapter 25:1-12

It's difficult to know what to do when you find no fault in a man accused of a crime that never really happened. Paul was being punished in prison, but it was baffling to those who were in authority, because they found no charges to lay at his feet. Paul, being aware of the law, once again uses his Roman citizenship to try and get a fair trial. Festus, the governor answers, *"You have appealed to Caesar? To Caesar you shall go!" (vs. 12)*

Paul was a bright man who frustrated his accusers with his knowledge of the law and the Word of God. Quite frankly, they just did not know what to do with him. Because of his Roman citizenship, they thought twice about how they would deal with Paul. Behind the scenes, God is unfolding his plan and purposes. When we are on an uncharted course, we cannot clearly see the path ahead of us. We must then take on the mindset that Paul had, knowing that whatever road he traveled, nothing could separate him from God. *"Who shall separate us from the love of Christ? Shall tribulation, or distress, or persecution, or famine, or nakedness, or peril or sword?" (Rom. 8:35)* When we are under the umbrella of God, we can go down any road, fully convinced and equipped by Him and His love.

Prayer: Father, thank You that nothing can separate us from You or Your love.

Reasonable Doubts

"But when I found that he had committed nothing deserving of death, and that he himself had appealed to Augustus, I decided to send him. I have nothing certain to write to my lord concerning him."

Acts 25:25,26a

Read Acts Chapter 25:13-27

When Festus replaced Felix, he had extra pressure from the Jews to reopen Paul's case. In doing so, he thought it would appease the Jews. The problem was, there was no evidence of a crime, and Paul was a Roman citizen. Such mind boggling problems for a new governor. Festus writes a letter, which was the required thing to do. In detail, he was supposed to document the accounts, accusations, and crimes, if any. Again the problem was, there was no evidence and there was nothing to incriminate Paul. Festus writes his closing thoughts in the letter to King Agrippa, **"Therefore I have brought him out before you, and especially before you, King Agrippa, so that after the examination has taken place I may have something to write. For it seems to me unreasonable to send a prisoner and not to specify the charges against him." (Acts 25:26,27)**

Festus had reasonable doubts about any wrongdoing by Paul, and he was not about to go it alone in deciding the outcome of Paul's fate. While everyone else was trying to reason together regarding Paul's situation and then come to conclusions, no doubt Paul was busy in his prison cell writing his own letters--which we still glean from today.

Prayer: Father, thank You that we rest safely in Your care.

Almost Is Not Enough

"Then Agrippa said to Paul, 'You almost persuade me to become a Christian.'"
Acts 26:28

Read Acts Chapter 26:1-28

As Paul was giving his defense before Agrippa, his testimony was getting a little too close to Agrippa's heart. Agrippa had to end the conversation and move on to another business agenda item. We never know just how powerful our testimonies can be. When we preach the gospel we must be aware that there is power in its message. The gospel can change anyone from being a pauper to a prince. Unfortunately for Agrippa, the Word was "almost" persuasive, but not enough to change his hardened heart. For those who come to Christ must have the faith to believe. That is what Agrippa lacked; he lacked faith to believe. *"But without faith it is impossible to please Him, for he who comes to God must believe that He is, and that He is a rewarder of those who diligently seek Him." (Heb. 11:6)*

Living an "almost" life will never be enough; God has such a deeper plan for our lives, filled with His rich love and passion. Paul left the "almost" life behind on the road to Damascus. This is why he could speak so boldly before the Jews, governors, and kings. For his once "almost" life had been transformed into one of the most committed Christian lives we will ever read about. Christ is more than enough for anyone. Are you living an "almost" life? If so, you are living a sparse one. You may want to examine your heart and let God's Word persuade you to live the "enough" life.

Prayer: Father, thank You for the "more than enough" life we have in Christ.

Such As I Am

"And Paul said, 'I would to God that not only you, but also all who hear me today, might become both almost and altogether such as I am, except for these chains.'"
Acts 26:29

Read Acts Chapter 26:29-32

How did Paul do it? Such confidence flowed from his life! He was able to stand before kings and boldly share his faith and even go a step further and say, *"I would that you be just as as I am."* It was Paul's heart, totally sold out and fully devoted to Christ. To some it may sound like Paul was bragging and that he thought people should be just like him. Paul's true heart was a heart submitted to Christ. Paul could say what he said because he imitated Christ. *"Imitate me, just as I also imitate Christ." (1 Cor. 11:1)*

Paul was a mentor to many, a true hero in the faith. Do you ever wonder if someone is modeling their life after you? There is no doubt that someone is--it could be a child, a grandchild, a niece or nephew, a neighbor or a friend. They are looking at you and imitating your example. They are depending on you to stand tall through the storms of life. There is a certain pressure from knowing that our lives are being watched. Paul was comfortable with who he was in Christ, and he knew that there was no benefit in living a compromised life. He lived and breathed Jesus Christ, and his heart wished that all others would be as committed as he was to Christ. Can you say the same?

Prayer: Father, thank You for the example of Paul and his ability to stand in the face of affliction.

_____

_____

_____

_____

_____

_____

_____

Hope

"Now when neither sun nor stars appeared for many days, and no small tempest beat on us, all hope that we would be saved was finally given up."
Acts 27:20

Read Acts Chapter 27:1-20

Once again the officials were in a quandary as to what to do with Paul, thus his request to appeal to Caesar was granted. So off to Rome Paul goes, as a prisoner aboard a ship. The trip had become difficult. They had to change ships and encountered various hardships while aboard. At one point, the trip had become so difficult that all hope was lost. This would be what we call a dark night of the soul. It is a fearsome thing to lose hope; for in doing so, we lose sight of who God is.

In the face of this trial, Paul stood up and spoke boldly before those aboard ship. *"Now I urge you to take heart, for there will be no loss of life among you, but only of the ship. For there stood by me this night an angel of the God to whom I belong and whom I serve, saying, 'Do not be afraid, Paul; you must be brought before Caesar; and indeed God has granted you all those who sail with you.'" (Acts 27:22-24)* When we are in the midst of life's difficulties, we can be assured that God will be with us, and those who are facing affliction will look to us for guidance. Why? Because, *"His hope does not disappoint." (Rom. 5:5a)*

Prayer: Thank You Lord for the precious gift of hope.

Shipwrecked

"And the soldiers' plan was to kill the prisoners, lest any of them should swim away and escape. But the centurion, wanting to save Paul, kept them from their purpose, and commanded that those who could swim should jump overboard first and get to land."
Acts 27:42,43

Read Acts Chapter 27:21-44

The soldiers were in a pickle. Because of the shipwreck, some of the prisoners might try to escape and if a prisoner escaped, the soldiers would be held liable. However, the centurion saw the bigger picture, sparing the life of Paul. It's amazing how the Lord works in moments when all odds are against us. Being shipwrecked meant being totally dependent upon heavenly resources.

It is clear that God ordains times in our lives when we too will find ourselves shipwrecked, when our only option is to go completely overboard into the unknown sea of trust. Our dependency is on nothing other than God and His sovereign will in our lives. This, friends, is when the heavens declare His glory. When we are at our worst, He is at His best. He is God and as His children we can put our trust in Him no matter how desperate our circumstances become. If today you sit shipwrecked, you must know that the God of ALL circumstances is awaiting you to put what little strength you have, fully into His hands, where He will be able to save you, just as he saved Paul and the prisoners. What a glorious thing it is to see God move in moments of despair!

Prayer: Father, thank You for ordaining difficulties so that we can see You work.

Divine Direction

"They also honored us in many ways; and when we departed,
they provided such things as were necessary."
Acts 28:10

Read Acts Chapter 28:1-16

Paul's shipwreck experience provided "UN"expected opportunities. The people on the island of Malta were intrigued with Paul's ministry. Some thought he was a god. However, in time, they learned that it was Paul's God who received the glory for the miracles and healings that took place. God often allows detours in our lives to accomplish His purposes. God loved the people on the island of Malta and divinely orchestrated that Paul and the soldiers and prisoners would land there.

At times, we too land on uncharted territory. We wonder why we are where we are, and how it is that we got there. *"A man's steps are of the Lord; how then can a man understand his own way?" (Prov. 20:24)* It would behoove us to take inventory of what God may be doing, even when we are in the midst of peculiar places. Such as when our car breaks down or we miss a plane and are delayed. Know that God is in control and is divinely directing our steps. The shipwreck experience provided Paul a chance to share Jesus and find some rest. The people of Malta were so blessed by Paul's visit that they provided for the needs of the travelers before they set sail to Rome. Isn't it amazing how the Lord works through our shipwreck experiences?!

Prayer: Father, thank You for Your divine direction.

From Persecution To Protection

"Then Paul dwelt two whole years in his own rented house, and received all who came to him, preaching the kingdom of God and teaching the things which concern the Lord Jesus Christ with all confidence, no one forbidding him."
Acts 28:30,31

Read Acts Chapter 28:17-31

As we come to a close in the book of Acts, we are reminded of God's sovereignty in the life of the believer. Paul who once persecuted the church, now protects it. He ministered to the body of Christ even while he was chained. We see here that Paul is now finally in Rome where he stood before the officials and was never convicted of a crime. From the verse today, we know that Paul was under what they call "house arrest," but this did not stop him from doing what he was called to do. Paul ministered to all who came his way, and it is recorded that while he was a prisoner in Rome, he wrote the following books: Ephesians, Philippians, Colossians, and Philemon.

When we investigate Paul's example, it should compel us to be better Christians. If we could have even a quarter of his passion, we could be better ambassadors for Christ. The end of Paul's life is not recorded in the Scriptures, but ancient tradition shares that Paul eventually was martyred for his faith in Christ. Like many of our "fathers of the faith," there is no doubt that Paul lived for the eternal, *"Choosing rather to suffer affliction with the people of God than to enjoy the passing pleasure of sin." (Heb. 11:25)* What a testimony to the power of God!

Prayer: Lord, give us more passion!

The Just Shall Live By Faith

"For in it the righteousness of God is revealed from faith to faith;
as it is written, 'The just shall live by faith.'"
Romans 1:17

Read Romans Chapter 1:1-17

*I*t was faith that we needed when we first believed, and it is faith that we live by everyday. We walk daily with the Lord and need to have the mindset of seeing the invisible. We have to put off old ways and by faith, put on new garments, believing God for what at times seems impossible. The awesome truth about living by faith is that we are tapping into heavenly resources. We are no longer dependent on our meager means, but we now depend greatly on the "UN"limited resources that faith in God can bring.

Faith is the essence of our relationship with God, without it we can't please God. *"But without faith it is impossible to please Him, for he who comes to God must believe that He is, and that He is a rewarder of those who diligently seek Him." (Heb. 11:6)* As the years have gone by, we have been tested in the area of faith, and many times we have failed. Many times we have prayed that God would help our unbelief. It has been evident that even the gift of faith comes from His heart. He allows us to be tested and in the end we choose the way of faith, because if we did not need faith, we would not know God.

Prayer: Lord, help us to believe You and to continue to live by faith.

Without Excuse

"For since the creation of the world His invisible attributes are clearly seen,
being understood by the things that are made, even His eternal power and
Godhead, so that they are without excuse."
Romans 1:20

Read Romans Chapter 1:18-32

Every year when we go on vacation, as we enter the June Lake Loop, we are in awe of His majesty. The incredible beauty of the mountains and lakes reflects His unique craftsmanship and we always say, "How can someone deny there is a God?" This verse clearly defines that man is without excuse, because God is revealed in His own creation. When our daughters were born, it too became clear that God is the creator of life. He has divinely orchestrated every cell in the human body and has uniquely created each individual.

There are times in one's life when he or she is faced with the decision to believe in God. Many will deny His power, but they are without excuse. Whether they receive Him now, is their choice. For Scripture says that *"'As I live, says the Lord, every knee shall bow to Me, and every tongue shall confess to God.' So then each of us shall give account of himself to God." (Rom. 14:11,12)* This verse clarifies that we are without excuse.

Prayer: God, help us to honor You with our whole heart.

_____
_____
_____
_____
_____
_____
_____
_____
_____
_____

Judgment Can Bring Condemnation

"Therefore you are inexcusable, O man, whoever you are who judge, for in whatever you judge another you condemn yourself; for you who judge practice the same things."
Romans 2:1

Read Romans Chapter 2:1-16

*J*esus said some interesting things in the Scriptures about judging. **"Judge not, that you be not judged. For with what judgment you judge, you will be judged." (Matt. 7:1)** This is powerful and very convicting. If we would all take inventory of our thoughts and our speech, we would be cautious about what we allowed to crowd our hearts and come out of our mouths. The truth is, we are all sinners and no one can stand on his own before God without being judged.

This is a difficult lesson to learn, and no one ever fully arrives at it in this life. But, we can grow as Christians and be mindful of what the Word of God says. Often, we have been convicted when we felt like judging someone who was judging another. It is not a pleasant thing to hear someone talk negatively about another, thus it should remind us to try and reflect the person of Jesus Christ. It's so much easier when we allow the Holy Spirit to work in that person.

Prayer: Father, thank You for Your mercy.

Circumcision Is Of The Heart

*"But he is a Jew who is one inwardly, and circumcision is that of the heart,
in the Spirit, and not in the letter; whose praise is not from men but from God."*
Romans 2:29

Read Romans Chapter 2:17-29

God knows a heart better than anyone, and He is not impressed with hearts that are religious only in deed. Unless a heart is truly devoted to God, circumcision is of no avail. True circumcision is that of the heart. There are many who are faithful to practice religion outwardly, but inwardly there is no passion or fervency for the Lord.

We have often seen this in our own hearts. In an effort to please God we can be legalistic and try to follow the law, missing the entire point. It's only when our heart is truly passionate and devoted to God that we rest safely in His will. This reminds us why God called King David, "a man after His heart." *(1 Sam. 13:14)* Even though David often failed God, in his own emptiness he always turned his heart to the One who would circumcise it. If you're having a difficult time in your walk with God, it could be that your heart has been far from Him. You need to strip off the religious garments and allow Him to have your heart.

Prayer: Father, forgive us for the times when our hearts have been far from You.

_____
_____
_____
_____
_____
_____
_____
_____
_____
_____
_____

There Is None Righteous

"As it is written: 'There is none righteous, no, not one;'"
Romans 3:10

Read Romans Chapter 3:1-20

*H*ave you ever heard the comment, "but so and so is such a good person"? The Scriptures clearly tell us that even our best works are not right. *"But we are all like an unclean thing, and all our righteousnesses are like filthy rags."* *(Is. 64:6)* Paul is bringing home the point, that unless God touches our crusty lives with the forgiveness of the blood of His Son Jesus, we are a lost people. Even the sweetest of old ladies has a sinful nature.

Oh, how our flesh wants to believe that we are of some good. Yet in it we fail daily; how appropriate it is to communicate the need for salvation, for without it, we are lost. The blood of Jesus Christ, God's Son, is the price that has been paid for our unrighteousness; this costly gift should not be neglected. In all that Christ did, He still takes no credit for being good. *"Why do you call Me good? No one is good but One, that is, God." (Matt. 19:17)* When we see ourselves for what we are, it brings with it, the humility that we need to live this life before a good and holy God.

Prayer: Lord, continue to show us daily, that we must die to self.

_____
_____
_____
_____
_____
_____
_____
_____
_____
_____

Falling Short

"For all have sinned and fall short of the glory of God."
Romans 3:23

Read Romans Chapter 3:21-31

$\mathcal{J}$ ust when we think we have arrived and can't be tempted by sin, we find ourselves falling short and sinning again. This is frustrating and heartbreaking, because in ourselves we can never be free from the tyranny of sin. Our common denominator is that we all sin. The beautiful hope about our weaknesses is that there is provision for those who walk in righteousness through faith. It is our Redeemer, Jesus. ***"Being justified freely by His grace through the redemption that is in Christ Jesus." (Rom. 3:24)***

All have sinned and fallen short
From His glory we all do fall
Precious blood He's given us
To redeem us from that sin
Mercy and grace flow from His heart
We fall on our face before His throne
In faith we believe and follow Him,
Our hope lies in Him alone.
TLR

Prayer: Lord, thank You for forgiveness of sin.

_____

_____

_____

_____

_____

_____

_____

_____

Justified By Faith

"For if Abraham was justified by works,
he has something to boast about, but not before God."
Romans 4:2

Read Romans Chapter 4:1-12

We are justified by faith and not by any works that our flesh can glory in. Oh how the flesh loves to rise up and take credit for spiritual victory. God is not impressed with our flesh, for in it dwells no good thing. God is impressed with faith, because without faith it is impossible to please Him and believe that He is God. *(Heb. 11:6)*

Having faith means that we are trusting God for things that are invisible. Faith will help us to trust God for the impossible and to believe Him for direction in our lives, even when it seems uncertain. Coming to the end of ourselves and submitting our will to His is difficult, because we battle our flesh. When we do come to the end of ourselves, we find rest as we trust God for our future. This is what Abraham did, and he was justified by faith and became the father of all who believe!

Prayer: Lord, for all the times we have and will falter in faith, please forgive us, then strengthen us.

Promises Produce Performance

*"And being fully convinced that what He had promised
He was also able to perform."*
Romans 4:21

Read Romans Chapter 4:13-25

Abraham was the father of faith, known for believing God for the impossible. How did Abraham acquire such faith? It was his love for God and a trusting heart to simply believe that God would accomplish what He promised He would do. Perhaps this is why Abraham was called the friend of God. *"And the Scripture was fulfilled which says, 'Abraham believed God, and it was accounted to him for righteousness.' And he was called the friend of God." (Jas. 2:23)*

We have many loyal friends who follow through with their promises, and these are mere mortal people. So...why should it surprise us that God keeps His Word? God's promises always produce performance. Even when it is the eleventh hour and things seem impossible, He comes through. Are you in the midst of waiting? If so, be of good cheer because He is about to come through.

Prayer: Lord, thank You for being a "promise keeper."

His Hope Does Not Disappoint

"Now hope does not disappoint, becuase the love of God has been poured out in our hearts by the Holy Spirit who was given to us."
Romans 5:5

Read Romans Chapter 5:1-5

*I*t has been said that a hopeless heart is a heart that has almost stopped beating. Being without hope can be a near death experience. The world is full of disappointed people, and it's a wonder how people in this life exist without the hope of God. Even as believers we sometimes lose heart and hope, but we know "Who" to turn to and when we do, we have His hope which will not disappoint.

The dictionary describes the word "hope," this way; "hope" means to expect, look forward to, to anticipate. All these descriptions are optimistic. When we have His hope, we have His heart and an eternal perspective. Having hope keeps our hearts beating, anticipating what God can do in what may appear to be a hopeless or desperate situation.

Prayer: Lord, Your precious gift of hope spurs us on.

_____
_____
_____
_____
_____
_____
_____
_____
_____
_____
_____
_____

Christ Dies For Sinners

"But God demonstrates His own love toward us,
in that while we were still sinners, Christ died for us."
Romans 5:8

Read Romans Chapter 5:6-21

Are there loved ones in your life who don't know the love of God? Take heart friends; God's love is still towards them, even if they have not yet found faith. As we reflect back to our days, prior to receiving Christ as our Savior, we are reminded of the many people that God placed in our path to pray for us and share Christ with us. We are ever thankful that God's love and patience towards us did not run thin, waiting for us to respond to His call. So many people played a role in bringing us to Christ and somehow in God's sovereignty, it led to our eventual salvation.

Instead of looking with despair at loved ones who don't know Christ, look at them with the love of God and put feet towards your faith. God is able to save the most crusty of hearts. God is working despite the seemingly unsettled feelings that come with having loved ones who have not yet responded to the call of salvation. We must remember that Christ died for sinners, while they were yet sinners.

Prayer: Lord, thank You for demonstrating Your love towards us, even before we knew You.

Freedom

"Therefore do not let sin reign in your mortal body,
that you should obey it in its lusts."
Romans 6:12

Read Romans Chapter 6:1-14

*T*his entire chapter speaks of putting away the old man, which means being dead to sin and alive in Christ. How do we reconcile the fact that we were once dead because of sin, yet now we are alive because of Christ? First, we must be aware that there is freedom from sin in Christ. This is not to say that we don't have a sinful nature anymore. What this means is that we have an advocate through Jesus. If we are truly a new creature in Christ, we won't be at peace with God if we allow sin to dwell in our bodies.

We must remember the bondage that we were once under because of sin. Remember how it was to be separated from Christ? We can backslide into bondage if we continue to exercise a so-called liberty to practice sin. It is not worth sacrificing our freedom in Christ to enjoy the temporal numbness of gratifying the flesh. If you find yourself practicing sin, you already know how it separates you from Christ. Confess your sin to God and put off the old man. *"If we confess our sins, He is faithful and just to forgive us." (1 John 1:9)*

Prayer: Father, thank You for freedom.

_____
_____
_____
_____
_____
_____
_____
_____
_____

The Gift

"For the wages of sin is death,
but the gift of God is eternal life in Christ Jesus our Lord."
Romans 6:23

Read Romans Chapter 6:15-23

We often take for granted the beautiful gift of salvation and eternal life that we have received. Too often we find ourselves comfortable in this life, forgetting that this is not our home. We have been spared the wages of sin; it would have cost us everything if Christ had not come into our lives.

The Gift Of Eternal Life

Before I believed my wages were death
For all my sin apart from Him, my life was lost
In debt I was to a lie, I almost spent eternity
But by His Spirit He drew me in
To a life filled with this gift, freely given
No one could pay for eternity, His blood He gave
For every sinner who would ever believe
The wages have been paid, You are set free
Let's remember the price that He paid
To spare our lives from the eternal grave.
TLR

Prayer: Father, thank You for giving Jesus as a ransom for our sins.

_____

_____

_____

_____

_____

_____

_____

_____

In Me Dwells No Good Thing

"For I know that in me /that is, in my flesh/ nothing good dwells;"
Romans 7:18a

Read Romans Chapter 7:1-20

Years ago we heard Sandy MacIntosh share a message about writing her daughter a letter as she was sending her off to college. The letter went something like this, "To my lovely, beautiful daughter who I love so much; you amaze me with your beauty and your talent, and I am honored to be your Mother. You are brilliant and full of life and vigor, and I know you will exceed in all that you do. But I need to share with you this one truth; despite all these wonderful things that I see in you as your Mother, you need to know this, *'In Your flesh dwells no good thing.'"* * Wow!!! If that doesn't stop you in your tracks and make you think!

This is what our heavenly Father is saying to us in this verse. Look my children; I love you and have a purpose for your life. I can help you reach your potential and become the godly person I intend you to be. But we must settle this, and you need to understand that this cannot be done in the realm of the flesh. This reminds us of the words of Jesus when He said, *"Watch and pray, lest you enter into temptation. The spirit indeed is willing, but the flesh is weak." (Matt. 26:41)* We should understand this and realize that apart from God, we can do nothing.

Prayer: Father, thank You for Your truth.

_____

_____

_____

_____

_____

_____

_____

_____

* Used with permission.

O Wretched Man

"O wretched man that I am! Who will deliver me from this body of death?
I thank God--through Jesus Christ our Lord!"
Romans 7:24,25a

Read Romans Chapter 7:21-25

𝒫aul speaks a spiritual truth here. He is trapped in a body of flesh with a sinful nature, yet realizes that he is a spiritual man too, because of Jesus Christ. It's difficult to reconcile our sinful nature with our new nature in Christ. Paul does a good job with it in these verses.

Wretched Man

O wretched man that I am
Who can save me from this sin?
I am caught up in this body of decay
O wretched man that I am
Painful it is to live in this flesh
This body I cannot understand
O wretched man that I am
Thank God for Jesus who gave His life
A ransom He paid to reconcile a life from this sin
O wretched man that I am
Found clean now by Him.
TLR

Prayer: Thank You for forgiveness and reconciliation.

_____
_____
_____
_____
_____
_____
_____
_____
_____

New Life Free From Sin

"There is therefore now no condemnation to those who are in Christ Jesus,
who do not walk according to the flesh, but according to the Spirit."
Romans 8:1

Read Romans Chapter 8:1-17

Being a new creature in Christ has some great advantages. For instance, we are free from the accusation of sin. Even though we still have a sinful nature and can fall short of the glory of God, we are no longer condemned. True Christians do not practice sin, they walk in the Spirit. Again clarifying that when one is born again by the Holy Spirit, one cannot be comfortable walking according to the former ways, such as living for the flesh.

We remember when we first got saved; our hearts were renewed and refreshed by our new found relationship with the Lord. It wasn't long though, before the enemy tried to bring up all our past sin. This verse was an eye-opener and brought such comfort to our souls. We now know that all of our past was washed and even our future failings. Christ is able to keep us. When we fall short, we need to confess and move forward in our faith, trusting that He can keep us from condemnation.

Prayer: Father, help us to walk in the Spirit.

All Things Work Together For Our Good

*"And we know that all things work together for good to those who love God,
to those who are the called according to His purpose."*
Romans 8:28

Read Romans Chapter 8:18-39

The word that stands out in this verse is "all." Let's meditate on this verse for a moment. Is it really saying that everything both good and bad are working together for our good? It's hard to fathom in our finite minds how this can be.

Just yesterday we spoke with a dear sister whose daughter was in a car accident. The car was totaled. The car had just been purchased a month before, and now the family would be without a vehicle. As we shared and discussed the details surrounding the accident, we could already see how God was at work; her daughter and friend walked away from the accident alive! We could have been making funeral arrangements instead of rental car arrangements. Even though it will be difficult without a vehicle, it will be exciting to see how God will provide for this family. It's an incredible privilege to be a child of God. It makes us feel sorry for those who are not in Christ, who don't have the hope we have.

If you are in a difficult situation now, just know that He is at work, working things out for your good. Yes, even the painful things are working together for good according to His purpose.

Prayer: Lord, thank You for working despite the difficulties that permeate our lives.

A True Evangelist

"I tell the truth in Christ, I am not lying, my conscience also bearing me witness in the Holy Spirit, that I have great sorrow and continual grief in my heart. For I could wish that I myself were accursed from Christ for my brethren, my countrymen according to the flesh."
Romans 9:1-3

Read Romans Chapter 9:1-13

Paul's deep passion for the Jews to know Christ remained a great burden upon his heart. He constantly agonized over their souls. Paul's heart-felt desire to share Christ with them, brought him to the point where he was willing to sacrifice his own salvation for theirs. As we have been meditating on these verses, we have been examining our own hearts and lives to see how deep our passion is for lost souls.

Paul was a true evangelist, one whom God called to be His voice. A true evangelist does not try to "sell" Christ to others, but instead demonstrates that he is willing to lay down his own life for what he believes. Today, we see such a mockery made of the Christian faith, displayed by the many phonies who proclaim Christ with their lips, but whose wallets are full. Paul's tenacity to share Christ was pure and motivated by a converted soul. When one has found the cure for sin, he wants to prescribe it to others and not just keep it for himself. Ask God to give you boldness to share your faith.

Prayer: Father, give us a passion that burns for lost souls and their salvation.

By Faith

"But Israel, pursuing the law of righteousness, has not attained to the law of righteousness. Why? Because they did not seek it by faith, but as it were, by the works of the law. For they stumbled at that stumbling stone."
Romans 9:31,32

Read Romans Chapter 9:14-33

Once again we are reminded that God is pleased by faith. However, one can follow all the rules and regulations of the law and still have a heart that is far from the truth. As we see over and over again in Scripture, those who seek righteousness by following the law fail.

The problem with some Christians is that Christ is about eighteen inches from where He should be. They follow Him with their heads and not their hearts. Thus, they stumble in their faith. God is not pleased with mechanical faith; He is pleased by genuine faith. Genuine faith believes that He is God and seeks Him with a sincere heart of devotion.

Prayer: Father, help our hearts to stay genuinely devoted to You.

Simple Salvation

"That if you confess with your mouth the Lord Jesus and believe in your heart
that God has raised Him from the dead, you will be saved."
Romans 10:9

Read Romans Chapter 10:1-13

$\mathcal{T}$he salvation message is so simple that most people miss it. In this verse, we see just how simple it is. One has only to confess with their mouth the Lord Jesus and believe in their heart that God has raised Him from the dead. The two key words are ***"confess and believe."*** It's interesting how this simple message gets right down to the nitty-gritty of the heart.

If our heart is not committed to believing that Jesus is Lord, surely we won't have a heart to confess Him. It's important that we understand that salvation comes as a result of our faith, and is not contingent upon anything but faith. Once again we see that God is impressed with nothing else other than true devotion from a sincere heart.

Prayer: Father, please help us to represent You well.

_____
_____
_____
_____
_____
_____
_____
_____
_____
_____
_____
_____

Beautiful Feet

"How then shall they call on Him in whom they have not believed? And how shall they believe in Him of whom they have not heard? And how shall they hear without a preacher? And how shall they preach unless they are sent? As it is written: 'How beautiful are the feet of those who preach the gospel of peace, who bring glad tidings of good things!'"
Romans 10:14,15

Read Romans Chapter 10:14-21

𝒯hese verses speak of the importance of sharing the salvation message. We see here that each one of us has the responsibility to share the Good News of Jesus Christ. We also see the importance of supporting missionaries. Our church has been so blessed to be a part of supporting world missions in a very simple way. Each week we have a team of people who serve at our missions' coffee and food table. These faithful workers cook and serve a feast to our congregation like you would not believe! There is everything from donuts to fish tacos. All food served is strictly donated; from week to week, the team never knows what will come in. All proceeds are by donation too. As a result, $46,000 has been donated to world missions this past year.

These people have beautiful feet, and they make it possible to bless the beautiful feet that are serving in the mission fields all over the world. Even though some are called to stay, we can all "reap the harvest" by supporting those that are sent.

Prayer: Father, open our hearts to the "beautiful feet" ministries of world missions.

God Needs No Counselor

"For who has known the mind of the Lord? Or who has become His counselor?"
Romans 11:34

Read Romans Chapter 11

We live in a world where everyone seems to need a counselor. Secular folks seek out therapists and psychologists to try to get to the root of life's problems. As humans, we lack the full understanding of the issues of the heart and the difficulties that arise in life. It is refreshing to know that as believers, we have full access to the throne of the great and Mighty Counselor, God.

God needs no counselor! Why? Because He has all the answers. We could "strain our brains" and never come up with even an ounce of the insight and wisdom that God possesses. He is the creator of everything. No one can really know His mind and though we try, we can never be His counselor. We should always seek counsel from our Heavenly Father because He is the great and Mighty Counselor.

Prayer: Father, thank You for being our Counselor.

_____
_____
_____
_____
_____
_____
_____
_____
_____
_____
_____
_____

Living Sacrifice

"I beseech you therefore, brethren, by the mercies of God, that you present your bodies a living sacrifice, holy, acceptable to God, which is your reasonable service."
Romans 12:1

Read Romans Chapter 12:1-8

Webster's dictionary defines the word "beseech" as to beg, to implore, to demand, and to plead. Paul is beseeching us to present ourselves holy, which is our reasonable service. Since Christ gave Himself as a living sacrifice, we too can offer up our lives in return. In this verse, there are three things that stand out:

- *Present - to offer or give up*
- *Holy - to consecrate, set apart*
- *Sacrifice - forfeit, surrender, to give up*

Lately, we have been challenged on every side to step up in our service and our sacrifice to the Lord. Sometimes we wonder, how much more can we give? But then we see Jesus on the cross and realize that our small sacrifices pale in comparison to His. We realize that it takes a heart of true devotion to even begin to offer an acceptable sacrifice. The Lord also repays our sacrifice; He is in debt to no man. So even in our sacrifice, He is giving.

Prayer: Father, help our lives to be an acceptable sacrifice to You.

Christian Behavior

"Let love be without hypocrisy. Abhor what is evil. Cling to what is good."
Romans 12:9

Read Romans Chapter 12:9-21

There have been countless studies done on the behavior of man. Psychologists and therapists are always trying to comprehend and explain the nature of man. In this chapter, Paul clearly outlines the steps of behavior modification for the believer. Our Christian behavior should reflect a life that does not conform to the ways of the world, but rather is transformed by the renewing of our mind. *(vs. 2)* When our mind is transformed, our heart is too. Here is an outline from our verse today on how to have successful Christian behavior:

- *Let love be without hypocrisy. Be sincere in our love of Christ and others.*
- *Abhor what is evil. Be repulsed by the evil of this world.*
- *Cling to what is good. Guard with your heart all that is pure, holy, and good.*

Our Christian behavior is the only Bible that some will ever read. As ambassadors for Christ, we want to represent the Lord well. The result will be a fruitful life, filled with peace and a proper heavenly perspective.

Prayer: Father, thank You for giving us the faith to believe You for these things.

Put On The Lord Jesus Christ

"But put on the Lord Jesus Christ,
and make no provision for the flesh, to fulfill its lusts."
Romans 13:14

Read Romans Chapter 13

The words "put on" mean to plant, position, and place. This is what Paul is describing when he says to "put on the Lord Jesus Christ." Paul communicates the importance of being ready for salvation's call. Being ready is the fruit of putting on the Lord Jesus Christ. While waiting for His return, we are to walk properly and be a living testimony of Jesus Christ.

We are to avoid the worldly temptation to feed our fleshly appetites and make no provision for the flesh. This takes action and obedience on our part; it takes looking ahead and avoiding potential temptations and opportunities to sin. One example is using the internet. We are well aware that there is potential harm on the web; therefore we should have a filtering system on our computers. This will keep out the things that may be harmful to us or family members. When we put on the Lord Jesus Christ, we obey the Bible's exhortation to imitate Him.

Prayer: Father, help us to honor and obey You.

An Accountable Plan

"So then each of us shall give account of himself to God."
Romans 14:12

Read Romans Chapter 14

Any accountant knows what an accountable plan is. It is there to provide accountability--explanations and accurate reporting. An accountable plan helps when a company is going through an audit. It provides a paper trail of the company's history. Whether we realize it or not, we too have an accountable plan in place. We will one day have a spiritual audit, where we will give an account to the Lord of what we have done with our lives. We shudder to think of the works and deeds in our own lives that will go unrewarded because we chose to respond in our flesh.

Another point in this verse is that we should not judge our brethren; it is not our job to judge them. Rather, we should focus on our own lives, knowing one day we will all give an account for our actions. Keeping account of our own lives should be enough to remind us that we are not our brother's judge or accountant. We won't answer for him, just as he will not answer for us. So if you have been keeping a record of others' wrongs, get out your shredder and dispose of those things that should not be named among us. An accountable spiritual plan will keep our hearts in check and leave a good spiritual trail. The day will soon come when we receive our very own spiritual audit. Thank God that our salvation is not contingent upon an accountable plan based on our own works.

Prayer: Father, help us to focus our hearts completely on You and not our brethren.

_____
_____
_____
_____
_____
_____

Christ, The Ultimate Model Of Self-Sacrifice

"For even Christ did not please Himself; but as it is written,
'The reproaches of those who reproached You fell on Me.'"
Romans 15:3

Read Romans Chapter 15:1-13

$\mathscr{P}$aul starts this chapter with an exhortation to self-sacrifice. Paul is reminding the church at Rome that dying to self has its merits. As our verse today indicates, Christ is the ultimate model of self-sacrifice, all reproaches fell upon Him. It's not easy to take the higher road of sacrificial living, but it is always right. Loving an unloving neighbor or family member cannot be done by the strength of the flesh. It's only accomplished by the empowering of the Holy Spirit.

When we place Christ and the cross before us, we can follow His example in living a life of personal sacrifice. Are there areas in your life that Christ is calling you to sacrifice? It could be something as simple as making a financial sacrifice for His kingdom or as difficult as loving an unloving person. Whatever it is, know this--it pleases the Lord when we follow His example in laying down our lives for the gospel's sake.

Prayer: Father, help us to step up our sacrifice for Your kingdom.

The Inclusive Heart Of God

"That I might be a minister of Jesus Christ to the Gentiles, ministering the gospel of God, that the offering of the Gentiles might be acceptable, sanctified by the Holy Spirit."
Romans 15:16

Read Romans Chapter 15:14-33

No doubt there were mixed emotions within the Jewish church concerning the salvation of the Gentiles. In today's verse, Paul clarifies his own motives and clearly illustrates the inclusive heart of God. We too can behave like the early church and want Christianity to include only those whom we see fit. We may be shocked when an "undeserving sinner" enters into a new found relationship with God and gains the same access that we have to His throne. God's inclusive heart moves beyond any race, gender, or people, and extends mercy to all who believe. *"There is neither Jew nor Greek, there is neither slave nor free, there is neither male nor female; for you are all one in Christ Jesus." (Gal. 3:28)*

Paul's passion for souls serves as an example to us today to move beyond any prejudices we might have. Knowing that God has an inclusive heart should motivate us to have one too.

Prayer: Father, help us to represent Your inclusive heart well.

Greetings

"Greet one another with a holy kiss. The churches of Christ greet you."
Romans 16:16

Read Romans Chapter 16:1-16

    Paul's heartfelt love, affection, and appreciation are woven throughout the greetings in this chapter. There are 26 different names mentioned in these greetings. There is no doubt that all the individuals mentioned played a significant role in Paul's personal life and ministry.

    If we evaluated our own lives, we too would think about those people whom God has used to impact our lives. A holy kiss was something that the early church practiced; it was a symbol of love and unity. Paul wanted to make it clear that love was the motive behind his greetings. Paul's example of love is a model to us to extend love to those around us. When you love someone, you gain access to their heart. This allows you to influence them for the good. This was Paul's motivation; we should make it ours.

    Prayer: Father, help us to show love to Your people and greet one another in love.

_____
_____
_____
_____
_____
_____
_____
_____
_____
_____
_____

Benediction

"Now to him who is able to establish you according to my gospel and the preaching of Jesus Christ, according to the revelation of the mystery kept secret since the world began."
Romans 16:25

Read Romans Chapter 16:17-27

*P*aul closes this chapter with an exhortation from the Lord. God is able to establish you. Paul speaks of the mystery of the gospel, because God's complete plan of salvation was at first hidden, but in Jesus Christ it has been revealed. The mystery of the gospel was first revealed to the Jews and now the Gentiles. The fact that God would establish the Roman church was a blessing to all.

Paul's love for both Jews and Gentiles is reflected in this benediction. The thought that Christ would unify the believers thrilled Paul's heart. It thrills our hearts to know that Christ brings the message of hope through the gospel and establishes harmony among people who would otherwise be divided. Are you in need of being "established" today? If so, know this: He is able to establish you in Christ Jesus.

Prayer: Father, thank You for Your universal heart towards sinners.

_____
_____
_____
_____
_____
_____
_____
_____
_____
_____
_____
_____

Letter Of Concern & Correction

"To the church of God which is at Corinth, to those who are sanctified in Christ Jesus, called to be saints, with all who in every place call on the name of Jesus Christ our Lord, both theirs and ours."

1 Corinthians 1:2

Read 1 Corinthians Chapter 1:1-9

First Corinthians is Paul's response to a letter that he received from the house of Chloe concerning some contentions that had arisen in the church at Corinth. Paul begins his response by reminding the church who they are in Christ. Paul reminds them that holiness comes from being in Christ and has nothing to do with the works of their flesh. It is clear in this passage that Paul had a special affection and love for the church at Corinth. Paul founded the church during his second missionary journey. Therefore, it must have been heartbreaking for him to learn of the many problems in the young church.

Paul used the word "sanctified," which means consecrated or set apart. The church had been sanctified by Jesus. However, changes were needed in their daily lives and in their devotion to the Lord. When we come to Christ, He sees us as clean now and forever, but in our flesh we are a work in progress. We are not perfect in the flesh, but we are being perfected. The church needed correction and Paul will address the many issues that ailed the church as we travel through this book.

Prayer: Father, like Paul, we pray for boldness to live for and love You.

Divisions Divide The Body

"For it has been declared to me concerning you, my brethren,
by those of Chloe's household, that there are contentions among you."
1 Corinthians 1:11

Read 1 Corinthians 1:10-31

The word "contention" means conflict. There was indeed conflict in this young church that the apostle Paul loved. The church had taken their eyes off the true leader, Jesus Christ, and instead put them on human leaders. Many of the members of the church were divided regarding whom they followed. *"'I am of Paul,' or 'I am of Apollos,' or 'I am of Cephas,' or 'I am of Christ.'" (vs. 12)* When we look to man, we become divided by man's opinions. Paul reminds the church that Christ is not a divider; He unites.

Division can destroy a church, and those caught up in the division will be devoured. Division is among the seven things that God hates. *"Yes, seven are an abomination to Him...And one who sows discord among brethren." (Prov. 6:16,19b)* We need to examine our hearts and make sure that we are not being divisive in our spirits. Contentions begin with things like bickering over small details. If we don't stop, it will spread like a virus throughout the church, and slowly the church will become infected. Paul will outline in the chapters to come a prescription that will cure the unhealthiness of a church that is sick with division.

Prayer: Father, keep our hearts pure before You and our church free from the tyranny and destruction of division.

_____

_____

_____

_____

_____

_____

_____

Faith In The Power Of God

"That your faith should not be in the wisdom of men but in the power of God."
1 Corinthians 2:5

Read 1 Corinthians Chapter 2:1-5

Each individual needs to come to the full realization that our faith is dependent upon the power of God and not men. Paul did not come to the Corinthians with man's wisdom, but rather by the preaching of Jesus Christ.

The Corinthian church had lost sight of their true power; they had taken their eyes off of Jesus and put them onto men. They began to glory in their own strength and spiritual gifts. As we grow in Christ, we must learn to guard our egos. We may learn some powerful truths, then foolishly start to think it's because we are special and have an edge over others regarding spiritual matters. Paul clears it all up in this passage. Man's wisdom brings futility, God's wisdom brings fruit.

It can be a humbling thing to find yourself bowing before the Almighty, yet when we do, we gain His power and His perspective. Then we become that vessel fit for honor--something that God can use to bring glory to Himself.

Prayer: Father, thank You for Your power and Your truth.

_____
_____
_____
_____
_____
_____
_____
_____
_____

Spiritual Mystery Revealed

"But as it is written: 'Eye has not seen, nor ear heard, nor have entered into the heart of man the things which God has prepared for those who love Him.' But God has revealed them to us through His Spirit."
1 Corinthians 2:9,10a

Read 1 Corinthians Chapter 2:6-12

$\mathcal{B}$eing a child of God has benefits that we sometimes forget. God reveals to us spiritual mysteries and the matters of His heart. When we take the time to ponder the mysteries of God, it is so exciting to witness and be included in the things He has prepared and reveals to us.

For over 27 years we have walked with God, yet we are still amazed at the daily revelations of His spiritual truths. *"Blessed be the Lord, who daily loads us with benefits, the God of our salvation!" (Ps. 68: 19)* If you're feeling a little spiritually bankrupt, then it's time to remember who you are in Christ. It's time to set your heart on the things of the kingdom and allow Him to unfold and reveal His wondrous riches to you. What an inheritance we have in Jesus Christ.

Prayer: Father, thank You for the benefits that You give us daily.

The Mind Of Christ

"For Who has known the mind of the Lord that he may instruct Him?'
But we have the mind of Christ."
1 Corinthians 2:16

Read 1 Corinthians 2:13-16

*H*ave you taken the time lately to ponder the riches that you have in Christ? He has given us a spiritual inheritance that is like a trust fund that never ends. He has revealed the mysteries of His kingdom unto us. We are joint heirs with Him. He also calls us His friends. Wow! If this doesn't motivate us, what will? *"No longer do I call you servants, for a servant does not know what his master is doing; but I have called you friends, for all things that I heard from My Father I have made known to you." (John 15:15)*

Life sometimes seems to take more than it gives; we struggle with busy schedules and find ourselves juggling the daily pressures of life. We often feel spent and unappreciated, as if no one really cares. This passage reaches out and reminds us that in all of the uncertainties of this life, one thing remains true. God loves us and has given us His Son, Jesus Christ; we have His mind and His thoughts and His perspectives. These are things that the world cannot offer us. These are the riches we receive at Christ's expense.

Prayer: Father, thank You for the reminder that we have all we need in Jesus.

Grow Up

*"For where there are envy, strife, and divisions among you,
are you not carnal and behaving like mere men?"*
1 Corinthians 3:3

Read 1 Corinthians Chapter 3:1-4

The Corinthian church behaved as though they did not have spiritual judgment. They were immature in their faith, arguing over petty disputes, behaving like "mere men" of this world. This surprised Paul. He thought they should have been a little farther along in their faith. The strife and division among the church reflected lives lacking spiritual nutrition. Whether they were ready or not to receive Paul's rebuke, it was time for the Corinthian believers to grow up.

We should always be moving forward in our faith as believers. This means that we should not be comfortable with a carnal life. Living between two worlds is contrary to our faith and will stunt our growth, and soon causes us to become stagnant. We are not perfect, but we are being perfected. If your spiritual life seems stagnant, it's probably because you have drifted away from a life that is progressing forward in faith. We too need to take heed of Paul's admonishment and grow up!

Prayer: Father, help us to continue to move forward in our faith.

We Are On The Same Team

"For we are God's fellow workers; you are God's field, you are God's building."
1 Corinthians 3:9

Read 1 Corinthians Chapter 3:5-23

Too often in the body of Christ we lose sight of the goal. The goal is God and believing in His Son, Jesus Christ. Then why do we spend so much time forgetting why we do what we do? It's a pity when you think about it. Our true purpose is to please the heart of God by living lives that reflect renewed and converted hearts. All those who are true teammates win because in the end, God wins. Of course, the end as we know it is really the beginning of eternal life with Jesus Christ.

Paul, like any good coach, reminds the team that all have a part in the body of Christ. Anyone who is not united will cause division and hinder the work of the entire team. We are at our best when we keep an eternal perspective and do our part in the body. Then we bring great glory to our heavenly Father. Heaven is cheering us onward, so let's not lose sight of our eternal goal.

Prayer: Lord, thank You for reminders like this one--to be team players.

Each One's Praise

"Therefore judge nothing before the time, until the Lord comes, who will both bring to light the hidden things of darkness and reveal the counsels of the hearts. Then each one's praise will come from God."
1 Corinthians 4:5

Read 1 Corinthians Chapter 4:1-13

We oftentimes become consumed with trying to please those around us. We worry and fret over what they might think of us. All the while our Lord patiently waits for us to come to Him, to glorify Him. Paul mentions the importance of having hearts that will please God. We are stewards of the mysteries of God. A steward is someone who has been given the responsibility of an overseer. We are overseers of the mysteries of God; a steward should be found faithful.

Our aim as stewards is to please our Master. It's not our job to evaluate or assess others around us. That job belongs to God; He will bring to light the hidden things of darkness. We have so much more peace when we have the right perspective regarding where our praise should go. It is comforting to know that ultimately God is the judge, and that He will judge even our praise. It makes you want to stop worrying about what others think and just *"Praise The Lord!"*

Prayer: Father, forgive us for the many times we have sought to please man and not You.

_____

_____

_____

_____

_____

_____

_____

_____

_____

_____

227

A Mentor's Heart

"Therefore I urge you, imitate me. For this reason I have sent Timothy to you, who is my beloved and faithful son in the Lord, who will remind you of my ways in Christ, as I teach everywhere in every church."
1 Corinthians 4:16,17

Read 1 Corinthians Chapter 4:14-21

*I*n this passage, Paul reflects the heart of a mentor. It is a powerful statement when he says, "Imitate me." How could Paul speak with such confidence? Some may interpret Paul's words to be a little overconfident. The truth is, Paul placed his confidence in Jesus Christ. Paul lived by the words he often encouraged others to live by--words like, *"I can do all things through Christ who strengthens me." (Phil. 4:13)*

Whether we believe it our not, when we mentor someone, people are watching and evaluating our conduct and behavior. It's not that intimidating if we take on Paul's mindset. He was focused on the one thing that would keep him moving forward in his faith--Jesus. Healthy sheep beget healthy offspring when they have a devoted and exemplary leader to follow. Paul deemed it important enough to send his disciple Timothy to encourage the Corinthian church in their walk. Think about it! Timothy was sent so that they could see with their own eyes how they should model their faith. Who's watching your life? What do they see? Can you say, "Imitate me because, I imitate Christ?"

Prayer: Father, help us to reflect and imitate Paul's heart for mentoring and discipleship.

_____
_____
_____
_____
_____
_____
_____
_____
_____

Sexual Immorality

"It is actually reported that there is sexual immorality among you,"
1 Corinthians 5:1a

Read 1 Corinthians Chapter 5:1-8

*A*pathy was prevalent in the church at Corinth, and it broke Paul's heart. He could not believe incest was reported as one of the problems within the church. Apparently, a young man in the fellowship was engaged in sexual immorality with his stepmother, and nothing was said or done about it. It can be easy to overlook someone's sin, because we don't want to confront or offend. If sin is not dealt with, it will cause infection and spread like wildfire.

Unfortunately, the Corinthians had a distorted view of how to deal with the sin. They ignored it, thinking it would either go away or that somehow it would stop. Untamed sin will never stop. It must be dealt with, and the church has a responsibility to confront it. If there is sincere repentance it will be obvious, but if not, it will affect the entire church, keeping the fellowship from receiving God's full blessing.

Prayer: Father, we pray that You would help the church not to practice sin.

_____
_____
_____
_____
_____
_____
_____
_____
_____
_____

Immorality Severs Fellowship

*"But now I have written to you not to keep company with anyone named a brother,
who is sexually immoral, or covetous, or an idolater, or a reviler, or a drunkard,
or an extortioner--not even to eat with such a person."*

1 Corinthians 5:11

Read 1 Corinthians Chapter 5:9-13

Paul's words may appear harsh, but immorality is an evil sin. Immorality in the church quenches God's Spirit. Paul lists a few other things that sever the special gift of fellowship we have with one another. If you have ever been in a situation where you have tolerated sin in the life of a brother or sister, then you probably already know how taxing it is, both emotionally and spiritually. It seems that their sin has the power to dominate our thoughts and time and keeps us from serving God with a whole heart.

So how do we approach a member of the church who is living a rebellious life? We should approach them with love and truth. We need to clearly communicate the Scriptures to them, and let them know we care about their souls; but we can't allow their preoccupation with sin to infect the church. They should be encouraged to repent and until they do, they should take their sin outside of the fellowship. We should also make it clear that they are welcome to return when they are ready to obey the Lord. Remember, the prodigal son had to leave his father's house to practice sin.

Prayer: Father, we pray for repentance and restoration for those who are prodigals.

Scarcity Of Righteousness

"Dare any of you, having a matter against another, go to law before the unrighteous, and not before the saints?"
1 Corinthians 6:1

Read 1 Corinthians Chapter 6:1-11

*P*aul warns the church at Corinth that taking legal action against a brother is a poor witness to the world. Instead of taking the higher road and allowing the Holy Spirit the opportunity to police the conscience of the offending brother, the church took matters before the local courts. They allowed Satan to pull the strings. The results were defamation of character and making a mockery out of Christianity.

When the church behaves like the world, we "dim the light" of our witness for Christ. The Corinthians lost sight of the fact that the world was watching their behavior. Their conflicts were being taken to pagan courts and their inability to work out their difficulties reflected serious division within the church. Paul rebukes the church for their immaturity and reminds them that God is the judge, and that one day, even the church will judge matters. So, stop fighting! What Paul was saying is leave the issue in God's hands and He will avenge you.

Today, Christians often try to "milk" the legal system. They get into a minor accident and claim injuries that aren't really there. This is a sin that should not be tolerated. A church that tolerates evil is a church devoid of the Spirit of God.

Prayer: Father, correct Your church; bring us back to You.

Bought At A Price

"For you were bought at a price; therefore glorify God in your body and in your spirit, which are God's."
1 Corinthians 6:20

Read 1 Corinthians Chapter 6:12-20

The price tag for our sins was the shed blood of Jesus Christ. So don't practice sin. When a believer brings immorality into their relationship with Christ it doesn't just affect them, it affects Christ. There are serious consequences for illicit sexual sin. They begin with separation from the Lord and bondage to sin.

The price was paid already; we were redeemed from the slavery of sin. You really have to wonder where a heart is at when there is no conviction in response to sin. At a recent retreat, the speaker spoke about sin saying, "Sin has its price tag. Sin will take you farther than you ever wanted to go. Sin will keep you longer than you ever wanted to stay. Sin will cost you more than you ever wanted to pay." We cheapen the grace of God and the price He paid for our sins when we discount His will for our lives. If you are even thinking about practicing sexual immorality, think again. Like Joseph, flee from temptation; and as we resist the devil, he shall flee from you.

Prayer: Father, thank You for Your redeeming power. Keep our hearts pure before You.

Marriage God's Way

"Nevertheless, because of sexual immorality, let each man have his own wife,
and let each woman have her own husband."
1 Corinthians 7:2

Read 1 Corinthians Chapter 7:1-9

After Paul had addressed the concerns that came from the house of Chloe, he focused on the list of questions he received from the church. The Corinthians had a few distorted views about marriage. Some believed they would be considered more spiritual if they remained single, living a life of celibacy. Others who were already married, thought it would be spiritual to abstain from sexual intimacy in marriage.

Paul clarifies how God sees singleness and marriage. To get right to the point he says, listen! If you are being tempted sexually, you probably should seek the Lord for a wife or a husband. He also admonishes married Christian couples to take care of the marriage bed, lest they be tempted. God ordained marriage, and He is pleased to bless the marriage relationship. Many couples have difficulty in their marriages because of past sins or because they may have been sexually abused as a child. God is able to give a fresh, clean start in marriage, but you have to trust in Him. Marriage God's way, is marriage at its best.

Prayer: Father, for all the marriages that are hurting or suffering, we pray for help and healing.

Marriage Vows

"Now to the married I command, yet not I but the Lord: A wife is not to depart from her husband. But even if she does depart, let her remain unmarried or be reconciled to her husband. And a husband is not to divorce his wife."
1 Corinthians 7:10,11

Read 1 Corinthians Chapter 7:10-40

Our world today is very much like the times of the church at Corinth. It doesn't seem like we should have to remind believing couples to remain in their marriages, but sadly, it is necessary. There are many who lift hands up to our Lord in church, yet despise their marriage relationship. They have forgotten their marriage vows made before God. The truth is, if they would submit their hearts in true devotion to God, He would cleanse their hearts and give them His perspectives.

The prescription here is that Christian couples should remain married. When a Christian couple divorces, you have to wonder whether they have stopped following Christ. If a divorce is necessary, they should remain single. We have seen all sides of this over the years in counseling. The couples that choose to follow God's instructions usually persevere and climb over the hurdles that were in the way of a successful marriage. Are you having difficulty in your marriage today? Remember, if you allow Christ His proper place, then you have all the ingredients for a healthy marriage.

Prayer: Father, we intercede on behalf of marriages that need Your help.

Knowledge Puffs Up, Love Edifies

"Now concerning things offered to idols: We know that we all have knowledge.
Knowledge puffs up, but love edifies."
1 Corinthians 8:1

Read 1 Corinthians Chapter 8:1-6

$\mathscr{P}$aul clears the air about a misconception going on in the minds of some of the Corinthian believers. Some believers felt that because God was the only true God, any meat offered to idols was okay to eat. Other weaker or younger believers in the faith were stumbled by even the thought of eating something that had been sacrificed to idols.

The point of this passage is love! Love overrules knowledge, because knowledge unchecked puffs up. In other words, knowledge has no lasting value if it fails to be seasoned with love. Too often folks with a little more education in spiritual matters, take it to the extreme and become prideful. It's difficult to receive from someone who is puffed up, because their pride diminishes their purpose. When we are dealing with younger and weaker brethren, we need to remember that we too were once at a place of vulnerability. Be sensitive to the Spirit, and you can teach by example.

Prayer: Father, help us not to forget where we came from.

Don't Stumble Your Brother

*"But beware lest somehow this liberty of yours
become a stumbling block to those who are weak."*
1 Corinthians 8:9

Read 1 Corinthians Chapter 8:7-13

To many, liberty means freedom and independence, but some often use their liberty to the extreme. Christians know that liberty means freedom from sin through devotion to God. As Paul admonished us earlier in this chapter, sometimes we need to take the higher road when it comes to our personal liberty and instead, choose love and devotion.

The weaker brothers were stumbled by the stronger believer's liberty to eat foods offered to idols. Paul's admonishment was for the stronger brethren to refrain from their liberty so as not to stumble their younger and weaker brethren. Again the issue is love and consideration. Paul sums up this whole idea in the book of Philippians. ***"Let nothing be done through selfish ambition or conceit, but in lowliness of mind let each esteem others better than himself." (Phil. 2:3)*** We should never be so selfish in our position to not consider our brethren. Think about your life and your liberties. Is there something you are taking to the extreme without considering your brethren?

Prayer: Father, help us to consider our brethren and take the higher road.

God Pays His Servants

"For it is written in the law of Moses,
You shall not muzzle an ox while it treads out the grain.'"
1 Corinthians 9:9

Read 1 Corinthians Chapter 9:1-18

Apparently there were several questions to Paul concerning ministers and their right to be paid for their work. Paul clarifies that a minister does indeed have the right to be paid, for it is how God provides for him. These questions no doubt arose when certain church members became irritated that ministers were being compensated, for they did not see their service as work. This was a sensitive issue in our household when Mike first entered full-time ministry. We were humbled when we received our first paycheck from the church. After a while, we realized it was God's provision for us to do His work. We also soon realized that you don't punch a time card when you are in full-time ministry. You are simply available 24/7. God provides resources, and He provides rest for ministers, just as He provided for the priests in the Old Testament.

Perhaps you too, at one time, have wondered why ministers are paid... Perhaps you have even judged ministers regarding their lifestyles. Maybe you have even thought, my tithes are paying for these things. May we remind you that all we have belongs to the Lord; so if the Lord chooses to provide for that minister, we too should support it. We also believe that ministers should not take advantage of the ministry. Pastor Chuck Smith taught us long ago, "Don't live above the people; don't live below them. Do your best to live among your congregation."

Prayer: Father, thank You for Your provisions to Your people and for Your ministers.

Identify With Others

"I have become all things to all men, that I might by all means save some."
1 Corinthians 9:22b

Read 1 Corinthians Chapter 9:19-27

$\mathcal{B}$efore an ambassador of the United States visits another country, they generally spend a lot of time learning about the people they are visiting. Nothing can be more of a turn off than someone invading your territory with their "guns loaded," trying to impart change. It doesn't work. You must be able to relate to the people you are ministering to.

Paul understood the importance of relating to those he ministered to. He took the time to learn their customs and he even adopted some of their practices in order to establish relationship. It was after he showed that he cared for them in the practical sense, that he demonstrated his concern in the spiritual sense. In relating to others, he never compromised his faith. He just took the time to listen, learn, and live his faith before them. This is why Paul's evangelical ministry reached many for Christ. It's a sad commentary on the church at large today to hear about ministers who come with their guns loaded and their offering bags open, then share an unloving gospel message to a people who might otherwise believe. Are you having difficulty making a difference in the lives that surround you? Choose love, and learn about the people you want to bring to Christ.

Prayer: Father, help us to communicate Your universal language of love.

_____

_____

_____

_____

_____

_____

_____

_____

_____

Take Heed Lest You Fall

"Therefore let him who thinks he stands take heed lest he fall."
1 Corinthians 10:12

Read 1 Corinthians Chapter 10:1-13

There is the temptation to believe that because we have been justified by faith that we no longer are vulnerable to sin. Paul warns the Corinthians that they need to practice self-examination. This wise saying is true, *"If not for His grace there go I."* It is always easy to see the sin in others, and yet forget how far God has brought us.

It's interesting to watch how we respond to the sins of others. We often become irritated and agitated at the very things that we ourselves did or even still do. Paul also warns the believer to "take heed lest he fall." "Take heed" means to listen, pay attention, observe, and take note. Over the years, we have seen many folks succumb to the same sin they have judged others for. Jesus had some interesting thoughts about this passage. *"And why do you look at the speck in your brother's eye, but do not consider the plank in your own eye?" (Matt. 7:3)* So let's take Paul's advice! Listen! Pay attention! Take note! If you see a brother erring, pray first. Examine your own heart, and be prepared with Scripture and a loving attitude before you approach the erring brother.

Prayer: Lord, help us to see through Your eyes.

239

Do All To The Glory Of God

*"Therefore, whether you eat or drink, or whatever you do,
do all to the glory of God."*
1 Corinthians 10:31

Read 1 Corinthians Chapter 10:14-33

Paul had a distinct anointing from God to spread the gospel message of Jesus Christ to people of different cultures. Here, Paul encourages us to, *"Do all things to the glory of God."* Keeping Paul's admonishment at the forefront of our hearts will help us to be better ambassadors for Christ.

We recently moved into our new church facility, and it has been a rather huge responsibility caring for it. The facility requires constant care and upkeep. We and our staff have been challenged with the increased workload. The Lord has been so gracious in giving us a wonderful facility, and we should be gracious stewards in caring for it. We are reminded to take care of it with joy and thanksgiving. It is a privilege to serve the Lord. *"And whatever you do, do it heartily, as to the Lord and not to men." (Col. 3:23)* When we have this perspective, we can change a negative attitude into a positive one.

Prayer: Father, help us to glorify You in all that we do.

_____

_____

_____

_____

_____

_____

_____

_____

_____

_____

_____

A True Coach

"Imitate me, just as I also imitate Christ."
1 Corinthians 11:1

Read 1 Corinthians Chapter 11:1-16

The word "imitate" means to emulate or duplicate; to try to be like. Some might consider Paul's statement egotistical. Nothing could be further from the truth. Paul modeled his life after Christ. He followed Him with fervor, coupled with faith and a humble spirit. He was all that he could be in Christ because he served Him with all of his heart, soul, and mind.

Any good coach cuts to the chase and brings home truth. There is no mistaking what a coach is thinking because he tells it to you, the way it is. What Paul clearly communicates in this verse is simply, follow me because I follow Christ. There are so many people who need discipleship and coaches to model after. Not long ago, a young man sat in our office and said these words, "I don't know how to be a Christian. Would you show me?" Oh, would we show him? We would be glad to show him! "Come follow us, because we follow Christ," were our words. Is there someone in your life who needs a coach? You can be a coach, just as Paul was a true coach for Jesus. Consider the people in your life and start leading them to Jesus.

Prayer: Father, help us to follow You with Paul's heart.

The Lord's Supper

"And when He had given thanks, He broke it and said, 'Take, eat; this is My body which is broken for you; do this in remembrance of Me.'"
1 Corinthians 11:24

Read 1 Corinthians Chapter 11:17-34

*I*n this verse, Paul reminds us of the importance of honoring the Lord's Supper. Apparently, there were many who were violating the "heart" of communion. Some were being selfish and self-centered, displaying disrespect. The Lord's Supper was intended to unite all believers in the bond of love.

Paul steps up his reproof in this chapter. In fact, he clearly communicates his disappointment. *"Shall I praise you in this? I do not praise you." (vs. 22b)* The chapter goes on to say that we should examine ourselves before we receive communion. Communion is a privilege and it symbolizes the Lord's death on the cross for our sins. It should not be taken lightly. Communion is one of our most favorite times, set aside for reflection. It reminds us of Jesus' great sacrifice, exactly as it was intended to do.

Prayer: Father, help us to remember and respect what Your Son Jesus did for us.

To Be Uninformed Is To Be Ignorant

"Now concerning spiritual gifts, brethren,
I do not want you to be ignorant."
1 Corinthains 12:1

Read 1 Corinthians Chapter 12:1-11

The word "ignorant" means uninformed; and it is obvious that the Corinthian church was uninformed about spiritual gifts. There were certain gifts among them which they exalted above others, such as speaking in tongues. This gift was elevated so much above the others that some believed those exercising the gift of tongues were more spiritual.

Today there are still many who are ignorant concerning spiritual gifts. Why? Because they simply don't read the Scriptures for themselves. They rely on the teachings of men. It's a tragedy to see some of the results that take place because of misinformation. Many people have fallen prey to parading their gifts rather than using them to glorify God. This has put both doubt and discouragement into the hearts of many. We can quench God's Spirit by being puffed up or not being open to His leading concerning spiritual gifts. In contrast, the Spirit of God is gracious and loving and orderly. When we follow His lead, we see harmony in the gifts that He bestows.

Prayer: Father, we pray that You would help us to be informed.

As The Spirit Wills

"But one and the same Spirit works all these things,
distributing to each one individually as He wills."
1 Corinthians 12:11

Read 1 Corinthians Chapter 12:11-31

This verse is such a comfort to us! It is obvious that it is God who distributes spiritual gifts through the avenue of His Holy Spirit. There has been too much division in the body of Christ over the gifts of the Holy Spirit. It seems that the biggest controversary comes with the gift of tongues. Many who have received the gift of tongues feel superior to those who do not possess the gift. This was a problem in the Corinthian church as it is today.

Paul brings us back to the essence of truth. It is the power of the Holy Spirit who distributes the gifts as He wills. If it is so important that everyone has the same spiritual gifts, it would be emphasized in Scripture. Declaring that all must speak in tongues is very much like saying that all should have the gift of administration! If that were so, can you imagine the chaos that would occur when everyone runs around telling others what to do? It would be a disaster as well as very boring. It is a restful place when we realize that we can operate in the Spirit using the spiritual gifts God gives us to glorify Him as He wills. That is simple and amiable.

Prayer: Father, help us to glorify You with our gifts.

Love, The Greatest Gift

"Though I speak with the tongues of men and of angels, but have not love,
I have become sounding brass or a clanging cymbal."
1 Corinthians 13:1

Read 1 Corinthians Chapter 13:1-7

Action speaks louder than words is what Paul is saying in this verse. All the parading of spiritual gifts and boasting mean nothing compared to having and demonstrating love. Have you ever witnessed someone, who you totally respected spiritually, behave in an ungodly manner? We will never forget the time when we were in a bank in another city. To our shock, we saw a well-known Bible study teacher literally screaming at a bank account representative. At first, we were shocked and of course quickly passed judgment on that person. Then quietly the Holy Spirit began to minister to us that we too, at times fall short of showing love.

Love is a universal word that we all understand, and we see it shown in different ways. Love for the most part is something that we all need and we can all give, especially those filled with the Holy Spirit. Is there someone in your life today that needs to be shown love? Why not sound off with a random act of kindness? You will be the better for it, and it will reflect Jesus.

Prayer: Father, thank You for the greatest gift of all.

His Love Never Fails

"Love never fails. But whether there are prophecies, they will fail; whether there are tongues, they will cease; whether there is knowledge, it will vanish away."
1 Corinthians 13:8

Read 1 Corinthians Chapter 13:8-13

There is so much in this life that is temporal and will one day fade away. Paul reminds the Corinthian church that one of the very things that seemed most important among them, the gift of tongues, would one day vanish. So what's left when everything else is gone? It's His love that remains.

Love is a universal language that we all understand. Though all is taken away from us, we can survive if we have love. Love changed the course of history. It came down in the form of Jesus when He bore the cross for our sins. Love should be the motivating factor behind all that we do as Christians. When we find ourselves running on empty in the area of love, we need to ask God to empower and fill us with His agape love. There are times when God calls us to turn the other cheek for love's sake. It's at these times we need to rely on Him for insight and the supernatural gift of love. Are you having difficulty loving today? Choose His love that never fails.

Prayer: Father, empower us with Your agape love.

_____

_____

_____

_____

_____

_____

_____

_____

_____

_____

Seek To Exhort

"Pursue love, and desire spiritual gifts,
but especially that you may prophesy."
1 Corinthians 14:1

Read 1 Corinthians Chapter 14:1-19

The Corinthian church had spent so much time parading spiritual gifts, such as the gift of tongues, that Paul now gives them a new and proper perspective. The gift of tongues is a gift that primarily edifies the person who speaks in tongues. Unless there is an interpretation and an order to the interpretation, it should be kept in private. In contrast, the gift of prophecy edifies the hearers. It includes edification, exhortation, and comfort.

Like the Corinthian church, we often lose sight of our eternal purpose. However, we should never lose sight of Jesus and the greatest gift of all, love. We should clothe ourselves with love and pursue it with passion, knowing that it will touch our lives as well as the lives of those we come in contact with. When we prophesy, we build up and remind others of God's Word. This promotes growth in our relationship with the Lord and has a long-lasting effect.

Prayer: Father, empower us with Your love and give us the gift of prophecy.

_____
_____
_____
_____
_____
_____
_____
_____
_____
_____
_____

God Is A God Of Order

"For God is not the author of confusion but of peace,"
1 Corinthians 14:33a

Read 1 Corinthians Chapter 14:20-40

Among the difficulties and divisions that were present in the Corinthian church was the lack of order within church meetings. People were not only speaking in tongues, without an interpreter, but the speakers were competing with one another and speaking out of turn. This led to confusion. The women would yell across the room trying to make sense of what was being said. The way it is described, it must have looked somewhat like a circus show.

Paul brings the Corinthian church back to order and reminds them that God is not the author of confusion. We need to take a look at our own lives and reevaluate what is important. Sometimes we find ourselves behaving like the Corinthian church. We are all about "showing off our spiritual talents," but we are not spiritually good to anyone because we lack order and priority. If your life seems upside down, perhaps God is saying, "Let Me give you peace in your confusion. Let Me help to prioritize what's most important." Take out a piece of paper and write down your priorities and stick with them. You will be amazed at both the spiritual and practical accomplishments you make.

Prayer: Father, help us to keep our priorities in order, especially our devotion to You.

A Hope For Our Future

"If in this life only we have hope in Christ,
we are of all men the most pitiable."
1 Corinthians 15:19

Read 1 Corinthians Chapter 15:1-34

Among the many divisions and warped interpretations of the fundamentals of the Christian faith, the Corinthians struggled with the idea of resurrection. Paul clearly articulates that Christ did indeed rise from the dead. Because of His resurrection, we have hope and confidence that we too will be with Him in the eternal.

Imagine what our purpose would be if Christ had not risen from the dead. We would have no hope for our future and as Paul said, we would be "most pitiable." We as believers not only have the benefits of the blessings of Christ in this life, but we have an eternal hope that keeps us moving forward in our faith. This is what separates us from the unbelieving world.

A Future and A Hope

Day by day we journey on this road called life
With the promise of a future both blessed and bright
We seek to serve our Savior, a living hope He is
With His help we won't be captive by our faults or sins
We will live above our troubles, our future is in His hands.

Yesterday is a tutor; we can't live in the past
Today His Spirit is with us, today He has good plans
A future and a hope He has for all who will believe
God's thoughts are good towards us, from Christ we do receive
At the end of life's journey we will forever be
With our blessed Savior, Jesus Christ of Calvary.
TLR

Prayer: Thank You for the hope we have through the resurrection.

A Living Lighthouse

"Therefore, my beloved brethren, be steadfast, immovable, always abounding in the work of the Lord, knowing that your labor is not in vain in the Lord."
1 Corinthians 15:58

Read 1 Corinthians Chapter 15:35-58

Have you ever thought of yourself as a living lighthouse? This verse reminds us of the importance of being steadfast in our Christian walk. The immovable lighthouse is a steady source of security for ships that depend on its beacon to guide them safely ashore. We too are living lighthouses who help guide the lost to safety.

This verse also reminds us that our labor for the Lord is not in vain. One day we will be rewarded for our faith and our steadfastness in the Lord. Our continued work and immovable faith aids us when the storms of life come our way. Although we may be tested, weathered, and at times feel worn, we still stand as living lighthouses to those who need to see Jesus. Just the other day, a couple from our church had a longtime friend die suddenly. The wife of the deceased man called the couple because they were the only "lighthouses" she had ever known. Their steadfastness in the Lord was her beacon of hope when she found herself in the midst of a storm.

Prayer: Father, help us to remain firm and immovable in our faith.

_____

_____

_____

_____

_____

_____

_____

_____

_____

_____

Diligence In Giving

"Now concerning the collection for the saints, as I have given orders to the churches of Galatia, so you must do also: On the first day of the week let each one of you lay something aside, storing up as he may prosper, that there be no collections when I come."
1 Corinthians 16:1,2

Read 1 Corinthians Chapter 16:1-4

*I*n the Old Testament, there were specific guidelines regarding the amount of tithes and offerings to give. It was very clear that the tithe belonged to the Lord. The New Testament speaks of giving too, but it reflects a more personal and intimate responsibility. We are to give cheerfully. ***"So let each one give as he purposes in his heart, not grudgingly or of necessity; for God loves a cheerful giver." (2 Cor. 9:7)***

In these verses, Paul communicates that we all have a responsibility to give; it is something we should plan ahead to do. Paul did not want money to be an issue when he came to the church. He also took responsibility to be accountable. He did not want to be alone with the gift, but requested that someone from the church accompany him to Jerusalem. What a joy it is to partake in the giving of our firstfruits to God! Our personal integrity in giving defines our love for God and helps us to understand that all we have comes from Him. If you are having trouble giving to God, follow the simple steps mentioned in these verses. Plan ahead, lay something aside, and give cheerfully. God will honor it and bless you for honoring Him

Prayer: Father, thank You for allowing us to give.

Opportunities & Obstacles

"But I will tarry in Ephesus until Pentecost. For a great and effective door has opened to me, and there are many adversaries."

1 Corinthians 16:8,9

Read 1 Corinthians Chapter 16:5-24

Paul is wrapping up his first letter to the Corinthians and concludes his thoughts with some personal disclosure. He speaks of desiring to come to the church at Corinth, if the Lord permits. The one thing Paul was sure of in his personal life, was that God had opened some incredible doors for him to minister the gospel. Paul was also keenly aware that with the opportunity to minister, came obstacles.

Have you ever stopped for a moment and realized that with each opportunity to minister the gospel comes an obstacle? We should be aware that the enemy awaits any opportunity to detour God's Word. We should also be aware that God goes before us, and although we may be discouraged by Satan, we will not be destroyed. Paul understood spiritual attacks were part of the business of doing God's will. He also understood that God went before him in his battles. There is no doubt that Paul was acquainted with the battle and equipped with God's Word. The Scripture, *"No weapon formed against you shall prosper,"* (Is. 54:17a) helped Paul to press forward in faith and finish what God had called him to do.

Prayer: Father, strengthen us for the battle, and remind us that You go before us.

_____
_____
_____
_____
_____
_____
_____

God Of All Comfort

"Blessed be the God and Father of our Lord Jesus Christ, the Father of mercies and God of all comfort, who comforts us in all our tribulation, that we may be able to comfort those who are in any trouble, with the comfort with which we ourselves are comforted by God."
2 Corinthians 1:3,4

Read 2 Corinthians Chapter 1:1-11

$\mathcal{N}$o one understands a difficulty more than someone who has walked the road before--a person who has lost a loved one, a woman who has had a miscarriage, a person who has lost a business, or gone through an unwanted divorce. When we receive comfort from the Lord during a time of suffering, He will call us to comfort others in the future.

It is refreshing to be ministered to by someone who understands and cares. Paul experienced much suffering in his ministry and was then able to comfort others and encourage them in their times of affliction. So when you feel as though no one cares or understands, know this: The God of all comfort awaits the opportunity to pour out His lovingkindness and mercy over you.

Prayer: Father, for those who are in need of comfort, we pray they will trust You in a new way today.

Preserved, Agreed & Secured

"Now He who establishes us with you in Christ and has anointed us is God,
who also has sealed us and given us the Spirit in our hearts as a guarantee."
2 Corinthians 1:21,22

Read 2 Corinthians Chapter 1:12-24

*T*he word "sealed" means preserved. The word "given" means agreed, and the word "guarantee" means security or deposit. The words are powerful and give us a greater understanding of the depth of what Paul was saying in these verses.

So often we struggle with believing God really loves us , and that we will make it to the finish line. These verses are comforting because they remind us that God is in charge. Our salvation is not determined by what we can offer, but by what He has already preordained, agreed to, and secured. Our part is to believe Him and receive Him with a pure heart. A life that has been touched by God will demonstrate a changed life and reflect the marks and characteristics of a Christian. So if you are struggling to believe that God can work in and through you, know this: He has already established you in Christ and will complete the work that He has begun in you. *"Being confident of this very thing, that He who has begun a good work in you will complete it until the day of Jesus Christ." (Phil. 1:6)*

Prayer: Father, thank You that our salvation is not dependent upon what we can do, but it is dependent upon what You have already done.

True Repentance, Fervent Love

"Therefore I urge you to reaffirm your love to him."
2 Corinthians 2:8

Read 2 Corinthians Chapter 2:1-11

*I*n Paul's first letter to the Corinthians, he addressed an issue of sin. There had been a young man in the fellowship who was in an incestuous relationship with his stepmother. *"It is actually reported that there is sexual immorality among you, and such sexual immorality as is not even named among the Gentiles--that a man has his father's wife!" (1 Cor. 5:1)* Paul had written to the church and given them instruction in disciplining the young man.

It is believed this is the same young man mentioned in I Corinthians 5:1. He now had repented from that sin and the church was in a quandary as to what to do next. Paul encourages them to forgive him and reaffirm their love. Sin separates us from God and intimate fellowship with our brethren. Repentance brings us back into a right relationship with God and should also restore our relationship with the brethren. When someone has sinned, too often we hold that sin against them. The sign of a true child of God is repentance, what we do when we are confronted with sin. If there has been genuine repentance before God and the brethren, then we ought to forgive. It reminds us of Peter's words, *"And above all things have fervent love for one another, for 'love will cover a multitude of sins.'" (1 Pet. 4:8)* Are you having trouble forgiving an offending brother? Look for the signs of true repentance, and then put on fervent love.

Prayer: Father, give us discernment in this area and give us Your agape love.

God's Favorite Fragrance

"For we are to God the fragrance of Christ among those who are being saved and among those who are perishing."
2 Corinthians 2:15

Read 2 Corinthians Chapter 2:12-17

*H*ave you ever thought of your life as a fragrance? Most of us have a favorite fragrance that we enjoy wearing. Certain fragrances remind us of someone. For instance, my grandmother always wore White Linen by Estee Lauder. Although she is home with the Lord now, whenever someone wears that fragrance, it reminds me of her.

To God we are the fragrance of Christ, and that is a blessing. While we often see only our weaknesses, God sees our completeness. Our life is a sweet smelling aroma offered up as a fragrant sacrifice. We are also a fragrance among those who are being saved and among those who are perishing. We may never fully understand the impact that we have on others because of Christ. To some we are a sweet fragrance and to others an aroma they would rather forget. So if your favorite fragrance is getting low, remember that you carry an unending supply of God's favorite fragrance, "Christ." So pour it all over your life, then all those you come in contact with will be reminded of Him.

Prayer: Thank You that even when our lives stink, You fragrance them with Christ.

_____

_____

_____

_____

_____

_____

_____

_____

Our Sufficiency Is From God

"And we have such trust through Christ toward God. Not that we are sufficient of ourselves to think of anything as being from ourselves, but our sufficiency is from God."
2 Corinthians 3:4,5

Read 2 Corinthians Chapter 3:1-6

The word "sufficient" means adequate or competent. This verse is freeing to the heart and soul. We know that in our flesh dwells no good thing and at times it's hard to believe that we will make it to the finish line. If we had to place our sufficiency in ourselves, we would fail; but since our sufficiency is in God, we have faith and are encouraged to move forward towards the finish line.

Paul called himself chief among sinners. ***"This is a faithful saying and worthy of all acceptance, that Christ Jesus came into the world to save sinners, of whom I am chief." (1 Tim. 1:15)*** We come to Christ with our broken and battered lives, offering what little faith we have. Then, our precious Lord gently pours His grace over our lives and gives us a reason to live. No wonder Paul spoke boldly about things like sufficiency. He lived daily with the pain of his past, but made the choice to live above the circumstances that could weigh him down. Has the enemy tried to make you a captive of your past? If so fight back, because our sufficiency is in God.

Prayer: Father, we thank You. Although in our flesh dwells no good thing, in our spirits through You, we are adequate.

Mirror Of Glory

"Be we all, with unveiled face, beholding as in a mirror the glory of the Lord,
are being transformed into the same image from glory to glory,
just as by the Spirit of the Lord."
2 Corinthians 3:18

Read 2 Corinthians Chapter 3:7-18

Most of us look into a mirror several times a day. For some reason, we are compelled to examine ourselves. Sometimes we don't like what we see; we see that we are aging. Time bestows no favors on our mortal bodies. Unlike the mirror that presents bad news, the mirror of the Lord looks beyond the flesh. It reflects glory--the glory of the Lord.

We are all a work in progress. We will never achieve perfection in this life, but we are being perfected as we are transformed into His image. Paul encourages the Corinthian church that the Spirit is transforming them into His image, doing an "extreme makeover." As they look into the mirror of the Holy Spirit, they should see the glory of the Lord. As believers, we carry with us the same Holy Spirit who reflects Himself through our lives and shines forth the glory of the Lord. If you have been looking in the mirror and aren't impressed with what you see, take the veil off and see the truth--the glory of the Lord surrounds you. No matter what our size, age, or weight, He can glorify our lives.

Prayer: Lord, when we look in the mirror, help us to see You.

"*But*"

*"We are hard-pressed on every side, yet not crushed; we are perplexed,
but not in despair; persecuted, but not forsaken; struck down, but not destroyed--"
2 Corinthians 4:8,9*

Read 2 Corinthians Chapter 4:1-15

The word "but" is mentioned three times in these verses. The word "but" changes things. It means nevertheless; on the other hand; yet; although. As Christians, we are sometimes called to go through many hardships for the gospel's sake. As Paul mentions in these verses, we can be hard-pressed, perplexed, and even at the point of despair. But as God's children, we can live above the circumstances that try to keep us down.

It's amazing to see God's peace upon His children. While the world looks for hope in temporal things, we are called to believe God for what is eternal. In the midst of the storms of life, God is our refuge. All through the Bible, we see that the word "but" changed the perspective of God's children through the storms. David had an understanding of what the word, "but" meant. In Psalm 139 he speaks of the handiwork of God in creating His children. ***"But behold, O Lord, You know it altogether." (Ps. 139:4b)*** Are you having a difficult time? Reflect on our God and the meaning of the word, "but."

Prayer: Father, thank You for controlling the circumstances that permeate our lives.

_____
_____
_____
_____
_____
_____
_____
_____
_____
_____

Renewed Day By Day

*"Therefore we do not lose heart. Even though our outward man is perishing,
yet the inward man is being renewed day by day."*
2 Corinthians 4:16

Read 2 Corinthians Chapter 4:16-18

Doctor's visits, high blood pressure, thyroid disease and the law of gravity do no favors for these bodies that are dying, day by day. One could really be discouraged if they put their entire hope and trust in outward appearances and these physical bodies. They just aren't made for eternal things. On the other hand, to those who believe and have faith in Christ, we understand these words that Paul spoke. Seeing the invisible, the eternal, and the transforming power of our Lord--keeps us moving forward in our faith as we are renewed day by day.

Paul nails it in the first part of this passage, "Do not lose heart." When we look at the circumstances, our heart fails. What happened to our young and vibrant bodies? How did we get here so soon? Time bestows no favors to these aging bodies; all the plastic surgery and age defying products can't change the inevitable. We all have an appointment with death, but "Do not lose Heart." The inward man, the person of your heart, is being transformed and rejuvenated daily. This is what changes our perspective and gives us back our hope.

Prayer: Father, forgive us for dwelling too much on appearances and these earthly bodies. Help us to keep focused on the eternal.

_____
_____
_____
_____
_____
_____
_____
_____

Heavenly Habitation

"For we know that if our earthly house, this tent, is destroyed, we have a building from God, a house not made with hands, eternal in the heavens. For in this we groan, earnestly desiring to be clothed with our habitation which is from heaven,"
2 Corinthians 5:1,2

Read 2 Corinthians Chapter 5:1-11

Heavenly Habitation! Sounds like a retreat center--well it is. As we comfort a congregation member who has cancer and is terminally ill, or a person who has just lost their beloved soul mate, these words of Scripture bring hope and encouragement to those who are suffering. As we ponder the thought of a Heavenly Habitation, it brings new zeal for the eternal. We put so much thought and stock into this life and fail to remember that we are just pilgrims passing through.

So if you're dreaming about the perfect vacation, start saving for it now! Put aside those things that are temporal and start investing in your future. The beautiful thing about heaven is that it offers an eternal timeshare. We've heard it said that even if you put the most incredible minds together and let them try to imagine the greatness of heaven, they would not even scratch the surface of its vast majesty and magnificence. Yes, we like Paul groan earnestly, desiring to be clothed with our Heavenly Habitation.

Prayer: How great is Your love! So much greater than our infinite minds can imagine.

New Creation

"Therefore, if anyone is in Christ, he is a new creation;
old things have passed away; behold, all things have become new."
2 Corinthians 5:17

Read 2 Corinthians Chapter 5:12-21

We come to Christ with beaten and broken lives marred by our sinful nature. Then He pours out His forgiveness and washes and cleanses us from sin. Our old nature takes a back seat to our new nature in Christ, and all things become new. As we progress in our faith, we realize that we still have sinful natures. Yet, a child of God can never be comfortable living for the flesh.

Oftentimes, when we feel a little discouraged about life and our walk with God, we should look back and remember how far He has brought us. We are not the same as when we first believed. We are a new creation. The enemy is the one who seeks to confuse us and turn us away from God. A true child of God does not exercise the option of turning away, even though he may be tempted by Satan. The Apostle Peter had this to say when Jesus confronted him about his faith: **"Lord, to whom shall we go? You have the words of eternal life." (John 6:68b)** If you are in a quandary and wrestle with doubts as to whether you are a new creation, believe God for the invisible and know that it is His good pleasure to work in and through you.

Prayer: Thank You for the encouragement found in Your Word, and the promise of being a work in progress.

_____
_____
_____
_____
_____
_____
_____
_____

Live For Today

"Behold, now is the accepted time; behold, now is the day of salvation."
2 Corinthians 6:2b

Read 2 Corinthians Chapter 6:1-10

$\mathcal{G}$od has given salvation to those who believe. Thus, Paul was exhorting the Corinthians to step up and let God help them with their difficulties. Although they had failed miserably, evidenced by the strife and divisions among them, Paul knew that if they would turn their hearts and faith towards God, He would help them to rise above their adverse circumstances.

There is no better time than today to make things right before God. It is always a mistake to put off what should be done today. There is urgency in Paul's words that time is short. We don't know what tomorrow will hold, so live today fully for the Lord. Learn from your mistakes and listen to the full counsel of God. There is no more acceptable time than now. If we knew we had only 24 hours to live, we would take Paul's words to heart. The Corinthians had wasted too much time focusing on the divisions and not on God and the peace He offers. Today, what are the things in your life that are hindering you from fully committing yourself to God? Lay them aside and get back in the race. Run with purpose, knowing that you have salvation in God, the only One who can rescue you from the storms of life.

Prayer: Father, help us to live today as if there were no tomorrow.

_____
_____
_____
_____
_____
_____
_____
_____

Equally Yoked

*"Do not be unequally yoked together with unbelievers.
For what fellowship has righteousness with lawlessness?"
2 Corinthians 6:14a*

Read 2 Corinthians Chapter 6:11-18

The Corinthians had become interested in what the false teachers were saying and neglected the truth of God's Word. Paul admonished them to break fellowship with those who were not like-minded. Too often believers fall prey to the snare that Satan sets for them. The most common area of deception involves those who yoke themselves in relationships that lead to marriage with an unbeliever. How difficult it is for them, after the fact! They miss out on the unity that like-minded hearts can have. The truth is, light and dark just don't mix. They have two entirely opposing worldviews, and those who try to mix the two must compromise.

Being equally yoked is paramount to a healthy relationship. Many times young people will come our way and want approval to marry an unbeliever. We always refer the couple to today's passage in Scripture to validate God's desire for them. God's truth often comes as a disappointment, and they are now faced with a decision affecting the rest of their life. The times when folks have compromised God's principles, and have not listened, they soon realize they have made a severe mistake. We should listen with attentive ears to God's Word. *"My son, give attention to my words; incline your ear to my sayings." (Prov. 4:20)*

Prayer: Father, help us to pay attention to the warnings You give us in Your Word.

_____

_____

_____

_____

_____

_____

Cleansing Power

"Therefore, having these promises, beloved, let us cleanse ourselves from all filthiness of the flesh and spirit, perfecting holiness in the fear of God."
2 Corinthians 7:1

Read 2 Corinthians Chapter 7:1

*W*hen we realize that God has surrounded our lives with His protection and affection, it helps us to receive His correction. The many divisions and problems that the Corinthian church had, no doubt, left them a little spotted and in need of a spiritual bath. Paul steps up his admonishment in this verse to allow the cleansing power of the Lord to wash them from their sins and give them a fresh start.

Sin has a way of creeping up on us, and if we are not careful and watchful, we might find ourselves drifting away from God and His truth. In the Old Testament, David wrote often about the cleansing power of God. He knew, too well, the cost of compromise and the separation from God that came with it. Thankfully, David knew how to get back home and take a spiritual bath. *"Who may ascend into the hill of the Lord? Or who may stand in His holy place? He who has clean hands and a pure heart..." (Ps. 24:3,4a)* Are your hands dirty today? Have you been at a place of separation from God and His people? Receive God's correction, and get back under His umbrella of protection and affection.

Prayer: Father, thank You for Your cleansing power and for the refreshment that comes from it.

_____

_____

_____

_____

_____

_____

_____

_____

_____

Sorrow Leads To Repentance

"Now I rejoice, not that you were made sorry, but that your sorrow led to repentance. For you were made sorry in a godly manner, that you might suffer loss from us in nothing."
2 Corinthians 7:9

Read 2 Corinthians Chapter 7:2-16

Paul did not take pleasure in having to write a second letter of correction to the Corinthian church. It is never easy to confront others about their sins. Paul was fully aware of the lessons that God had taught him and did not despise teaching them to others. There are times in all of our lives when we are corrected by the Lord. In His still small voice, He speaks volumes to a heart that needs to be broken. A broken and contrite heart leads to repentance and God loves it. *"The sacrifices of God are a broken spirit, a broken and contrite heart--these, O God, You will not despise." (Ps. 51:17)*

Sorrow leads to repentance, and that is a good thing. We learn the best when we are broken. Our brokenness is a sweet sacrifice to the Lord, for in it He can work great things in our lives. The Corinthians experienced many conflicts and division, but when they were confronted with truth, they received it as from the Lord. If you are going through a season of sorrow because of sin, know this: Sorrow can produce repentance. Repentance leads to a contrite spirit, and this pleases the very heart of God.

Prayer: Father, thank You for restoring our hearts.

_____

_____

_____

_____

_____

_____

_____

_____

_____

Do You Want To Be Rich?

"For you know the grace of our Lord Jesus Christ, that though He was rich,
yet for your sakes He became poor, that you through His poverty might become rich."
2 Corinthians 8:9

Read 2 Corinthians Chapter 8

$\mathscr{I}$f we were to ask most people if they would like to be rich, the consensus for most would be "yes!" There is an interesting word in this verse, "might." It means may or could. It seems that the verse is open-ended, leaving the decision up to the reader. Paul is declaring something powerful in this verse. He is appealing to those who understand that true riches are not gained by material wealth or substantiated by what our investment portfolios might say.

In God's economy, every believer has the potential to become rich. This should appeal to everyone's heart. God's riches came at Christ's expense, and those who invest in Him will reap an eternal reward. The eternal riches that we have in Christ are not bound by what the Dow Jones is doing, or what the current interest rate is. If you have been feeling like a pauper, perhaps it's time for you to look at your spiritual portfolio and start reinvesting in your eternal account. No amount of money or personal wealth will give you the joy that comes from the One who became poor, so that you might become rich.

Prayer: Father, help us to remember that all we have comes from Thine hand.

Prepared Giving

"Therefore I thought it necessary to exhort the brethren to go to you ahead of time, and prepare your generous gift beforehand, which you had previously promised, that it may be ready as a matter of generosity and not as a grudging obligation."
2 Corinthians 9:5

Read 2 Corinthians Chapter 9:1-5

The Corinthian believers had promised to give, but had not yet followed through. Perhaps they were hesitant because of the false accusations that were made against Paul. Apparently, the false teachers had been accusing him of pocketing the contributions. Paul clears the air within the church by reminding them that he had sent men with the most upright of character to collect the gift for the poor Macedonians.

We at times can be covetous with our money, as if we were responsible for gaining our wealth. This verse reminds us to plan ahead in our giving and to keep the Lord first in mind. Do you prioritize your paychecks in advance but leave the leftovers to God? With this check we will pay this, and with that check we will pay that. And if there is anything left then we will consider what we can give to God. This strategy never works, because when we don't honor God first, there is never enough. If you are having financial difficulties or are hesitant in your giving, perhaps it's time to start "preparing" to give in advance. We have put this into practice, and it's amazing how God honors our giving. In the beginning, it is a challenge, but it is such a blessing to give.

Prayer: Father, thank You for the privilege to give.

Indescribable Gift

"Thanks be to God for His indescribable gift!"
2 Corinthians 9:15

Read 2 Corinthians Chapter 9:6-15

After admonishing the Corinthians to be prepared in their giving and to give with a cheerful heart, Paul closes this section of his letter with appreciation to God for His indescribable gift--His Son, Jesus Christ. The word "indescribable" means beyond description. This means that nothing compares to the gift we have in Jesus. At times we can get so caught up in this world and place too much emphasis on the things that are perishing. We often lose sight of the priceless gift we have in Jesus. Sometimes it takes a trial in our life to remind us that we are rich in Christ.

Through His riches, He makes a pauper, a prince. This is what is so amazing about our Lord! As our lives swiftly pass before us, we find it even more true that we are rich because of Christ. *"That in the ages to come He might show the exceeding riches of His grace in His kindness toward us in Christ Jesus." (Eph. 2:7)* Are you desperate today? Do you need a touch from God? Tap into His indescribable gift, Jesus. You will see that His sacrificial gift brings you the peace you need.

Prayer: Father, thank You for Jesus.

Holy Battle

"For the weapons of our warfare are not carnal but mighty in God for pulling down strongholds, casting down arguments and every high thing that exalts itself against the knowledge of God, bringing every thought into captivity to the obedience of Christ."
2 Corinthians 10:4,5

Read 2 Corinthians Chapter 10:1-6

*P*aul did not fight spiritual battles in the realm of the flesh. He understood that there was a greater source to look to. The source is Christ, and through Him strongholds and every kind of evil are brought down. There is obedience in turning our hearts and thoughts over to the Lord in times of testing. We often succumb to the fiery darts of the enemy, only to find that we become despondent. We need to take Paul's admonishment to "bring every thought into captivity to the obedience of God."

We never know when we will be hit by the attacks of the enemy. Even after a victory, we are still vulnerable; this usually takes place when we are tired, weary, and worn. It's at these times that our faith is tested. However, if we are in the Word, we will come to that place where we fully submit to God and do battle through the power of His Son, Jesus Christ. He is already victorious. He fought the battle on the cross and when it was finished, every stronghold of the enemy was defeated and cast down. If you are tired, weary, or worn, find rest and peace at the cross of Christ.

Prayer: Father, thank You for finishing the fight.

Glory In The Lord

"But 'He who glories, let him glory in the Lord.'"
2 Corinthians 10:17

Read 2 Corinthians Chapters 10 & 11

$\mathcal{P}$aul had his detractors, so he was careful when giving his credentials to make his boast in the Lord. While others compared themselves to one another and measured their success by their own judgments, Paul understood that his calling and success could only be measured by what God had done for him.

We live in a world that demands credentials, degrees, and accomplishments that verify we have earned our way up the ladder of success. This may be true in the business world, but not in light of the gospel of Jesus Christ and His eternal perspective. Truly, we can only boast in the Lord. Everything that we are, is based on what Christ did for us, and not on what we have done for ourselves. Some have trouble with this kind of thinking but if you study it, you will agree that the gospel is inclusive, inviting everyone to join in with equal opportunity. He is the centerpiece of our very being, and we can all have true success as we center our lives around His accomplishments. We are happiest when we give the glory to the One who poured out His life as a drink offering for us. Truly, our boast is in the Lord!

Prayer: Lord, may all the glory go fully to You.

_____
_____
_____
_____
_____
_____
_____
_____

Visions & Revelations

"It is doubtless not profitable for me to boast.
I will come to visions and revelations of the Lord:"
2 Corinthians 12:1

Read 2 Corinthians Chapter 12:1-6

*P*aul had a right perspective and proper balance when it came to sharing his spiritual experiences. Apparently Paul received visions and revelations from the Lord, however he did not focus on the experience; instead he focused on Christ. Too often we hear about those who claim they have had prophetic visions and dreams but sadly focus on the experience rather than on the Lord. There were many false teachers in Paul's day who promoted false doctrine and led people astray. Paul's heart--to keep the main thing, the main thing--is evident in this verse.

There is nothing wrong with dreams and visions; we just need to keep a right perspective and glorify the Lord in the midst of them. Recently, we heard about a group of individuals who prophesy and tell people their future. The focus is on the person, and their own self-promotion rather than the Lord. This is the kind of thing that Paul avoided. He was careful not to confuse experience with fact. Paul knew, beyond a shadow of doubt, that Jesus was Lord; he simply chose to focus on the Lord and His message and not the messenger. We can all learn a lesson from Paul and limit our boasting to the Lord.

Prayer: Father, help us to stay focused on You.

Strength In Weakness

"Therefore I take pleasure in infirmities, in reproaches, in needs, in persecutions, in distresses, for Christ's sake. For when I am weak, then I am strong."
2 Corinthians 12:10

Read 2 Corinthians Chapter 12:7-21

Do you have a thorn in your flesh? Is there a physical buffeting in your life that won't go away? Maybe it's not physical pain, but maybe it's emotional pain. Paul was acquainted with a thorn in his flesh. In this chapter, he prayed three times for God to remove it. God spoke to him and told him, *"My grace is sufficient for you, for My strength is made perfect in weakness." (vs. 9)* Only God can use pain to bring us closer to Him. In the years we have walked with the Lord, we find there is always something a little uncomfortable in our lives. If it's not a physical infirmity, then it may be a financial hardship, a sick relative, or a hurting congregation member. At times it's even been another person who has brought us great pain.

Paul had a good grip on God's strength, being made perfect in his weakness. It was his weakness that kept his heart humble and focused on His Savior. We often forget how empty our lives would be without our loving Lord. Our weaknesses keep us thirsting for more of Him and less of ourselves. If you're having a difficult time, ask God to give you Paul's heart of taking pleasure in the pain. How can one find pleasure in pain? It's when we trust Him in the midst of our pain that we find His amazing strength.

Prayer: Father, thank You for weakness and for Your strength.

Examine Yourselves

"Examine yourselves as to whether you are in the faith. Test yourselves. Do you not know yourselves, that Jesus Christ is in you?··unless indeed you are disqualified. But I trust that you will know that we are not disqualified."
2 Corinthians 13:5,6

Read 2 Corinthians Chapter 13:1-6

The Corinthians were examining Paul's life to see if he was qualified to speak for God. Now Paul asks them to examine their own lives. The word, "examine" means to scrutinize, and look carefully. We too should look carefully at our own lives before passing judgment on others. Jesus spoke about this in the gospels. *"Judge not, that you be not judged. For with what judgment you judge, you will be judged; and with the measure you use, it will be measured back to you."* *(Matt. 7:1,2)* Ouch! This one hurts. For if we look, even for a moment at our own lives, we will see that without God's grace, we too would be disqualified.

Jesus Christ is our Qualifier and His grace alone is sufficient for us. Imagine how Paul must have felt, being questioned about his qualifications. No doubt he was a little disturbed. However, the wisdom in his answers to the Corinthians reveal his clear understanding that Christ is the One who qualifies each one of us.

Prayer: Father, thank You for Scriptures like this, that remind us to examine our own lives.

Be Of One Mind

"Finally, brethren, farewell. Become complete. Be of good comfort, be of one mind, live in peace; and the God of love and peace will be with you."
2 Corinthians 13:11

Read 2 Corinthians Chapter 13:7-14

Paul concludes this letter with a benediction and an admonishment to let the Lord's peace reign among the brethren and to be of one mind. Perhaps this was the greatest need of the Corinthian church, the need to be like-minded. If they focused on Jesus, the centerpiece for their purpose, it would finally bring them to a place of unity. There were so many problems and much confusion among the Corinthian church, but they had questions, and they asked them. This tells us they were willing to learn. God's continued grace was bestowed upon the Corinthians, just as it is given to us today.

Are you having difficulty finding peace and unity in your life or church? It's time to take the Bible's teachings and apply them to your life. It's hard to understand how God works it all out, but He does! He is working in us a better plan, as we draw nearer to Him.

Prayer: Father, thank You for the many lessons in this book.

275

Pure & Simple

*"But even if we, or an angel from heaven, preach any other gospel
to you than what we have preached to you, let him be accursed."*
Galatians 1:8

Read Galatians Chapter 1:1-10

The gospel of Jesus Christ is pure, and we should cling to the purity of its truth. There is always a counterfeit around the corner, seeking to pervert the message of Christ. Like Satan's other tactics, he mixes truth with lies. The Galatians had fallen for the lies and had perverted the message of Christ. Paul writes to correct them, pointing out that if anyone, including himself or an angel preaches any other gospel, let him be accursed.

Jesus is more than enough! Sometimes people have a difficult time believing it. They get confused by the piety of cults and man-made religions. People look for other paths to salvation, such as by works or following man's rules. Nevertheless, the simple and pure gospel message of Jesus Christ has turned the whole world upside down; it remains constant and unchanging. *"For God so loved the world that He gave His only begotten Son, that whoever believes in Him should not perish but have everlasting life." (John 3:16)*

Prayer: Father, thank You that You remain the same.

_____
_____
_____
_____
_____
_____
_____
_____
_____

The Gospel's Revelation

"But I make known to you, brethren, that the gospel which was preached by me is not according to man. For I neither received it from man, nor was I taught it, but it came through the revelation of Jesus Christ."
Galatians 1:11,12

Read Galatians Chapter 1:11-24

The miracle of salvation comes only by the revelation of Jesus Christ. Paul is testifying to this in these verses. No man can give salvation; man can preach the gospel, but even that gift comes from God. Paul recounts his former conduct and how he vehemently persecuted the church and tried to destroy it. But God had different plans for Paul's life. After his conversion, Paul would spend the rest of his life serving the same church he once persecuted. He put the same passion into his ministry as he once did in his misdirected attack against the church.

What is your purpose in life? Are you who you want to be? From time to time, we need to ask these questions; we need to examine our lives to see if the gospel, that once converted our hearts, is the most passionate thing in our life. If not, we need God's mercy and grace to get us back to the place where we once believed. Paul's life serves as an example to us. If he could put his past behind him, we can too. Live in the present with hope for the future and a fervor for the gospel, knowing that all has been given to us by Jesus Christ.

Prayer: Father, thank You for salvation and the awesome revelation of the gospel.

_____
_____
_____
_____
_____
_____
_____
_____
_____

Enemies Among Us

*"And this occurred because of false brethren secretly brought in /who came in
by stealth to spy out our liberty which we have in Christ Jesus, that they
might bring us into bondage/."*
Galatians 2:4

Read Galatians Chapter 2:1-10

It's hard to believe that within the body of Christ there can be false teachers—those who by definition are enemies of the gospel. These enemies of the gospel come in secretly and pose as believers, while their motives are to undermine the freedom and liberty we have in Christ. Paul was not moved by these enemies; he was able to identify them immediately. Paul had a clear-cut commitment to the only One who can bring salvation, Jesus Christ.

Just a few weeks ago, some individuals secretly came into our church to graffiti their message in the men's bathroom. Their message was exactly like the one Paul speaks of in this passage. They seek to use the Bible or the Word of God to handcuff the Holy Spirit's work. The truth is, some may fall for their tactics, but their fruits reveal their true sinful nature. Jesus Christ came to free us from bondage, not to strangle us and bring us under the law. If you feel a heavy yoke upon you, it's not from our Lord. Take Paul's advice and don't submit to it, not even for a moment.

Prayer: Father, thank You for the freedom we have in Christ.

Crucified With Christ

"I have been crucified with Christ; it is no longer I who live, but Christ lives in me; and the life which I now live in the flesh I live by faith in the Son of God, who loved me and gave Himself for me."
Galatians 2:20

Read Galatians Chapter 2:11-21

Just a few weeks ago we saw the movie, "The Passion of the Christ." It was difficult to watch the reenactment of our Lord's crucifixion and His death. But the clear picture of His sufferings brought to light how powerful today's verse really is. Without His crucifixion, we would not have life; we would still be caught up in the oppression of sin. God's love is pure and holy, and has brought the believer the saving power of His Son, Jesus Christ.

It's an awesome thing when we, in our hearts, ponder the incredible privilege it is to be crucified with Christ. This means we are a new creation, and our old nature no longer has dominion over our lives. We have a new ruler, and it's the Holy Spirit of God and His Son, Jesus. It is because of His great love for us that He humbly gave all He had, so He would be all we would ever need.

Prayer: Father, thank You for sacrificing Your Son Jesus for our sins.

_____
_____
_____
_____
_____
_____
_____
_____
_____
_____
_____

Walk In The Spirit

"Are you so foolish? Having begun in the Spirit,
are you now being made perfect by the flesh?"
Galatians 3:3

Read Galatians Chapter 3:1-14

The Galatians were in need of reproof from Paul. They had veered offtrack and began to take matters into their own hands. Their new found freedom in Christ was being misdirected into works of the flesh. There is the strong temptation for all of us to operate in the realm of the flesh. We try to impose works to justify ourselves, only to find out that we have quenched the work of the Holy Spirit in our lives.

No doubt, as we grow in Christ and get comfortable with Him, we oftentimes lose the flavor and leading of the Spirit's work. We get caught up in the "do's and don'ts" and the bondage of works. How boring and disappointing this kind of relationship must be to our Lord! He wants a personal and fresh Spirit-filled relationship with His people. Have you been feeling the bondage of operating in the flesh? If so, ask for a fresh anointing from God and His Holy Spirit. Continue to walk by faith, and as you do, you will continue to walk in His Spirit.

Prayer: Father, help us to understand the importance of demonstrating our works without quenching Your Spirit.

Justified By Faith

"Therefore the law was our tutor to bring us to Christ, that we might be justified by faith. But after faith has come, we are no longer under a tutor."
Galatians 3:24,25

Read Galatians Chapter 3:15-29

The law had its purpose and played a vital role in demonstrating our desperate need for a Savior. The law proves to us that we are sinners and that we cannot live by the law alone. In God's sovereignty, He saw man's need for a redeemer, so He gave His Son Jesus as an offering and atonement for our sins. Now those who believe in Jesus, they are justified by faith and are no longer bound by the law. Why does faith play such an important role in our justification? Because the Scriptures say, *"But without faith it is impossible to please Him, for he who comes to God must believe that He is, and that He is a rewarder of those who diligently seek Him." (Heb. 11:6)*

Jesus brought us freedom from the bondage of sin and freedom from the law. Although the law served a purpose and was part of God's plan, it is Christ to whom our freedom is really attributed. God also wants man to have an up close and personal relationship with Him and not a mechanical relationship based on the law. He desires that man should live by complete faith and trust in His Word.

Prayer: Father, thank You for Jesus and the gift of being justified by faith.

281

Abba Father

"And because you are sons, God has sent forth the Spirit of His Son into your hearts, crying out, 'Abba Father!'"
Galatians 4:6

Read Galatians Chapter 4:1-16

Intimacy is what our verse speaks of today. We need a close personal relationship with God the Father, through the Spirit of His Son, Jesus Christ. Many people who have had poor relationships with their earthly fathers, have difficulty with their relationship with God the Father. Today's verse demonstrates His heart towards us, as He reveals His great love by sending His Son. The word "Abba" means "daddy," and that is how He wants us to see Him. If you struggle with Him as God the Father, there is no need to stuggle any longer. He extends His hand of mercy and His heart of love to you today. The Father invites you to draw a little closer to deepen your personal relationship with Him.

Abba
Abba, Daddy, Papa too
Holding out Your arms to all who come to You
Inviting them to come closer, closer to You
Forgiving and forgetting our sins You do
As we come, come a little closer to You
Abba, Daddy, Papa too
Giving us Your Spirit through Jesus Your Son
Clearing up the clutter in our lives
And You making us one.

Prayer: Abba, thank You for being our Daddy and Papa too.

Spiritual Growing Pains

"I would like to be present with you now and to change my tone;
for I have doubts about you."
Galatians 4:20

Read Galatians Chapter 4:17-31

Paul was like a spiritual parent who was away from his children. As soon as he was gone, the children stumbled into mischief and fell prey to false teachers. When Paul learned of this, he wrote them concerning their faith. Because they fell prey to the attacks of the enemy, they stunted their growth. Paul had to be sharp and direct when rebuking them about their errors. No parent takes pleasure in disciplining their children, but most will tell you, discipline is necessary for growth. As the Galatians received Paul's reproof, no doubt they felt pain, much like growing pains.

Paul was not afraid to speak his mind to his spiritual children. However, like most parents who sometimes doubt whether their children will make it to the finish line, Paul had his doubts too. Nevertheless, like a good father, he rose to the occasion to teach truth. Perhaps, today you are experiencing spiritual growing pains. Don't despise them; learn from them as Paul learned from Christ, the error of his ways.

Prayer: Father, help us to receive correction and give it lovingly, when needed.

_____
_____
_____
_____
_____
_____
_____
_____
_____
_____
_____

With Freedom Comes Responsibility

*"For you, brethren, have been called to liberty; only do not use liberty
as an opportunity for the flesh, but through love serve one another."*
Galatians 5:13

Read Galatians Chapter 5:1-15

The gift of freedom comes at a cost! Our forefathers fought for the freedoms we now enjoy in our nation. Many of them risked and sacrificed their lives for the freedom we have today. Christ also gave His life that we might enjoy Christian liberty, no longer being bound by the law; we are set free from sin. Unfortunately, we sometimes take our liberties for granted and use them as an opportunity to sin. In our verse today, Paul makes it clear that we should not flaunt our liberty as an opportunity to sin. However, we should use our liberty as an opportunity to do good by serving one another in love.

With freedom comes responsibility, and the privileges we enjoy should not be discounted by imposing the law upon others. It's amazing how some try to burden others with the heavy yoke of the law, while they themselves are not willing to abide by them.

Prayer: Father, help us to reflect Your heart of Christian liberty in our lives.

Fresh Fruit

"But the fruit of the Spirit is love, joy, peace, longsuffering, kindness, goodness, faithfulness, gentleness, self-control. Against such there is no law."
Galatians 5:22,23

Read Galatians Chapter 5:16-26

After encouraging the Galatians to walk in the Spirit and not in the flesh, Paul now begins to reveal the benefits that come from walking in the Spirit. The work of the Holy Spirit in the life of the believer brings forth fresh fruit. Fresh fruit is appetizing and everyone likes to enjoy its benefits.

On the other hand, rotten fruit is not very appetizing and illustrates what walking in the flesh looks like. The result of walking in the flesh, produces an unfruitful life that does not refresh anyone. The Galatians were in need of this reminder, just as we are today. Walking in the Spirit is evidence that the Holy Spirit is working in our lives. Are you having difficulty with the fruits of the flesh? Then ask God to annoint you with a renewed empowering from His Holy Spirit. The results will produce fresh, spiritual fruit.

Prayer: Father, keep our hearts empowered by Your Spirit so that we might walk in Your Spirit.

Self-Deception

"For if anyone thinks himself to be something, when he is nothing, he deceives himself. But let each one examine his own work, and then he will have rejoicing in himself alone, and not in another. For each one shall bear his own load."
Galatians 6:3-5

Read Galatians Chapter 6:1-5

The word "deception" means fraud or con, and that's exactly what we do when we compare and judge ourselves to others. This deception is easy to fall prey to, especially when we see others fall. The truth is, as human beings we are capable of any and all sins. Somehow, when we see that others have chosen the wide road to sin, we think to ourselves, "I would never do that." What we should really do is first, go into prayer for the wayward brethren, then examine our own lives to see if we are truly walking in the faith.

We are warned in Scripture to take heed--that means to pay attention. ***"Therefore let him who thinks he stands take heed lest he fall." (1 Cor. 10:12)*** When we examine our lives and meditate upon God's Word, it becomes clear that we were lost in our sins, and now we are saved by His mercy and His grace. So the only thing that makes us anything is Christ Himself, the One worthy of all honor and praise.

Prayer: Father, it's hard to look closely at our lives, but it is fruitful when we do.

Don't Grow Weary, But Do Good

"And let us not grow weary while doing good, for in due season we shall reap
if we do not lose heart. Therefore, as we have opportunity, let us do good to all,
especially to those who are of the household of faith."
Galatians 6:9,10

Read Galatians Chapter 6:6-18

In these verses, Paul admonishes us to not grow weary in doing good. This is a problem we all face. Sometimes it feels like all we do is give and do good without much reward. The truth is, anything we do for the Lord is noted by Him, and like the farmer who plants and waits for his harvest, in time, we too will reap if we faint not. The word "weary" means exhausted, fatigued, or drained. When we feel this way, we need to ask ourselves where we are receiving our strength? If we are trying to do good deeds and love in our own human strength, we will ultimately fail.

However, when we walk in the Spirit as we learned in chapter 5, we will possess a renewed sense of God's presence and His empowering to do all He puts before us--yes, even love the unlovely. We are happiest when we give our lives away. There is a certain joy that comes from looking after and caring for people, especially our brethren. Are you feeling tired, weary, and worn? Don't give up. Instead, do something good for someone else. In due season, you shall reap an extra portion of God's love and grace.

Prayer: Father, help us to have Your strength when we are weary.

Every Spiritual Blessing

"Blessed be the God and Father of our Lord Jesus Christ,
who has blessed us with every spiritual blessing in the heavenly places in Christ..."
Ephesians 1:3

Read Ephesians Chapter 1:1-12

The unique mark on a believer's life is not the material wealth he or she possesses in this world, but rather the true riches one has in Christ. While the world invests in financial portfolios and building up treasures, the child of God invests in the eternal rewards that will never fade away. There are overwhelming pressures to succeed by accumulating personal wealth and power in this life. It's amazing that people actually sacrifice their marriages and families for these "idols." When security is measured by what is in the bank, we see how hopeless and helpless this world is without Jesus Christ.

On the other hand, those who know Christ have spiritual portfolios that continually reap a large and growing return. As this life slips by, we see even more clearly how empty this life is apart from Christ. What a joy it is to know that we persevere in our pilgrimage with Jesus, not as paupers but as Princes and Princesses in His kingdom. Christ has given us a rich inheritance and every spiritual blessing. Because of this, we don't have pressure, instead we have His peace. Have you forgotten about the spiritual blessings you have in Christ? Today, be reminded of the wealthy portfolio of heavenly treasures that await you as a child of God.

Prayer: Father, thank You for the blessings we have in Your Son Jesus.

Guaranteed Inheritance

"In Him you also trusted, after you heard the the word of truth, the gospel of your salvation; in whom also, having believed, you were sealed with the Holy Spirit of promise, who is the guarantee of our inheritance until the redemption of the purchased possession, to the praise of His glory."
Ephesians 1:13,14

Read Ephesians Chapter 1:13-23

$\mathcal{T}$he Holy Spirit is like the engagement ring that the bride receives from her bridegroom as a promise, until the day he comes and takes her in marriage. He is the guarantee of our inheritance; He seals the deal, so to speak. The word "inheritance" means legacy, birthright, or bequest. It's an awesome thing to think about; we have been given a spiritual inheritance from God Himself.

Here Comes The Bridegroom

With this ring I thee wait
Until You come from those pearly gates
To take me as your bride
I hear Your footsteps, You're getting close
I will be ready to depart
Here comes the bridegroom
Tell everyone that He wants them too
To join Him at the marriage supper
A feast like no other
The Holy Spirit is the seal
That He is coming and will reveal
His incredible love, an inheritance
To all, to all who will respond to His call
Come quickly my King and my Lord
Until then I will wear the promise
You gave sealed by Your Spirit
For You I await.   *TLR*

Prayer: Father, thank You for the guarantee of Your Holy Spirit.

_____

_____

_____

Alive In Christ

"But God, who is rich in mercy, because of His great love with which He loved us, even when we were dead in trespasses, made us alive together with Christ (by grace you have been saved), and raised us up together, and made us sit together in the heavenly places in Christ Jesus,...."
Ephesians 2:4-6

Read Ephesians Chapter 2:1-10

When the first man, Adam, came into the world, he brought the tyranny of sin and death to the human race. Christ also came into the world, died and was buried, but He rose from the grave. Unlike Adam, Christ's death and consequent resurrection brough new life to those who believed. We were once dead in our sins, suffocating from the bondage and the oppression of sin. Then we were touched by grace and made alive in Him. If that wasn't enough, He went even further and gave us hope for our future and the promise of life everlasting.

As the world crumbles before our eyes, we must realize that the time for Christ to return for His church is near. With this realization comes purification and a renewed sense of His presence. Being alive in Christ means that we have His mind and His heart, and that He has revealed to us the mysteries of His kingdom. We are His friends. *"No longer do I call you servants, for a servant does not know what his master is doing; but I have called you friends, for all things that I heard from My Father I have made known to you." (John 15:15)*

Prayer: Father, thank You for Your love and the gift of life in Christ.

He Is Our Peace

"For He Himself is our peace, who has made both one,
and has broken down the middle wall of separation between us,"
Ephesians 2:14

Read Ephesians Chapter 2:11-22

We were once so close yet so far away from the peace that Jesus eventually brought us. In the temple area of Jerusalem, there was a wall of separation that kept the Gentiles from going past the Court of the Gentiles. If any Gentile would dare to go beyond the Court, they were in danger of a swift and sudden death.

Before Christ, God had made a covenant with the Jews. The Gentiles sat from a distance and watched without hope. But Christ broke down the wall of separation and through His precious blood, extended His hand to all who would believe. God's love is inclusive; it's not exclusive. Jesus brought peace and overcame the barrier that once drew a line that barred equal access to God. *"For God so loved the world that He gave His only begotten Son, that whoever believes in Him should not perish but have everlasting life." (John 3:16)*

Prayer: Father, thank You for Your inclusive love.

_____

_____

_____

_____

_____

_____

_____

_____

_____

_____

_____

Less Than The Least

"To me, who am less than the least of all the saints, this grace was given, that I should preach among the Gentiles the unsearchable riches of Christ."
Ephesians 3:8

Read Ephesians Chapter 3:1-13

Paul continues to share the gospel message about the grace of God through Jesus Christ. The wall of separation came down and God's grace fell on all those who would believe. Through his own life experiences, Paul knew better than anyone what God's grace meant. God's grace allowed Paul, who at one time persecuted the Christian church, to now preach the truth to the Gentile nations. Paul was humbled that God would use him in such a manner, and so he gave his all to preach salvation to any listening ears.

When we come to the end of ourselves, we too realize that we are the least among men. God unmasked the sin that once kept us in bondage and pours out the unsearchable riches of His grace.

> G - God's
> R - Riches
> A - At
> C - Christ's
> E - Expense

Christ paid the price with His blood, for a debt that we could not pay. This is what God's grace means.

Prayer: Father, thank You for Jesus, the gift of undeserved favor.

He Is Able

"Now to Him who is able to do exceedingly abundantly above all that we ask or think, according to the power that works in us, to Him be glory in the church by Christ Jesus to all generations, forever and ever. Amen."
Ephesians 3:20,21

Read Ephesians Chapter 3:14-21

Paul ends this chapter with a doxology of praise to God for His ability to do "exceedingly and abundantly above all" that we could ever dream or ask for. These verses remind us that God is infinite and able to do more than our finite minds could possibly imagine. As God's children, we need not fear Him since we have full access to His mighty throne. We can come boldly before Him, asking and believing by faith that He is able to do above all that we ask or think. *"Let us therefore come boldly to the throne of grace, that we may obtain mercy and find grace to help in time of need." (Heb. 4:16)*

There was a time when we had a specific need, known only to God. We leaned on our human understanding and looked to our own resources to provide for it. Because we could only see what we didn't have, it was hard to grasp that God could take care of the need. We learned a great lesson about trusting God when He provided exceedingly and abundantly more than we could have ever imagined. It was a true faith builder. Are you in need today? No matter how big or small it may be, just know that He is able.

Prayer: Father, thank You for providing, even when we feel poverty-stricken.

_____
_____
_____
_____
_____
_____
_____
_____

Body Ministry

"...from whom the whole body, joined and knit together by what every joint supplies, according to the effective working by which every part does its share, causes growth of the body for the edifying of itself in love."

Ephesians 4:16

Read Ephesians Chapter 4:1-16

God created our human bodies with such care. Each part of the body works so uniquely together for a purpose. Although we don't see the different functions of the body operating, we do know when it is not functioning as it should. The body of Christ also has a function. When it operates as it should, it builds up and blesses the other parts of the body. However when it doesn't, there is a schism which hinders its effectiveness and slows down the edification process.

Paul shared in the book of Romans the importance of body ministry. *"For as we have many members in one body, but all members do not have the same function, so we, being many, are one body in Christ, and individually members in one another. Having then differing gifts according to the grace that is given to us, let us use them: if prophecy, let us prophesy in proportion to our faith; or ministry, let us use it in our ministering; he who teaches, in teaching; he who exhorts, in exhortation; he who gives, with liberality; he who leads, with diligence; he who shows mercy, with cheerfulness." (Rom. 12:4-8)* Yes! Body ministry is important for all who are members of the body of Christ. Use your gifts wisely for the glory of God and the edification of the other members of His precious body.

Prayer: Lord, thank You for Your unique creation of the body.

_____
_____
_____
_____
_____
_____

Be Angry, But Do Not Sin

"Be angry, and do not sin': do not let the sun go down on your wrath."
Ephesians 4:26

Read Ephesians Chapter 4:17-32

As Christians, sometimes we are confused by the emotion of anger. For most of us, our first thoughts are that we are in sin. Trying to discern what is righteous anger and what is not, takes wisdom from God. However, what Paul is saying in this verse is that at times you will get angry. But, the key is not to allow that anger to swallow you up to the point of losing self-control and to the point of sin.

The second part of this verse warns us to not let the sun go down upon our wrath. When Terri and I were preparing for marriage, I received some wise counsel from my grandmother who said, "Michael, whatever you do, don't go to bed angry; finish it and make peace." There have been only two nights in the 27 years we have been married that we went to bed angry. Twice we allowed anger to fester in our hearts and let the sun go down upon our wrath, thus turning the incidents into sin. Those were the two toughest nights of our marriage. Hopefully, we learned from those dark nights of the soul. Keeping a lid on anger takes a humble heart that is willing to yield to God, even when we feel justified. Stop and yield your heart to God. You will be the better for it.

Prayer: Father, thank You that even when we fail You, forgiveness is there for the taking.

Let It Not Be Named Among You

"But fornication and all uncleanness or covetousness,
let it not even be named among you, as is fitting for saints;"
Ephesians 5:3

Read Ephesians Chapter 5:1-7

Being an ambassador for Christ means that wherever we go and whatever we do, we represent His name. If we yoke ourselves to the things of this world yet say we are Christians, we need to be aware that we are being poor ambassadors. The Ephesians lived in an area where sin abounded and there was much temptation, just like the world we live in today. So how do we keep ourselves from the temptations of the times we live in? Paul began this chapter with the answer! We are to be imitators of God; we are to behave as His dear children by walking in love.

There is the old cliché that goes like this, "We are the only Bible some will ever read." What type of witness for Christ are you projecting with your life? When we take the time to ponder the things of our Lord and the sacrifices He has made for us, we see in a brand new light the importance of reflecting hearts and lives that represent Him well. We need to be aware that we have a family name at stake.

Prayer: Father, help us to represent You well and let not evil be named among us.

Don't Speak Of Things Done In Secret

"And have no fellowship with the unfruitful works of darkness, but rather expose them.
For it is shameful even to speak of those things which are done by them in secret."
Ephesians 5:11,12

Read Ephesians Chapter 5:8-33

*S*ince we have come out of the darkness and into the light, we are no longer bound by the shameful works of darkness. Because of this, we should give no place or foothold to the evil practiced by those walking in sin and its shame. Paul reminded us in verse 8 that we were once in darkness, but now we are children of the light. The light we possess emanates from Christ who exposes the darkness and unmasks the lure and deception of sin.

Satan always tries to dress up darkness, but when exposed by the light of Christ, it is seen for what it really is--sin. Sin, when practiced, no matter how it is packaged will crowd Christ out of your life. Sin suffocates and separates us from the light. *"Awake, you who sleep, arise from the dead, and Christ will give you light." (Eph. 5:14)* Paul also admonishes us in verse 15 to "redeem the time, because the days are evil." The word "redeem" means to buy back or exchange. Have you been tempted to "speak of" or practice sin? If so, get back into the light of Christ and see sin for what it is.

Prayer: Father, forgive us for the times when we have shut the light of Christ out of our lives and have chosen the unfruitful works of darkness.

Children & Parents

"Children, obey your parents in the Lord, for this is right. 'Honor your father and mother,' which is the first commandment with promise: 'that it may be well with you and you may live long on the earth.'"
Ephesians 6:1-3

Read Ephesians Chapter 6:1-9

Obedience is a word that has a sacrificial meaning; it warrants both attention and promise. Children are commanded to obey their parents in the Lord. If they are obedient, they are promised a full and productive life. The word "honor" means respect and admiration. Even if the parents are nonbelievers, they should be respected for Christ's sake. However, this does not mean that a child has to comply with a parent who is asking them to do evil. In fact, verse 4 clearly articulates that fathers should not provoke their children to wrath, meaning parents should not be unreasonable in the correction of a child. Instead, they should seek to bring them up in the admonition and training of the Lord.

What about difficult parents and/or children who are hard to love or seem to challenge our very being? We need to remember that God is sovereign in all His ways, and He makes no mistakes. Your parents and your children were ordained by God and given to you. David wrote about this in Psalms. *"For You formed my inward parts; You covered me in my mother's womb." (Ps. 139:13)* This verse brings comfort and hope. We can believe God through times of testing, trusting that He knows what He is doing. So if you are in the midst of a challenge, take heart and heed God's Word, for in it is life and restoration.

Prayer: Father, thank You for helping us with both parents and children. Help us to honor, obey, and respect.

Armor Up

*"Put on the whole armor of God,
that you may be able to stand against the wiles of the devil."
Ephesians 6:11*

Read Ephesians Chapter 6:10-24

Soldiers do not go to war unarmed or without a battle plan. If they did, they would easily be defeated. Yet Christians often fail to put on spiritual armor before they go out into the world's battlefield. We can't stand on what we don't know, and we won't recognize the wiles of the enemy unless we are trained and have a battle plan. In these verses, Paul has laid out the Christian's battle plan. He gives step-by-step instructions on how to put on the whole armor of God and the reasons why the armor will protect us.

The word "armor" means protective covering, and that is what God's Word provides. We need to armor up daily, giving our commander-in-chief full attention and due diligence to fight the war and win. Armor covers us from the deceitful plots of the enemy who often come against us. For the Lord's Word declares *"For we do not wrestle against flesh and blood, but against principalities, against powers, against the rulers of the darkness of this age, against spiritual hosts of wickedness in the heavenly places." (vs. 12)* So if you have been defeated lately, follow the guidelines in these verses. Armor up for the battle, knowing that in doing so you will quench the fiery darts of the wicked one.

Prayer: Father, help us to recognize the importance of putting on the whole armor of God and preparing for the battle.

Work In Progress

"Being confident of this very thing, that He who has begun a good work in you will complete it until the day of Jesus Christ;"
Philippians 1:6

Read Philippians Chapter 1

There are so many projects that get started and never get finished. One of the difficulties of being a born-again Christian is the realization that we still live in temporal bodies prone to sin. It is important that we understand that our salvation is not dependent upon our accomplishments, but rather upon God's grace. This work was started in our lives the day we first believed. Although we can't always see or feel the changes, God is working faithfully in the lives of those who abide in Him.

Paul's gift of exhortation in this verse emphasizes that we can be confident, not in ourselves, but in the faithful and finished work of our Lord Jesus Christ. When we finally do come before our Lord, He will have completed the work He began in us. What a joy it will be when we are presented as a unique creation and completed work of our Lord! What Paul is saying here is, hang in there, don't be discouraged. God is able to finish the work He began--yes, even in spite of our shortcomings. We must remember King David. He sinned greatly against our Lord, and yes there was a cost. But David's sin brought him before the Lord, broken and repentant. God called David, "a man after His own heart," thus continuing the work He began in him.

Prayer: Father, thank You for the work of Your mighty hand.

Giving Up Our Right To Be Right

"Let this mind be in you which was also in Christ Jesus, who, being in the form of God, did not consider it robbery to be equal with God, but made Himself of no reputation, taking the form of a bondservant, and coming in the likeness of men. And being found in appearance as a man, He humbled Himself and became obedient to the point of death, even the death of the cross."

Philippians 2:5-8

Read Philippians Chapter 2

Every year I get the awesome privilege of going to the Calvary Chapel Pastors' Wives Conference. I just had the opportunity again to go and glean from so many that walk the same road as I do. Each year I like to come away with something that will be life changing and each year God is so faithful to meet me in a unique way. This year God touched me in a way that will require me to really humble myself. "Ouch," there's that "humble" word again!

A workshop that was entitled, "Doing The Right Thing When You Have Been Wronged," drew me in, and of course my first thoughts were, hum...this sounds interesting! Interesting was not the right word. How about CONVICTING?!!! Karen Johnson shared her own personal experiences of the suffering she had gone through in the past year. She had extreme physical suffering in addition to the regular duties of being a mother and a pastor's wife. Her testimony brought tears to our eyes as we identified with her stresses. However, none of us were prepared for her prescription for the pain that she had suffered. She said, "We must give up our right to be right." She used Jesus and the cross as her measuring stick. She quoted a saying that hangs on a picture in her home, "Pain plants the flag of reality in a rebellious heart." She ended her message with, "To know pain is to know the fellowship of His suffering." * ***That I may know Him and the power of His resurrection, and the fellowship of His sufferings, being conformed to His death..." (Phil. 3:10)*** That's it! He took the fall for us, and this should be enough to remind us to give up our own right to be right... If you're having pain and difficulty in your life, perhaps it's because God wants to reveal Himself to you in a deeper way. This is what He has shown me. Even if we have been wronged, we are free when we relinquish our "right to be right" to the Lord.

* Used with permission.

Indoctrination

*"Finally, my brethren, rejoice in the Lord. For me to write the same things
to you is not tedious, but for you it is safe."*
Philippians 3:1

Read Philippians Chapter 3

*P*aul begins this chapter by informing the Philippians of the importance of being mindful of God's Word. At Calvary Chapel we go systematically through the Word of God. Why? On each page of the Bible is the inspired Word of God, and it is there to remind us of God's truth. How soon we forget and need to be reminded! Satan is a clever deceiver. He loves to come with false teachings that are tantalizing to the ears. The Philippians needed to be warned again about the dangers of falling prey to the enemy's devices.

In the military, the word "indoctrination" means programming, instructing, coaching, and training. Boot camp is where much of the military's indoctrination takes place. Potential soldiers are subjected to a rigorous schedule of physical and mental endurance. This is necessary if a soldier is to stand against the plans and schemes of the enemy. As believers, we need to heed Paul's words that it is "safe" and spiritually profitable for us to be constantly reminded to beware of evil. Part of our indoctrination is to be in God's Word, in fellowship, serving, learning, and applying the truths we learn to our lives. This is why mid-week service, Bible studies, and prayer meetings are available. Have you been feeling spiritually weak, as though the enemy has won the battle? Not so! Get up and get back to the place where you first began. Indoctrination by the power of the Holy Spirit through God's Word is good, safe, and freeing.

Prayer: Lord, thank You for the power of Your Word and the opportunity to serve in Your platoon.

Prayer

"Be anxious for nothing, but in everything by prayer and supplication,
with thanksgiving, let your requests be made known to God;"
Philippians 4:6

Read Philippians Chapter 4

Anxious are my thoughts tonight
Worry is knocking at my door
If I open the door it will be dark
It will be hard to see the light

Uncertain is how I feel inside
About the things going on in my life
Divinely designed by You alone
To draw me to Your Holy Throne

At a loss for words, and what I should say
Your Spirit I pray will lead the way
Trusting You know all of my thoughts
The deepest parts of my heart

Thanksgiving is what I choose to do
My prayer requests I make known to You
It really doesn't matter, all of these things
When my mind is on You, Your peace You bring.   TLR

This poem was written after a disappointment. The disappointment caused a cloud of frustration to overwhelm my heart and worry to set in. The only thing that lifted the cloud was God's Word and its reminder to pray.

Prayer: Father, thank You that we can come before You with the cares that overwhelm our lives.

_____
_____
_____
_____
_____
_____

Before All Things

"And He is before all things, and in Him all things consist."
Colossians 1:17

Read Colossians Chapter 1

From the beginning, Jesus was there with the Father and the Holy Spirit. He was before all things. It's mind-boggling when we try to fathom the infinite mind of God. They say, "If you can get past Genesis, chapter 1, verse 1 and believe it, then the rest will be a breeze." *"In the beginning God created the heavens and the earth." (Gen. 1:1)* What an awesome God we serve! Like the song says, "He's got the whole world in His hands."

Jesus is above all powers and principalities of this earth. When we ponder this truth, it brings such comfort to our souls. We serve a God who is living and powerful, the creator of all things. What could possibly be bigger than Him? Nothing! Absolutely nothing! Take a minute and take inventory of your life. What are the things that seem too big, or make you fearful or doubt? Know that God is invincible and unconquerable. He is able to take care of what concerns you today. When we trust Him with our whole hearts, we can trust Him with our lives. *"He is before all things, and in Him all things consist,"* even those things that we desperately need. Stop! Look! Listen! He is God.

Prayer: Father, forgive us for the times we have tried to reason our faith with our finite minds.

_____

_____

_____

_____

_____

_____

_____

_____

Hidden In Christ

"Set your mind on things above, not on things on the earth.
For you died, and your life is hidden with Christ in God."
Colossians 3:2,3

Read Colossians Chapters 2 & 3

The world is so attractive until the reality of its emptiness is unmasked. Nothing satisfies--our fleshly appetites just want more. Perspective is what we need and that is why Paul encourages the church to set their minds on things above. At the moment we gave our lives to Christ, it was then that we died to this world. Nothing compares to Him. When we are abiding in Christ, we have a deeper understanding of the true meaning of the word "hidden," meaning we are literally buried in Christ. We still live in these earthly tabernacles and we are prone to sin. Sometimes we wander from our Lord, but ultimately we belong to the treasure chest of heaven. Our lives are no longer under the dictatorship of this world.

The word "set" means to position, place, and put. These are the actions we need to take when being lured away by the empty lusts of Satan. We are to place our minds on the heavenly things of God. Then we will be reminded that we are just pilgrims passing through this temporal place. Have you ever been in a conversation with a group of unbelievers? Their minds are totally set on this life. It's all about career, money, succeeding, and gaining. How fleeting this world is! Solomon who had every earthly pleasure said, "all is vanity." After experiencing all the worldly lusts and pleasures, his concluding thoughts were, *"Fear God and keep His commandments." (Eccl. 12:13b)* In the end, Solomon learned the truth about setting his mind on things above and what real treasure is.

Prayer: Father, thank You for the things that are above and hidden in Christ.

Unimpeachable Conduct

*"Walk in wisdom toward those who are outside, redeeming the time.
Let your speech always be with grace, seasoned with salt, that you
may know how you ought to answer each one."*
Colossians 4:5,6

Read Colossians Chapter 4

The early church was not highly thought of among nonbelievers. In fact, those outside of Christ thought the church was full of atheists who would not worship the gods of this world. Paul urged the church to be wise in their conduct and busy about the Lord's work. Watch your speech; let your words be gracious reflecting Jesus, with unimpeachable conduct toward one another.

"Unimpeachable" means impeccable, irreproachable, and blameless. "Conduct" means behavior, demeanor, and actions. Nothing is more shameful or embarrassing than a Christian's fall from grace. Although at times we do fail in our flesh, we must learn from our errors and ask God to empower us with His Holy Spirit to live godly lives before the watching world. When unbelievers are going through tribulation, it's often the Christian they seek for prayer or counsel. Yes, the world is watching, and we wait to give them the answer--Jesus, the only saving power for the soul.

Prayer: Father, thank You for Your impeccable love.

Passing The Test

*"But as we have been approved by God to be entrusted with the gospel,
even so we speak, not as pleasing men, but God who tests our hearts."
1 Thessalonians 2:4*

Read 1 Thessalonians Chapters 1 & 2

$\mathscr{P}$aul wanted to clear the air about the criticism that he and his co-laborers received for sharing their faith in Christ. Their motives were pure and their actions were above reproach.

Character is revealed through tests. Paul was well acquainted with tests; he took them often and in the end they revealed his heart as a true lover of Jesus. Paul bore the marks of living a true Christian life. The marks often came in the form of beatings, sufferings, and imprisonment.

It's been said, "Faith that cannot be tested, cannot be trusted." From time to time, we should ask ourselves, whose name do we wear in the face of affliction? Passing the test is not always easy, but when we are fully committed and fully armored in God's Word, we can be sure that when tested, we too will reveal the true marks of a Christian.

Prayer: Father, help us to honor You when we are being tested.

Caught Up

"For the Lord Himself will descend from heaven with a shout, with the voice of an archangel, and with the trumpet of God. And the dead in Christ will rise first. Then we who are alive and remain shall be caught up together with them in the clouds to meet the Lord in the air. And thus we shall always be with the Lord. Therefore comfort one another with these words."

1 Thessalonians 4:16-18

Read 1 Thessalonians Chapters 3 & 4

The rapture of the church is difficult to grasp with our finite minds. How is it that we can be changed in the twinkling of an eye? We must remember that God created us from the dust of the earth. If He could do that, certainly He can transform us at the blink of an eye. Recently while catching up on our e-mail, we marveled at how amazing it is that we can send a message via e-mail, and in moments it is on the other side of the world. Thinking about the rapture, we concluded, ***"Is anything too hard for God?" (Gen. 18:14a)*** Nothing, absolutely nothing, is too hard for God.

Paul wanted the church to be comforted and educated about the Lord's coming. He wanted to make it clear that the dead in Christ would indeed rise first, before those who were alive. We are living on the edge of some incredible times in these last days. As we see the nightly news and align it with Scripture, we should look up, for our redemption is near.

Prayer: Father, thank You for the clear-cut truth in Your Word.

The Day Of The Lord

"But concerning the times and the seasons, brethren, you have no need that I should write to you. For you yourselves know perfectly that the day of the Lord so comes as a thief in the night. For when they say, 'Peace and safety!' then sudden destruction comes upon them, as labor pains upon a pregnant woman. And they shall not escape. But you, brethren, are not in darkness, so that this Day should overtake you as a thief."

1 Thessalonians 5:1-4

Read 1 Thessalonians Chapter 5

We are children of the light! This means that God has revealed to us the hidden mysteries of His kingdom. One revelation is that we are not to be in darkness concerning the Day of the Lord. He is coming again, and while we don't know the day or the hour, we do know that He will come. Because we have been forewarned regarding the Day of the Lord, we should be careful not to fall asleep nor be complacent in our faith. We should be alert and watchful. Christ could come at any moment, and for Christians, His coming should not be a surprise.

Knowing His coming is imminent, we should live our lives in such a way that the world wants to know Jesus. The Day of the Lord for Christians is a celebration. We will finally and forever be with our Lord! **_"For God did not appoint us to wrath, but to obtain salvation through our Lord Jesus Christ." (vs. 9)_** But for the unbelieving world, the Day of the Lord will be a nightmare. Sudden wrath and destruction released by God's judgment will be unleashed upon the unbelieving world. Seize the moment, and share Christ while there is time and opportunity.

Prayer: Father, thank You for salvation. Please help us to be living testimonies of our faith.

Apostasy

"Let no one deceive you by any means; for that Day will not come unless the falling away comes first, and the man of sin is revealed, the son of perdition,"
2 *Thessalonians 2:3*

Read 2 Thessalonians Chapters 1 & 2

There are a few differing views on what "falling away" means. The Greek term commonly means a military rebellion. In the Bible, "falling away" means a spiritual decline and rebellion towards God. We see this rebellion today as we witness the compromise of God's Word taking place in this world. The recent decision among particular church denominations to not only allow, but ordain homosexuals in the church, is evidence of the outright rebellion towards God and His Word. Then there are the seeker-friendly church environments that water down the gospel, cutting out the blood and the cross. These gradual spiritual declines only help to pave the way for apostasy.

Paul urges us to stand fast in our faith. ***"Therefore, brethren, stand fast and hold the traditions which you were taught, whether by word or our epistle." (vs. 15)*** At Calvary Chapel, we are blessed to be taught the uncompromising Word of God. We are taught to hold fast to God's Word and not to waver from it. In these last days, it is so important that we don't compromise our convictions; for if we do, we set ourselves up for deception. Let's heed Paul's admonition to not be deceived.

Prayer: Lord, thank You for the strong foundation we have in Your Word.

Faithful Father

"But the Lord is faithful,
who will establish you and guard you from the evil one."
2 Thessalonians 3:3

Read 2 Thessalonians Chapter 3

As a Christian, do you ever feel that you just might not make it to the finish line? There are so many temptations and attacks from the enemy. We can easily buy into his lie that God has somehow removed His love from us, and that our salvation is dependent upon our ability to achieve. Today's verse clears up the deception of those feelings. "But the Lord is faithful!" Oh what beautiful words these are to a tired, weary, and worn soul. God will establish us and guard us from the evil one. These are comforting words!

God is a faithful Father who watches over the souls of His children. He knows what we can bear, and won't give us more than we can handle. This does not mean we are exempt from trials and tribulations; it means that He will equip us and strengthen us through them. The Thessalonians were under pressure and attack from wicked men, and so Paul is reminding them who is really in control. When our eyes are on our circumstances, we lose sight of the mighty power and omniscience of our Lord. In contrast, when our eyes are set upon our Lord, we see His power and we are enabled to live above the circumstances. We see His faithfulness and protection, and we are strengthened.

Prayer: Father, thank You for being a faithful Father.

The Purpose Of The Law

"But we know that the law is good if one uses it lawfully."
1 Timothy 1:8

Read 1 Timothy Chapter 1

In his letter, Paul encourages Timothy as a true son in the faith. He urges Timothy to correct the wrong thinking that was prevalent in the church. False doctrine was being taught and they were using the law as a platform to promote it. Paul wanted to clarify that the purpose of the law was to make sinners conscious of sin. *"Therefore by the deeds of the law no flesh will be justified in His sight, for by the law is the knowledge of sin." (Rom. 3:20)* Jesus puts an end to "works righteousness." So the law only points out our need for salvation by the grace of God.

Paul urged Timothy to fight the good fight when waging war on those who had strayed from sound doctrine. Paul was pretty frank about the seriousness of the sin committed by those who cause division by teaching false doctrine. *"I delivered them over to Satan that they may learn not to blaspheme." (vs. 20)* We must remember that the law, without love, kills. The new covenant we have in Christ brings life.

Prayer: Father, thank You that in the law, we see our desperate need for You.

Modesty Matters

"In like manner also, that the women adorn themselves in modest apparel, with propriety and moderation, not with braided hair or gold or pearls or costly clothing, but, which is proper for women professing godliness, with good works."
1 Timothy 2:9,10

Read 1 Timothy Chapter 2

The meaning of the word "modesty" has somehow been forgotten, even among the Christian community. The word "modesty" literally means humility. It appears that many women today have no conviction when it comes to wearing revealing or immodest clothing; they take no issue with the fact that they are stumbling their brethren. I have heard this said a number of times, "If men look, they have a problem!" This kind of attitude is irresponsible and it flies in the face of what we are taught in God's Word. The truth is, men do have a problem; by nature they are visually stimulated when they see a woman who wears immodest or provacative clothing, thus becoming stumbled.

Godly women need to look deep into what the Word says about beauty and modesty. We should examine ourselves to see if our hearts are in the wrong place. If the blouse is low enough to reveal even a little cleavage, it's too much. If the pants or skirt are too tight or short, it's too much. No doubt I may have offended some of you, but I would rather do that than have you offend a brother who is trying to live a pure and holy life before his Lord. As godly women, we need to have balance; there is nothing wrong with being fashionable, but it takes wisdom and creativity to look your best and still maintain modesty. If you find this convicting, then I'm sure the Holy Spirit wants to bring about some changes in your apparel. Finally, we need to heed Paul's admonition and concern ourselves with the things that count for eternity. Godly women should care about godly things and have a reputation for doing what is good.

Prayer: Father, help Your daughters to be sensitive to matters concerning modesty.

High And Holy Calling

"This is a faithful saying: If a man desires the position of a bishop, he desires a good work."
1 Timothy 3:1

Read 1 Timothy Chapter 3

The office of a bishop is a high and holy calling; the qualifications of an overseer are clearly articulated by Paul in this chapter. The standards are high and can only be met by living for and loving a Holy God. We have all seen or heard the devastating stories of those who have failed to meet these standards and have found themselves disqualified from ministry. The pain from falling is great, as is the pain that the body of Christ experiences.

We should not fear failure, but rather fear our heavenly Father, the One who is able to keep us from the evil one. When even small compromises seep into our lives, we soon find ourselves on the brink of capitulation and sin. Once a lady told us that she saw nothing wrong with pastors and their wives having an occasional drink. She asked us our opinion about it. We answered by saying, "If even just one drink stumbles our brethren, starting with you, it's not worth it." Those who serve among the body of Christ must be ever mindful of the presence of the Lord. Serving the Lord and His people brings more joy than any temporary moment of pleasure this world offers. It is a good thing to desire the office of a bishop, especially when we understand the calling.

Prayer: Father, keep our hearts pure and right before You.

Step Into Spiritual Shape

"For bodily exercise profits a little, but godliness is profitable for all things, having promise of the life that now is and of that which is to come."
1 Timothy 4:8

Read 1 Timothy Chapter 4

We live in a world that promotes physical exercise. Everywhere we look, we see ad campaigns that market the idea that exercise will give us healthier and fuller lives. There is some truth to this, but if we only seek to be "in shape" physically, we fail to see the bigger spiritual picture.

Stepping into spiritual shape means that we will have a healthier spiritual life by working towards the eternal goal--one that is lasting and will not fade away. If we would allot even a portion of the time that we spend trying to look and feel better, and instead invest it in the things of the Spirit, we would understand the deeper meaning of our verse today. The truth is, these bodies are fading away, and no matter how much we try to rejuvenate them, they are perishing. Paul wrote about this in his letter to the Corinthians. *"Therefore we do not lose heart. Even though our outward man is perishing, yet the inward man is being renewed day by day." (2 Cor. 4:16)* Let's step into spiritual shape by working on the inner person of the heart. This is something that has eternal value and is precious in the sight of God.

Prayer: Father, thank You that You renew our hearts day by day.

The Love Of Money

"But those who desire to be rich fall into temptation and a snare, and into many foolish and harmful lusts which drown men in destruction and perdition. For the love of money is a root of all kinds of evil, for which some have strayed from the faith in their greediness, and pierced themselves through with many sorrows."
1 Timothy 6:9,10

Read 1 Timothy Chapters 5 & 6

"Money, money, money, money!" That's how the song goes, and people still sing its tune today. Paul clearly communicates with the young Timothy, that the love of money produces all kinds of evil. Money has a way of stealing away our affections from the Lord. We often say, "If I won the lotto, I would give all the money to the poor, and I would buy the church whatever it needed." This kind of thinking is exactly what Paul is talking about. If the truth be known, having too much money would destroy most of us. We have all heard the stories of past winners of the lotto. While their bank accounts may be full, their lives are filled with sadness and the complications of having money.

God has created us so that we might depend upon Him for our provisions and be wise with what He has given us. The Scriptures have much to say about the love of money and the destruction that it brings. Contentment is what we should have when it comes to money. In Proverbs, Agur the son of Jakeh, writes about money with a wise and balanced attitude. ***"Two things I request of You (deprive me not before I die): remove falsehood and lies far from me; give me neither poverty nor riches--feed me with the food allotted to me; lest I be full and deny You, and say, 'Who is the Lord?' Or lest I be poor and steal, and profane the name of my God."*** *(Prov. 30:7-9)*

Prayer: Father, thank You that all that we have has been provided by Thine hand.

_____

_____

_____

_____

_____

Stir Up Your Gift

"Therefore I remind you to stir up the gift of God which is in you through the laying on of my hands. For God has not given us a spirit of fear, but of power and of love and of a sound mind."
2 Timothy 1:6,7

Read 2 Timothy Chapter 1

The words "stir up" mean to awaken, and to arouse. The young Timothy was like most of us and was prone to falling into the trap of doing nothing. You get the strong impression that Timothy even had a little fear when it came to using his spiritual gifts for the Lord. We too often succumb to the lie of the enemy and freeze in our faith, laying aside the gifts God has given us. Oftentimes, it's because we have been hurt. It may have been due to a sour remark or an unthankful attitude among those whom we serve.

Paul brings back to Timothy's memory what the gifts are for and from whom they came. God empowers us through His Holy Spirit and gives us gifts to be used for His glory. We must remove ourselves and our own egos when it comes to using them for the Lord. We need to die to self and our own fears in order to stir up the gifts God has given us, and serve Him with a whole heart. If we allow confusion and fear of people or their unloving comments to paralyze us, we lose sight of whom we serve. If you have laid down your spiritual gifts, it's time to take Paul's advice. Stir up the gifts God has given you! If you need help, ask the elders of the church to lay hands on you and pray for you. Get back in the race--this time to win!

Prayer: Father, thank You for awesome reminders like this one, to step up in our faith.

A Soldier's Heart

*"You therefore must endure hardship as a good soldier of Jesus Christ.
No one engaged in warfare entangles himself with the affairs of this life,
that he may please him who enlisted him as a soldier."*
2 Timothy 2:3,4

Read 2 Timothy Chapter 2

The Christian life is one of spiritual warfare; we fight an unseen battle each day. We are called to endure hardships, and to expect them as part of our normal daily lives. We are warned not to become entangled by the cares of this world, for if we do, we weaken our purpose and endanger our own spiritual safety.

Many of our young men and women are serving as good soldiers in Iraq. Each day they wake up to fight the battle for freedom. If they become entangled with the cares of this life, they may be caught off guard by the enemy and may even be captured or die. Having a soldier's heart means that we understand why we are enlisted into God's army. We must be alert, aware, awake, and live our lives in such away that we please Him. We can't let the discouragements of Satan to diminish our purpose. We must remain steadfast in our faith, fighting the good fight to win!

Prayer: Father, thank You for the example of being a good soldier in Your Word.

Perilous Times

"But know this, that in the last days perilous times will come: For men will be lovers of themselves, lovers of money, boasters, proud, blasphemers, disobedient to parents, un-thankful, unholy, unloving, unforgiving, slanderers, without self-control, brutal, despisers of good, traitors, headstrong, haughty, lovers of pleasure rather than lovers of God, having a form of godliness but denying its power. And from such people turn away!"
2 Timothy 3:1-5

Read 2 Timothy Chapter 3:1-9

These verses line up with the evening news! We are indeed living in perilous times. The world is in chaos and people are living lives that are contrary to God. Satan is pulling no punches as he seeks to devour and destroy lives. He does this by deceiving people to believe that there is no God and no accountability before Him. However as Christians, we do not need to fear these times; we just need to continue to walk by faith, believing God for our future. We need not fear Satan, because God is greater. *"You are of God, little children, and have overcome them, because He who is in you is greater than he who is in the world." (1 John 4:4)*

So how then should we live in these perilous times? We need to have our hearts totally devoted to God. He should be in the forefront of our lives and minds. We should abide in His Word daily to get the spiritual nutrition we need to be armed and ready. "To be forewarned is to be forearmed." Finally, we need to be busy redeeming our time for the Lord, looking for the coming of our Lord Jesus Christ.

Prayer: Father, though we live in perilous times, we are privileged to have You on our side.

_____
_____
_____
_____
_____
_____

Inspired By God

"All Scripture is given by inspiration of God, and is profitable for doctrine, for reproof, for correction, for instruction in righteousness,"
2 Timothy 3:16

Read 2 Timothy Chapter 3

The Word of God is literally inspired by His heart; He is the author of the Bible. Every page of the Bible bears the thoughts and intents of God our Father. This is why Calvary Chapels place such an emphasis on God's Word and the importance of learning it and hiding it in our hearts. God's Word is profitable for doctrine, meaning within its pages are the very principles for living the Christian life. God's Word corrects us when we are wrong or in sin, and brings us back to the place of abiding in Christ. God's Word gives us the instructions we need for righteous living.

The inspired Word of God speaks to us when no one else will. It cuts to the very heart of the matters of this life. *"For the word of God is living and powerful, and sharper than any two-edged sword, piercing even to the division of the soul and spirit, and of joints and marrow, and is a discerner of the thoughts and intents of the heart." (Heb. 4:12)* God's Word gives us the ability to believe God for the impossible and helps us to build our faith. *"So then faith comes by hearing, and hearing by the Word of God." (Rom. 10:17)* We should seek out the Word of God because it is His very voice that speaks to us. No wonder the prophet Jeremiah found God's Word to be his life-giving sustenance. *"Your words were found, and I ate them, and Your word was to me the joy and rejoicing of my heart." (Jer. 15:16)*

Prayer: Father, keep us ever so close to Your Word.

Preach The Word

"Preach the word! Be ready in season and out of season.
Convince, rebuke, exhort, with all long-suffering and teaching."
2 Timothy 4:2

Read 2 Timothy Chapter 4

*T*his is an exhortation to preach God's Word without reservation. We are to always be ready to give an account of God's Word. We should not be slack in this area, but rather be faithful in every season. No matter what storms come our way, we should remain steadfast, living above the circumstances of this life.

We are to convince, encouraging others to believe by living a truthful and prudent Christian life. We are to exhort, urging and encouraging others in their faith. We are to rebuke, admonishing and reproving when necessary. We are to be patient and long-suffering, waiting for fruit to come from our obedience. We are to teach, being so acquainted with God's Word that it pours from our lives and overflows into the lives of those around us. The time is short brethren. We need to wake up and start exhorting ourselves and others onward in the faith.

Prayer: Father, thank You for exhortations, like we find in our verse today.

_____

_____

_____

_____

_____

_____

_____

_____

_____

_____

_____

Christ Our Centerpiece

*"Grace, mercy, and peace from God the Father
and the Lord Jesus Christ our Savior."*
Titus 1:4

Read Titus Chapter 1

When we are preparing a special dinner, we always seem to work around the centerpiece; it sets the stage for the rest of the table. It would seem awkward to have a beautiful table without one. The centerpiece brings balance to the entire setting, adding a theme to the event. Christ is the centerpiece of our faith, and He should always be the main focus and motive behind our faith. When we are busy about the things of the Lord, we often lose sight of the very One which we represent. Paul brings into focus the adoration due our heavenly Father and His Son, our Lord Jesus Christ.

With Christ as our centerpiece, we inherit the beautiful gift of grace and peace that flows from the Father's heart. The word "centerpiece" means main attraction, pride and joy, showpiece, and focus. We need to take the time to reflect upon Christ as the center of our life, giving Him the glory and honor due His name. In the opening of his letters to the churches, Paul always seems to have the proper perspective. He always reminds us that Christ is truly our centerpiece.

Prayer: Father, thank You for Your Son Jesus, the centerpiece of our faith.

_____

_____

_____

_____

_____

_____

_____

_____

Divide, Devour & Destroy

"But avoid foolish disputes, genealogies, contentions, and strivings about the law; for they are unprofitable and useless."
Titus 3:9

Read Titus Chapters 2 & 3

There are three things the enemy has in mind when he attacks. Number one is to divide, meaning to split, to separate, to carve up. Number two is to devour, demolish, consume and overcome. Number three is to destroy. Satan's goal is to wipe out, to annihilate, and to tear down. As Christians, we need to be aware that his tactics are subtle. He often comes disguised in religiosity, but soon seeks to cause division among the brethren. Our intellect is often stroked by his cunning devices, and we buy into the same lie and worldly desire as Adam and Eve--the desire for more knowledge. Unfortunately, this knowledge puffs up and eventually causes disputes and contentions.

We should avoid such things and keep our focus on Christ. The times spent arguing over the unessential things of the faith are a waste, and God's Spirit is grieved. Paul writes about it here, saying "...they are unprofitable and useless." There are better things to devote our time to like God's wisdom and truth. We must be aware and alert concerning the subtle attacks of the enemy. *"Knowledge puffs up, but love edifies." (1 Cor. 8:1b)*

Prayer: Father, help our eyes to be open to Your truth.

Put It On My Account

"If then you count me as a partner, receive him as you would me.
But if he has wronged you or owes anything, put that on my account."
Philemon 17,18

Read Philemon

*O*nesimus was a runaway slave; he had left the house of Philemon, only to encounter the true freedom found in Jesus Christ. Paul now writes to Philemon asking him to receive Onesimus back, not only as a slave, but a brother. Paul truly believed that Onesimus had repented, so he offered to pay for any loss Philemon suffered due to Onesimus' departure. Paul could do this because he witnessed Onesimus' true conversion. We can take a lesson from Paul concerning forgiveness and paying the debt for someone else's wrong.

Our ultimate example however, is Jesus Christ who picked up the tab and unconditionally paid the debt of sin for the entire world. As Christians we should be quick to forgive, especially when a person has repented. Onesimus would return to Philemon with a new freedom--a freedom he didn't expect to receive. He would now be a better servant and a true brother in the faith. Is there something or someone in your life that owes you a debt? Put it on the Lord's account! He will repay the debt and you will be free from the bondage of a bitter and unforgiving heart.

Prayer: Father, help us to forgive, especially those who have repented from sin.

My Son

"You are My Son, today I have begotten You."
Hebrews 1:5a

Read Hebrews Chapter 1

*J*esus, the Son of God! We can only imagine how the Father must have felt when Jesus accomplished His work as the Messiah. His birth was a miracle from the beginning--divinely born to a young Jewish girl who believed God for what seemed the impossible. Later, Jesus sacrificed His life on the cross and paid in full, the debt man could never pay. Now Jesus sits at His rightful place, the right hand of the Father, who is well pleased with His Son.

In this first chapter of Hebrews, the writer explains why Jesus is above the angels by referring to Psalm 2:7. This Psalm reveals the Father's delight in the work of His Son. Jesus is above the angels because He is the Father's only Son. He is incomparable to any creation, because as God, He is superior to any created being. And now He occupies His rightful place at the right hand of God. *"But this Man, after He had offered one sacrifice for sins forever, sat down at the right hand of God." (Heb. 10:12)* As He sits at the right hand of God, He makes intercession for us. *"He always lives to make intercession for them." (Heb. 7:25b)* This knowledge should motivate us to glorify Jesus in all that we do. This also provides confidence for our daily living as Jesus intercedes for us, and sees us through the difficulties of this life.

Prayer: Father, thank You for Your Son, our Savior.

325

Drifting Away

"Therefore we must give the more earnest heed to the things we have heard, lest we drift away."
Hebrews 2:1

Read Hebrews Chapter 2

One day we were at the beach, settling in and finally getting into the water. We were having so much fun that we hardly noticed we had slowly drifted away from the spot where we had settled. That's how it is when we start making even tiny compromises in our faith. Like the current at the beach that caused us to drift away, we suddenly find ourselves wandering without direction. The writer of Hebrews warns us not to neglect the things which we have learned, even though they might seem repetitious.

Drifting Away

Drifting away we do
When our eyes aren't on You
Slowly we find ourselves afar
When all the while You are near

Drifting away we do
When our eyes aren't on You
Compromise takes us too far
When we lose sight of You

Drifting away we do
When eyes aren't on You
Lost and confused
Until we wander back to You

Drifting away we do
When our eyes aren't on You
Keep us ashore
Our minds stayed on You
So drifting away we won't wander far.
TLR

Prayer: Father, thank You for reminders like this one, to take heed lest we drift away.

An Evil Heart Of Unbelief

"Beware, brethren, lest there be in any of you an evil heart of unbelief in departing from the living God;"
Hebrews 3:12

Read Hebrews Chapter 3

*L*iving in a state of unbelief is a dangerous place to be. For if in our faith we don't believe, we are nothing more than a skeptic. In our verse today, we are warned that having a heart of unbelief is evil, which is sin. As Christians we are called to have faith and believe in God. *"But without faith it is impossible to please Him, for he who comes to God must believe that He is, and that He is a rewarder of those who diligently seek Him." (Heb. 11:6)*

We need to keep our faith alive, and we do that by heeding God's Word and staying in fellowship with Him. Too many times we see that folks slip away from God because they were too impatient for Him to work in their lives. The results have been devastating. We've seen this in the lives of young people who refuse to wait for God to bring them the right mate. They are impatient, so they seek out a mate by conforming to the world, only to find that they were deceived by Satan. It takes faith not to believe, so why not use our faith <u>to believe</u>? It pleases God for one, and it gives us assurance to know we are under His umbrella of protection. We need to be patient in our belief, knowing that God will answer. Sometimes God says "yes," sometimes God says "no," and sometimes God says "wait." The truth is, God <u>will</u> answer our heart's cry. We just need to believe that He is God, and set aside our doubts and unbelief.

Prayer: Father, help us with unbelief.

Sharper Than Any Two-Edged Sword

"For the word of God is living and powerful, and sharper than any two-edged sword, piercing even to the division of soul and spirit, and of joints and marrow, and is a discerner of the thoughts and intents of the heart."

Hebrews 4:12

Read Hebrews Chapter 4

The Word of God is living, meaning its words possess life. The Word of God is powerful and influential. The Word of God is sharper than any two-edged sword, and can be used as a weapon. It is piercing, knife-like, and able to cut to the very heart of the soul and spirit. The Word of God discerns the thoughts and intents of the heart. It knows and understands the matters of the heart.

These are the very reasons why we as believers should hide God's Word in our hearts--so that we might be able to stand on His truth. The Word of God should be an integral part of our daily lives. We all need to be admonished to stay close to God and His Word. Do you realize that others count on you to stand strong in His Word? The Word of God has the ability to change our perspective, and helps us to keep an eternal view. It exhorts us to live above the circumstances that so often handicaps our faith. Even one day without the Word can be detrimental to our spiritual health. So if you have been neglecting God's Word, you already know that He is calling you to return to the place where you will find His supernatural power to live the Christian life.

Prayer: Father, thank You for reminding us of the power of Your Word.

Time To Grow Up

"For though by this time you ought to be teachers, you need someone to teach you again the first principles of the oracles of God; and you have come to need milk and not solid food. For everyone who partakes only of milk is unskilled in the word of righteousness, for he is a babe."
Hebrews 5:12,13

Read Hebrews Chapter 5

Each day we all have one thing in common--we are given 24 hours. How we choose to use those 24 hours determines who we love to serve. For some, it's just getting through the workday; yet for others, it's making room in their schedules for hobbies or things of interest. Unless we, as children of God, make room for Him in our daily lives, we are probably growing in Christ at a snail's pace. The writer of Hebrews confronts this kind of lethargic thinking and exhorts the reader to grow up. "You should be teachers by now." This means that much time has been wasted, and it's because the approach towards God and His Word has been childlike. We should start managing our time with purpose, asking God to forgive us for our baby-like behavior, and start moving forward in our faith. It's time to grow up!

We were just recently on vacation in the Eastern Sierras. As we were traveling through a small town, we noticed that many of the churches had banners that read, "Forty Days of Purpose." How about 365 days a year and 24 hours a day of purpose? Yes, it's time to grow up! We need to make our days count for the Lord and for eternity by staying close to the God whom we say we love.

Prayer: Father, thank You for admonishments like these to "grow up."

Anchored In Christ

*"This hope we have as an anchor of the soul, both sure and steadfast,
and which enters the Presence behind the veil."*

Hebrews 6:19

Read Hebrews Chapter 6

Hope is one of the most beautiful words that we know. It means we can optimistically anticipate and expect that our Lord will do just what He has promised. As believers, our hope is secured in Christ, just like an anchor that securely holds a boat in place.

Anchored In Christ

Anchored in Christ we are
With a hope that is an anchor to our souls
Security is what this means
Our Savior will own

Hope is beautiful as we place it in Thee
Steadfast and sure to all who believe

Anchored in Christ we are
With a hope that is an anchor to our souls
Anxiously we wait for You
To come through

The storms they will come and go
But fear we need not, with Christ at the helm
We are safe even in the unknown.   *TLR*

Prayer: Father, thank You for the hope we have in You.

_____

_____

_____

_____

_____

_____

_____

_____

He Lives To Make Intercession For Us

*"Therefore He is also able to save to the uttermost those who come to God
through Him, since He always lives to make intercession for them."*
Hebrews 7:25

Read Hebrews Chapter 7

The saving power of Christ is an awesome thing, and it is highlighted by the fact that He is always making intercession for us. The finished work of the cross is enough. We are saved by God's grace, and the work He does in our lives is ongoing. The fact that Jesus is making intercession for us to His Father God means that He is our advocate.

Our Lord God is able to save to the uttermost, even those who may appear to be the farthest away from Him. This is why we should never give up on God and never give up on anyone, despite how far they may seem from Him. Our sanctification is not dependent upon our goodness or works, but rather on what Jesus Christ did for us on the cross. He freed us from the power of sin. Although we may still sin, we are not bound by sin, and we have Someone to go to with our sin. The Christian life is progressive and as we grow in Christ we should sin less. We will continue to be sanctified until finally we are glorified. We of course should never cheapen God's grace with unrepentance, for surely forgiveness and repentance go hand in hand.

Prayer: Father, thank You that through Your Son Jesus, You care for our souls.

331

Once And For All, To All Who Believe

"So Christ was offered once to bear the sins of many. To those who eagerly wait for Him He will appear a second time, apart from sin, for salvation."
Hebrews 9:28

Read Hebrews Chapters 8 & 9

*I*n the Old Testament, we see that many animal sacrifices were necessary for the atonement of man's sins. In the New Testament, we see that Christ was the ultimate sacrifice, coming in the form of a man. He is God and gave His life as a sacrifice for all who believe.

Christ's one time death <u>was</u> and <u>is</u> sufficient for salvation. Unlike the ritualistic and repetitive works of animal sacrifices, His one time death on the cross paid the penalty for sin. When we sin, we can now come boldly before God and ask for forgiveness through His Son, Jesus Christ. His love and blood covers our sins and sanctifies us. Jesus has given us a new covenant, the covenant of salvation that He promised, then fulfilled. When we think of the Old Testament saints and the repetitious rituals they had to endure, we find ourselves even more thankful for the precious new covenant we have in Christ.

Prayer: Father, thank You for Your Son and the new covenant we have through His death.

Draw Near

"Let us draw near with a true heart in full assurance of faith, having our hearts sprinkled from an evil conscience and our bodies washed with pure water."
Hebrews 10:22

Read Hebrews Chapter 10

This is an invitation to come before God, having the assurance that He has already paid a great price for our sins, and that we have full access to Him. In the Old Testament, the high priest always washed before he entered the Holy Place. Christ's blood is sufficient for cleansing. His blood washed away our sins, making it possible to go before Him and to have a personal relationship with Him.

In our verse today, we are encouraged to draw near to God. We should seek Him out and wholeheartedly desire to have fellowship with Him. ***"Draw near to God and He will draw near to you." (James 4:8)*** Sin has a way of creeping into our lives and separating us from our Father. But, we already know that a great provision has been made for our sins by the blood of Jesus. So let us come before Him in repentance, knowing that He has already washed and cleansed us, making it possible to draw near to Him. And with full assurance, He guarantees to meet us.

Prayer: Father, thank You that You guarantee to meet us whenever we seek You.

Hall Of Faith

"Now faith is the substance of things hoped for, the evidence of things not seen."
Hebrews 11:1

Read Hebrews Chapter 11

*F*or the Christian, the word "faith" means confidence, assurance, reliance, and devotion. Hebrews Chapter 11 is known as the "Hall Of Faith." On the walls of this hall hang the pictures and stories of those who have gone faithfully before us. Their examples are outlined one by one for us to glean from. Too often we think that we are the only ones who have had to believe God for the impossible. Not so! Many have gone before us, walking their own lives of faith, believing in God for the unseen. God in His infinite wisdom, allowed difficult and complicated situations to arise in the lives of our forefathers of the faith. Why? Because God wanted them to build trust in Him. So often, the only way we humans learn, is by seeing the invisible God do the miraculous.

Our faith in God and His Son Jesus is the substance and essence of what we believe. He builds our faith by proving that He is able to do all things. His omnipotence is the evidence that substantiates our faith. What impossible situation do you face today? What is the one thing that you believe God for? Revisit the stories of old, mentioned in this chapter, and let them jog your memory regarding God's faithfulness in times of testing.

Prayer: Father, thank You for being the evidence of things unseen.

_____

_____

_____

_____

_____

_____

_____

Maranatha Marathon

"Therefore we also, since we are surrounded by so great a cloud of witnesses, let us lay aside every weight, and the sin which so easily ensnares us, and let us run with endurance the race that is set before us, looking unto Jesus, the author and finisher of our faith, who for the joy that was set before Him endured the cross, despising the shame, and has sat down at the right hand of the throne of God."

Hebrews 12:1,2

Read Hebrews Chapter 12

The word "Maranatha" means the Lord cometh. The word "marathon" means long-distance race. Combine these words and it summarizes our verse today. We are in this race until the Lord takes us home. We should be looking unto Jesus, knowing that He is the originator of our faith, trusting Him that we will finish.

Any runner in a marathon knows that in order to reach the finish line, he must not be bogged down with extra weight. The runner travels light and with a focused purpose. He is well-trained and determined to finish well. He has a healthy diet, makes personal sacrifices, and denies his flesh so that he might accomplish his goal. The writer of Hebrews, like a good coach, encourages us to do the same. Let us remember why we are in the race. We must stay focused, and not skip our spiritual feedings such as daily devotions, church services, prayer, and fellowship. Keep a light touch on the things of this world, and remember that in His time we will finish the race well. So if you have veered off track, it's time to get back into the race--this time to win!

Prayer: Father, thank You for exhortations like this one to stay focused on You.

Be Content

"Let your conduct be without covetousness;
be content with such things as you have."
Hebrews 13:5a

Read Hebrews Chapter 13

In our verse today, we are admonished not to allow the bitter seed of covetousness to enter our hearts and affect our conduct. This is perhaps the most silent of sins, because it starts with a discontented spirit that critically assesses what we may or may not have. To top it off, we live in a world that encourages us to be self-indulgent. The problem with self-indulgence is that it is never enough. We always want just a little more than we have or can afford. So how do we reconcile this dilemma? We must first go to our Lord in repentance, thanking Him for what we do have. We then need to understand that there is nothing, or no one in this life that can satisfy our hearts the way He can.

Solomon, one of the richest men to ever live, had everything that the flesh could ever want. He had wisdom, wealth, power, a multitude of women, the best clothes, food and homes, yet it was not enough. In his closing thoughts in the book of Ecclesiastes, Solomon concluded this: *"Let us hear the conclusion of the whole matter: Fear God and keep His commandments, for this is man's all." (Eccl. 12:13)* True contentment can only be found and valued in Him; for He is able to lift us above the discontentments of this life and make us grateful for what we have, especially His unconditional love.

Prayer: Father, thank You for being all that we need to be content.

Listen

"So then, my beloved brethren, let every man be swift to hear, slow to speak, slow to wrath; for the wrath of man does not produce the righteousness of God."
James 1:19,20

Read James Chapter 1

If we would be as swift to listen as we are to speak, we would probably not be so misunderstood and confused. Listening is no doubt one of our greatest challenges; we often speak before we think. Consider these common scenarios: A wife is trying to communicate her needs to her husband, but he is just not hearing her. A husband expresses his frustration over his job, but his wife ignore his complaints. A child cries out to be heard, but everyone is just too busy to listen. Sadly, the consequences of not listening can have devastating results.

James reminds us of the importance of being quick to hear and slow to speak. This takes patience, and it takes a heart that is willing to step back and observe. Try it sometime; really pay attention to what others are saying. Look at them when they speak, and prayerfully consider how you might answer. God is always willing to listen to us, and we should be willing to listen to Him. This requires ears that are ready to hear. Hearing what God has to say is paramount in having a close, personal relationship with Him. ***"My sheep hear My voice, and I know them, and they follow Me." (John 10:27)***

Prayer: Father, help us to listen to Your still small voice, and to others we may be neglecting.

_____

_____

_____

_____

_____

_____

_____

Faith In Action

*"What does it profit, my brethren, if someone
says he has faith but does not have works? Can faith save him?"*

James 2:14

Read James Chapter 2

*J*ames might be misunderstood by those who think he is trying to say, we are saved by our works. This is not James' point. His exhortation is directed to those who might be complacent in their faith, believing that all they need to do is believe. James is saying that genuine faith produces genuine works. Later in the chapter, James states his concerns about this matter of faith and works. *"But someone will say, 'You have faith, and I have works.' Show me your faith without your works, and I will show you my faith by my works." (vs. 18)*

Paul wrote, *"Therefore we conclude that a man is justified by faith apart from the deeds of the law." (Rom. 3:28)* While this Scripture is so very true, some may mistake its intentions to mean that we don't have to put "feet to our faith." There are many examples of men and women in Scripture who had both faith and works operating in their lives. Abraham had incredible faith, but it didn't stay there; he moved forward in action. Abraham's faith produced a work in him so great, that he was willing to sacrifice his son Isaac on the altar for God. Are you experiencing a time in your life where your faith is apathetic or dead? If so, ask God to refresh your heart and begin serving Him.

Prayer: Father, thank You that our faith is alive, active, and working in us for You.

_____

_____

_____

_____

_____

_____

_____

The Taming Of The Tongue

"But no man can tame the tongue.
It is an unruly evil, full of deadly poison."
James 3:8

Read James Chapter 3

This verse is perhaps one of the most difficult to reconcile. For in reading it, there is a sense of hopelessness about conquering the spew of the tongue. Let's take a deeper look at what our verse is saying. No man can tame the tongue; this is true, for in our flesh dwells no good thing. One of the dilemmas concerning the tongue is that it is used constantly, and often words flow before wisdom does. It frequently takes a series of failures in our speech before we even begin to grasp the nature of its evil. When the words leave our mouth, we often wish we could take them back, but the damage is already done. The tongue is an unruly evil, full of deadly poison. It is unmanageable and full of fatal venom. The tongue has the ability to both bless and curse our Lord.

So how do we even begin to tame the tongue? We need to remember that, *"With God all things are possible." (Matt. 19:26)* When we sin with our tongues and have been convicted by the Holy Spirit, we should repent. We should ask God to help us to put a guard over our mouths. *"I said, 'I will guard my ways, lest I sin with my tongue; I will restrain my mouth with a muzzle,'" (Ps. 39:1)* We need to remember to keep our conversations Christ-centered, for in doing so there is safety. We should seek to use our mouths to edify others and not tear them down.

Prayer: Father, thank You for mercy; for we desperately need it, especially in our speech.

Life Is But A Vapor

"Whereas you do not know what will happen tomorrow. For what is your life? It is even a vapor that appears for a little time and then vanishes away."
James 4:14

Read James Chapter 4

We are not in control of our destiny in this life. We wake up everyday not really knowing what will come our way. We may have our own personal agenda, but life takes many twists and turns. It's almost as if God wants us to be in the dark about tomorrow, so we will trust Him for today.

Just Today

Just today, to live for You
Even in today, things can go awry
Life is uncertain, nothing for sure
Except for Your love, and life through Your Son

Just today, to live for You
When we worry about tomorrow, we are in debt to it too
Strength for this journey is what we need
We are dependent upon You for everything

Just today, to live for You
With the promise that You will provide a way
Keep us trusting You with all of our hearts
For this life is a vapor
And surely one day we will rest in Your arms, for eternity.
TLR

Prayer: Father, help us to live in the present and just for today.

_____
_____
_____
_____
_____
_____
_____

Fervent Prayer

"The effective, fervent prayer of a righteous man avails much."
James 5:16b

Read James Chapter 5

*O*ur prayer lives can often become ineffective when we allow them to become routine and mundane. Ritualistic and repetitive prayers are boring for both God and us. In our verse today, James reminds us that prayer is a privilege and we should approach it with fervent hearts. The word "fervent" means enthusiastic. Therefore, we should eagerly approach prayer with the expectancy that our prayers are being heard and will be answered.

When we really consider what our prayer lives mean to God and us, we should be motivated and excited to pray. We have the awesome privilege of going before the holy throne room of our Lord and making intercession before Him. He is always listening, and He too wants to respond with fervency. James finishes this verse with the reminder that, "fervent prayer avails much." So if you have been feeling like your prayer life is stagnating and lacking, be reminded and encouraged that God hears. He is waiting for you to come with anticipation and expectancy.

Prayer: Father, forgive us for the times we have come before You without expectancy.

Living Trust

"Blessed be the God and Father of our Lord Jesus Christ, who according to His abundant mercy has begotten us again to a living hope through the resurrection of Jesus Christ from the dead, to an inheritance incorruptible and undefiled and that does not fade away, reserved in heaven for you."
1 Peter 1:3,4

Read 1 Peter Chapter 1

A few years ago, we made arrangements to have a living trust prepared so that in the event of our death, our family would receive an inheritance. In the trust we stated our desires and wishes, and things are now set in order. The value of our living trust probably doesn't amount to much; eventually its material worth will fade away and will only be a memory. Jesus Christ, our Lord and Savior, is our Living Trust. His death and resurrection are part of the legacy He left to us; it is an inheritance that will not fade away. His Living Trust is not like any other; it is never ending, promising to be with us forever.

The word "inheritance" means birthright. We really don't deserve such an inheritance, but because we are God's sons and daughters, we immediately (upon spiritual conception) became heirs to His kingdom. Think about the things that you possess and may want to leave to your children. Despite their earthly value, nothing will compare to the Living Trust that you can leave them through Jesus Christ. The inclusive love of God shines brightly in our verses today. We are rich and wealthy beyond what any earthly inheritance could provide.

Prayer: Father, thank You for the incorruptible living trust You have left to all who believe.

His Marvelous Light

"But you are a chosen generation, a royal priesthood, a holy nation, His own special people, that you may proclaim the praises of Him who called you out of darkness into His marvelous light;"

1 Peter 2:9

Read 1 Peter Chapter 2

Sometimes we forget the darkness of the past we once walked in and the life that so desperately needed a Savior. When we responded to the call of His Spirit, we came out of darkness and into His marvelous light. The word "light" means illumination; in other words, the lights went on, and we could see and understand spiritual things.

We are His own special people, and we are called to proclaim the praises of Him who brought us out of darkness and into His marvelous light. Think about it for a moment. Where do you think you would be today if that light were not in your life? We know where we would be, and most likely that would be dead. We don't always see ourselves the way God does; we often see our failures and inability to avoid sin. God sees us as His kids, and like any good father He seeks to correct us when we err and return us to His path of righteousness. God sees the finished work that He has begun in us, and that's why we should proclaim His praises to this generation.

Prayer: Father, thank You for Your marvelous light.

_____
_____
_____
_____
_____
_____
_____
_____
_____

God Sees & Hears

"For the eyes of the Lord are on the righteous, and His ears are open to their prayers; but the face of the Lord is against those who do evil."
1 Peter 3:12

Read 1 Peter Chapter 3

Our grandson, Wyatt, was at our home last night. He is an active one year old, and it takes his parents' attentive eyes as well as ours to watch and keep him from danger. Our ears are constantly listening to Wyatt, as he babbles baby words trying to talk. We wouldn't want to miss a thing he has to say! In our verse today, Peter paints a picture that describes how God's eyes are upon His children and how He attentively listens to our hearts' cry.

We often feel as if we are alone in the difficulties of this life. There are times when we are hurting, and we don't think anyone sees or wants to hear our burdens. This verse poses an encouragement to those who are living right before God. We are encouraged that God does see and hear our prayers. He answers them too. *"Many are the afflictions of the righteous, but the Lord delivers him out of them all." (Ps. 34:19)* Peter finishes this verse by making it clear that the "face of God is against those who do evil." It may appear that people are getting away with their evil practices, but one day they will be accountable for their lives before God, and He will judge them.

Prayer: Father, thank You that we have an advocate in You.

_____
_____
_____
_____
_____
_____
_____
_____
_____

The End To All Things

"But the end of all things is at hand;
therefore be serious and watchful in your prayers."
1 Peter 4:7

Read 1 Peter Chapter 4

*I*t's been asked, "If you had only 24 hours to live, how would you live those 24 hours?" This is a good question to ponder. Peter is admonishing us as believers to live our lives in such a fashion that we expect Christ's return at any moment. Let's be serious about our relationship with God, and be watchful for His coming in both conduct and prayer. The end of all things should keep us looking at the eternal hope we have in Christ, and not the temporal things of this world.

Take some time today to evaluate your life. Take inventory of the things that are most important to you. Look closely at your heart; are you pleasing God with your whole life? Or are you a casual Christian, a sort of spectator in the faith? Peter closes this chapter with a reminder that God will judge His own. ***"For the time has come for judgment to begin at the house of God; and if it begins with us first, what will be the end of those who do not obey the gospel of God?" (vs. 17)*** We have been given much in Christ, so with it comes much responsibility. God wants our whole heart, not just a part of it. We need to be alert, living as if we were in the last 24 hours of this life.

Prayer: Father, help us to take heed to this admonishment to be serious and watchful.

_____
_____
_____
_____
_____
_____
_____
_____
_____

Let Go & Let God

"Casting all your care upon Him, for He cares for you."
1 Peter 5:7

Read 1 Peter Chapter 5

A few years ago some friends gave us a plaque that said, *"Good morning, this is God. I will be handling all of your problems today."* We worry, fear, and fret over things that are completely out of our control. If we would just go to God with our cares in the beginning, we would save ourselves so much unnecessary anxiety. We are human though, and God will allow us to come to the end of ourselves so that we will finally see how desperately we need Him.

Peter brings home this truth by reminding us that we need to cast our care upon the Lord, because He cares for us. We need to resign as chief executive officers of our lives, and let go and let God do what He does best. Furthermore, we are reminded in Romans 8:28 that *"All things work together for good to those who love God."* This means that even our troubles can work in our favor because Christ cares. There have been countless times in our lives when God has turned something bad into good. So in the event you have been trying to handle the difficulties of this life in your own strength, let go and give them over to the One who cares for you.

Prayer: Father, thank You that You are in charge. Help us to trust You.

Reminders

"For this reason I will not be negligent to remind you always of these things,
though you know and are established in the present truth."
2 Peter 1:12

Read 2 Peter Chapter 1

We all need to jog our memories from time to time. We have reminders all around us so we don't forget to do the things that are important. We have palm pilots, day planners, calendars, e-mail, and secretaries to provide daily reminders of our appointments. All these resources and still on occasion we forget.

As Peter nears the end of his life, his pervading thought is to remind the brethren of the importance of staying close and true to God's Word. Peter knows that we have this knowledge, but is compelled by the Holy Spirit to let these reminders be heard over and over again, as long as he has breath. The written word is so important, and Peter highlights this later in the chapter when he says that he is making efforts to leave behind reminders of the faith. *"Moreover I will be careful to ensure that you always have a reminder of these things after my decease."* *(vs. 15)* We can take a lesson from Peter and his reminders. He knew this life was temporal, for he lived in persecution and continually on the verge of death. But even in his suffering, the Holy Spirit was moving Peter to speak the praises of the One whom he would be with for eternity. What kind of heavenly reminders are you leaving behind for others to glean from?

Prayer: Father, thank You for the continual reminders of how precious our faith is.

Godly Deliverance

"And delivered righteous Lot, who was oppressed by the filthy conduct of the wicked."
2 Peter 2:7

Read 2 Peter Chapter 2

At first glance, our immediate reaction is to pass judgment on Lot for the poor decisions he made throughout his life. We think about the time in Genesis Chapter 13 when Lot chose what appeared to be the better land for himself. Or we think back to the time when he offered his daughters to the evil men of Sodom. To some of us, Lot was a lost soul who deserved God's wrath. However, in our verse today, we see that Lot was called righteous. He was an imperfect man who became a victim of his poor choices and the evil conditions that surrounded his life.

God called Lot righteous. Why? God knows the thoughts and the intents of the heart and judges them. When the time came to leave Sodom and Gomorrah, Lot obeyed and did not look back upon the corrupt city, but his wife did. As she was running out of Sodom, her flesh looked back to yearn for the carnal life she loved more than God. We are admonished in Scripture to *"Remember Lot's wife." (Luke 17: 32)* Remember that there is a cost for loving the world more than God. Lot's wife looked back and she became a pillar of salt. If God called Lot righteous, then we should take a second look at Lot's life. God did deal with Lot's inadequacies; he lost his wife and belongings, but in the end he did not lose His God whom he loved. We also see that his life is a reminder to us to keep a light touch on this world and its material offerings.

Prayer: Father, thank You that Your mercy is not contingent upon our mistakes.

God Is Free From The Tyranny Of Time

*"But, beloved, do not forget this one thing, that with the Lord one day is
as a thousand years, and a thousand years as one day."*
2 Peter 3:8

Read 2 Peter Chapter 3

For most of us, the clock is ticking and our lives revolve around time. We are in bondage to the hours of each day. Peter reminds us in this chapter that God is in control of time, and in fact He transcends time. *"The Lord is not slack concerning His promise, as some count slackness, but is longsuffering toward us, not willing that any should perish but that all should come to repentance." (vs. 9)* God's passion for souls is evident in this verse; He waits patiently for those to come to Him. Think about the moment when you first believed. Aren't you glad that God patiently waited until that decision was made? While it may appear that God is taking His "sweet time" to return for His church, He has perfect timing. He is not a slacker; in fact He is carefully awaiting the day when that last soul says, "Yes Lord!"

So how then should we live? We should live our lives believing that we are on the threshold of eternity. Many people lose heart and say, "They've been saying the Lord is going to return since my grandma was a young girl." Again, God has sovereignty and wisdom in delays; so many have come to the saving knowledge of Christ since grandma was a little girl. But, we should not take ease. Peter also reminds us that, *"The day of the Lord will come as a thief in the night." (vs. 10)* We should be watchful and prayerful, and not neglect the things of faith. *"And do this, knowing the time, that now it is high time to awake out of sleep; for now our salvation is nearer than when we first believed." (Rom. 13:11)*

Prayer: Father, thank You for being in control of time.

True Confessions

"If we confess our sins, He is faithful and just to forgive us our sins and to cleanse us from all unrighteousness."
1 John 1:9

Read 1 John Chapter 1

Next to John 3:16, this verse is one of our favorites because it reflects the true character of a loving and merciful God. This verse invites the believer to come before God to be washed and cleansed from sin. We should be mindful that sin severs our fellowship with God. *"If we say that we have fellowship with Him, and walk in darkness, we lie and do not practice the truth." (vs. 6)* We often plod along in our relationship with God with a "business-as-usual" attitude; this is a dangerous place to be. We easily begin to drift away, hardly noticing that we have strayed. The flesh left alone is destructive, and is in constant need of being brought under the subjection of the Holy Spirit.

The word "confession" means to admit that we were wrong and are truly repentant for our sins. God is faithful and just to forgive us and cleanse us. These are perhaps some of the most beautiful words in the Bible. If you are at a place in your life where you are feeling distant from God, it's time to reevaluate your heart, and examine where you are with God. If sin has been keeping you from having fruitful fellowship with Him, take time out for true confessions, and expect to be brought back to the place of walking in the Spirit.

Prayer: Father, thank You for Your mercy.

_____

_____

_____

_____

_____

_____

_____

_____

Passing Through

"Do not love the world or the things in the world."
1 John 2:15a

Read 1 John Chapter 2

The Christian life is a life of pilgrimage; we are simply passing through. On our pilgrimage, we can often lose sight of the eternal perspective and set our sights on the things of this world. Having a love for the world means that we have an appetite for evil. The lust of the eyes, the lust of the flesh, and the pride of life--these are the very things that keep us from loving our Father in Heaven.

How do we balance this out? Does this mean that God does not want us to be blessed in this life? If we look at the life of Abraham, the Father of all nations, we see that he was tremendously blessed with earthly possessions. It was God who blessed him, so we see that God does desire to bless His children. The balance comes in knowing where our blessings come from, and not allowing them to steal away our love from the Giver of these things. Like Abraham who was called "A friend of God," we are called to love God more than this world or anything it has to offer. John beautifully illustrates this point as he reminds us that we are just passing through. *"And the world is passing away, and the lust of it; but he who does the will of God abides forever."* *(vs. 17)*

Prayer: Father, help us to keep a light touch on this world.

We Shall See Him

"Beloved, now we are children of God; and it has not yet been revealed
what we shall be, but we know that when He is revealed,
we shall be like Him, for we shall see Him as He is."
1 John 3:2

Read 1 John Chapter 3

*I*n Corinthians, Paul wrote that now we only see in part. *"For we know in part and we prophesy in part. But when that which is perfect has come, then that which is in part will be done away." (1 Cor. 13:9,10)* We walk this life in faith believing God for the invisible. Yet, we know in our spirits that He is real because He has revealed Himself to us. One day we will know Him as He is, and we shall be like Him. John was expressing the hope that we have in knowing the One who holds our future.

When we consider our future in heaven with our beloved Lord, we know that this world holds nothing that will compare to the glory that will be revealed when we see Him. Consider for a moment what it will be like to be free from the tyranny of sin. We will no longer be plagued by these mortal bodies, but we will be renewed and we will be like Him. This hope purifies our hearts and minds, and that's why John encourages us. *"And everyone who has this hope in Him purifies himself, just as He is pure." (vs. 3)* So if your heart has been failing you, be of good courage, for we will soon be with our beloved Lord.

Prayer: Father, thank You that one day we will see You as You are.

Overcomers

"You are of God, little children, and have overcome them,
because He who is in you is greater than he who is in the world."
1 John 4:4

Read 1 John Chapter 4

There are many things that oppose the faith of God's children. John warns us in the previous Scriptures that we are not to believe every spirit, but rather test them to see if they are of God. In our verse today, we are encouraged to take heart. The Holy Spirit that dwells in us is greater than any evil spirit that the devil brings our way.

From the beginning, Satan has tried to advance his kingdom. Oftentimes he comes disguised as one of God's children. We should be aware of his tactics, and ask the Holy Spirit for wisdom and spiritual discernment. The message that stands out in today's verse is that we are overcomers because of the Holy Spirit, thus we will prevail over any attack that the enemy plots against us. In this chapter, John reminds us that we are not of this world. Since we are God's children, we have already triumphed over the evil of Satan. The Spirit of God is upon us, and this should cast out any fear that the enemy might use to paralyze our faith.

Prayer: Father, thank You for Your Holy Spirit and the wisdom we receive from You.

According To His Will

*"Now this is the confidence that we have in Him,
that if we ask anything according to His will, He hears us."*
1 John 5:14

Read 1 John Chapter 5

$\mathcal{D}$o you ever feel as though your prayers are ineffective? We have felt that way many times. However, answered prayer is not contingent upon how we feel, but rather on how we pray. John lays out clear guidelines on how to pray with confidence. We are admonished to pray according to His will. So in a nutshell, we can be confident that God hears our prayers as we pray accordingly. We should never feel as though our prayers fall on deaf ears. James emphasized the importance of our prayers to God when he wrote, *"The effective, fervent prayer of a righteous man avails much." (James 5:16b)*

God always answers prayers when we pray according to His will. This means that we are to entrust our prayers to His will, wisdom and sovereignty. In answering prayers, He sometimes says "yes," and He sometimes says "no," and He sometimes says "wait." We always seem to be glad when He says "yes," but we often struggle when He says "no," and we can hardly bear it when He says "wait!" Again, the whole point in praying to Him is so that our will becomes conformed to His. We are so thankful for the many times God has answered our prayers with a clear "yes!" and a definite "no!" We have also learned to be grateful for those times when it appeared as though God was silent, yet in His sovereignty He was delaying His answer by saying "wait!"

Prayer: Father, thank You for Your sovereignty in answering our prayers.

Imitate That Which Is Good

"Beloved, do not imitate what is evil, but what is good.
He who does good is of God, but he who does evil has not seen God."
3 John 11

Read 2 & 3 John

There are certain signs that reflect a life that loves God. The desire to do good and honor the Lord is the fruit of a true believer who understands the deeper things of God. There are also certain signs of a life that reflects evil. The desire to practice evil is also fruit of the flesh and reflects a heart that rejects God. John is writing to help the church discern the difference between lives that reflect good versus evil.

So often folks come in for counseling, and many yield to the biblical counsel they are given. Those who don't, go their own way and continue doing things according to the flesh. They often wonder why their lives are in continual turmoil and crisis. God promises blessings to those who walk in His counsel. ***"Blessed is the man who walks not in the counsel of the ungodly, nor stands in the path of sinners, nor sits in the seat of the scornful; but his delight is in the law of the Lord, and in His law he meditates day and night." (Ps. 1:1)*** We are admonished by John to imitate that which is good, and that's why discipleship and mentoring are so important. As we grow in Christ, we change and model Him for others to follow.

Prayer: Father, help our lives to reflect Your Son, Jesus Christ.

_____
_____
_____
_____
_____
_____
_____
_____
_____

The Love Of God

"Keep yourselves in the love of God,
looking for the mercy of our Lord Jesus Christ unto eternal life."
Jude 21

Read Jude

*I*n this short book, Jude asserts his up front, get to the point approach. After his greeting, Jude exhorts the church to contend earnestly for the faith. He warns about the imposters who have crept into the church, seemingly unnoticed. He denounces these ungodly men who turn from God's grace and deny the deity of the Lord Jesus Christ. It's hard to believe that such a thing can happen in the church; but over the years, that's exactly what has happened. Many false teachers and heretics have risen up and started cults, marketing the idea of Jesus, but ultimately denying His death and resurrection. From such, we should turn away!

Jude reminds the body of Christ to keep the main thing, the main thing. "Contend for the faith," means to put yourself forward, or to compete, stay focused and don't waver. The prescription he gives for living above life's circumstances is to keep ourselves in the love of God. What an awesome way to conclude his letter. He reminds us to stay close to the One and Only True God! Looking unto Jesus and being mindful of His merciful heart towards sinners, helps us to set our sights on the eternal. Living in the nearness of God's love will help us to keep His perspective.

Prayer: Father, thank You for reminders, like the one Jude gives, to keep ourselves abiding in Your love.

Behold The King Is Coming

"Behold, He is coming with clouds, and every eye will see Him, even they who pierced Him. And all the tribes of the earth will mourn because of Him. Even so, Amen."
Revelation 1:7

Read Revelation Chapter 1

$\mathcal{T}$he word "revelation" means unveiling or disclosure. The book of Revelation will reveal our Lord glorified. At His second coming, every eye will see Him and the entire universe will behold His glory. Those who pierced Him will mourn because they will see that He truly is the Messiah. Hearts will grieve because they rejected Him.

The entire universe will see our glorified Lord, and in that one moment, all eyes will understand that all the mocking and ridicule that Jesus endured was at the hands of man, who believed the lies of Satan. Today's verse coincides with Daniel's vision concerning the Lord's coming. *"I was watching in the night visions, and behold, One like the Son of Man, coming with the clouds of heaven! He came to the Ancient Of Days, and they brought Him near before Him. Then to Him was given dominion and glory and a kingdom, that all peoples, nations, and languages should serve Him. His dominion is an everlasting dominion, which shall not pass away, and His kingdom the one which shall not be destroyed."* *(Dan. 7:13,14)* We are in the midst of the last days, and at any moment Christ could come for His bride, the church. Are you ready? Can you hear His footsteps?

Prayer: Father, wake up Your church and purify our hearts.

_____

_____

_____

_____

_____

_____

_____

Blessings Of Faithful Living

"Be faithful unto death, and I will give you the crown of life."
Revelation 2:10b

Read Revelation Chapters 2 & 3

*J*esus was exhorting the church to faithfulness. In the midst of persecution, the church needed strength, encouragement, and hope. Every believer needs to persevere in the face of suffering. When the enemy is at our door, bombarding us with discouragement and doubt, it's no time to bow out. The battle belongs to the Lord, and He will equip us to endure under pressure. He is the Lord of our salvation, and His only requirement is faithfulness. Faithfulness is not something we can manifest in our own strength; faithfulness is entrusting God with our lives, believing Him for the invisible and the impossible.

The word "faithful" means to be true. It doesn't mean that we won't sometimes be fearful or have moments of discouragement. It simply means that we believe God will come through with what He has promised. There are blessings that come from faithful living, and Jesus speaks of giving "the crown of life" to those who are faithful unto death. If God calls us to suffer for Him, we must believe that He will equip us. *"He who calls you is faithful, who also will do it."* (1 Thes. 5:24)

Prayer: Father, thank You for Jesus and His faithfulness, even unto death.

He Is Worthy

"Then I looked, and I heard the voice of many angels around the throne,
the living creatures, and the elders; and the number of them was ten thousand
times ten thousand, and thousands of thousands, saying with a loud voice:
Worthy is the Lamb who was slain to receive power and riches and wisdom,
and strength and honor and glory and blessing!'"
Revelation 5:11,12

Read Revelation Chapters 4 & 5

Today's verses speak of God's redeeming love and His final victory through "the Lamb who was slain," Jesus Christ. There is no one worthy to open the scroll--no elder, no angel, no creature, only one--Jesus, the One who redeemed us by His blood. Jesus is the exalted One, and those who gather around the throne respond by worshipping Him.

When we see our Lord Jesus as He is--holy, anointed, and worthy of all praise--we are brought into a state of worship. Bowing before His holy throne, He is worthy; all of creation will acknowledge that He is Lord, to the glory of the Father in heaven. Paul writes about the glorified and exalted Christ. *"Therefore God also has highly exalted Him and given Him the name which is above every name, that at the name of Jesus every knee should bow, of those in heaven, and of those on earth, and of those under the earth, and that every tongue should confess that Jesus Christ is Lord, to the glory of God the Father."* *(Phil. 2:9-11)*

Prayer: Father, thank You for the privilege of worshipping You.

The Voice Of The Martyrs

"When He opened the fifth seal, I saw under the altar the souls of those who had been slain for the word of God and for the testimony which they held."
Revelation 6:9

Read Revelation Chapters 6 & 7

The opening of the seals represents the judgment of God. Jesus, the only One worthy to open the seals, reveals the beginning of sorrows. When the fifth seal is opened, we read that the martyrs cry out unto the Lord to avenge their blood. *"How long, O Lord, holy and true, until You judge and avenge our blood on those who dwell on the earth?" (vs. 10)* The saints were given a white robe and asked to be patient just a little while longer, for there are still some who will surrender their lives for their faith.

Like the saints at the altar who cried out unto the Lord for vengeance, we too often lack patience in the midst of a trial. We cry out for deliverance, but God's sovereign and eternal plan is working in us a far greater work. With suffering comes salvation, and God's eternal works are accomplished. Like every trial or testing of our faith, there comes an end to that trial. Today, are you in the midst of suffering? Are you crying out to the Lord asking, "How long?" He does have an answer for you; rest a little while longer. *"For he who has entered His rest has himself also ceased from his works as God did from His." (Heb. 4:10)* We need to let go of our wills, our works, our understandings, and lean on God. In the end, the Lord will bring everything into perspective and will accomplish His will in our lives.

Prayer: Father, thank You for that special place in Your heart for Your saints.

Woe, Woe, Woe

*"And I looked, and I heard an angel flying through the midst of heaven, saying with
a loud voice, 'Woe, woe, woe to the inhabitants of the earth, because of the
remaining blasts of the trumpet of the three angels who are about to sound!'"
Revelation 8:13*

Read Revelation Chapters 8 & 9

The word "woe" means anguish, despair, and affliction. The judgments of God are serious, and the fact that "woe" is mentioned three times, reflects the intensity and the seriousness of them. During the tribulation period, the inhabitants of the earth who remain will suffer great hardship and pain for their unbelief in God. There is a saying that we have heard over the years, and it goes like this: "If you can't live for Christ now, will you be able to live for Him during the days of tribulation?" According to these verses, it will be difficult, but we know from Scripture that there will be some who will respond to the call of God. Although these new believers will be saved, during the tribulation they may have to surrender their lives.

We should ponder the "woes" given in Scripture, because they are from the very heart of God and serve as a warning. Consider your life and those around you. Are you living for the Lord today? Or, are you vacillating between two worlds? We must remember that for an undisclosed time, there is an open window of grace for us. Sadly, one day it will close, and the world will desperately wish it were still accessible. Like the open door of the ark and Noah's invitation to get on board, we know that the day came when God shut the door of opportunity. Listen to the woe and its warning. Live today for Christ!

Prayer: Father, help us to stand holy before You, and to share our faith while we have this window of grace.

Even In Death, There Is Victory

"Now after the three-and-a-half days the breath of life from God entered them,
and they stood on their feet, and great fear fell on those who saw them."
Revelation 11:11

Read Revelation Chapters 10 & 11

Satan may think that he has his final victory when the two witnesses of Revelation are killed. We see how unbelievers will celebrate the death of the witnesses by giving gifts to one another. But as the party ends, God begins a new work as He breathes life into their bodies. Even in death, there is victory with God. We saw that as Jesus was crucified for the sins of the world. Satan may have thought he finally defeated Christ, but we know that He rose from the grave, conquering death, and more importantly conquering spiritual death.

The witnesses' resurrection brought great fear upon the people, as God called them up saying, **"'Come up here.'--In the same hour there was a great earthquake, and a tenth of the city fell. In the earthquake seven thousand people were killed, and the rest were afraid and gave glory to the God of heaven." (vss. 12,13)** The resurrection of the witnesses means life, because many will come to know the saving power of our Lord Jesus during "The Great Tribulation."

Prayer: Father, thank You for Your mercy. Even in death, we have victory through You.

_____

_____

_____

_____

_____

_____

_____

_____

The Mark Of The Beast

"He causes all, both small and great, rich and poor, free and slave, to receive a mark on their right hand or on their foreheads, and that no one may buy or sell except one who has the mark or the name of the beast, or the number of his name. Here is wisdom. Let him who has understanding calculate the number of the beast, for it is the number of a man: His number is 666."

Revelation 13:16-18

Read Revelation Chapters 12 & 13

Satan is a counterfeit, and he uses his chief counterpart, the Antichrist, who is nothing more then a created being. For a time, he will be charismatic and able to influence people to go to hell. However, one day he will be cast down and utterly destroyed. The Scriptures are clear in warning us about the Antichrist who will lead the world with deception and lies, causing them to take the mark of the beast. Six is the number of imperfection and the number 666 is the number of complete imperfection.

In the world we live in today, we see how folks are being groomed to take the mark of the beast. Like lambs to the slaughter, they will willingly take the mark if they don't yield their lives to Christ. A microchip has already been designed, that can be placed into a person's hand or head. This microchip has the ability to carry all personal information about an individual and can even be linked to one's bank account. We have a window of grace to share our faith with those who don't know about salvation through Jesus Christ. We have the cure for this ailment, therefore let's follow the commission. ***"And He said to them, 'Go into all the world and preach the gospel to every creature.'" (Mark 16:15)*** We need to wake up, get up, and go out!

Prayer: Father, give us Your heart for souls.

King Of Kings & Lord Of Lords

"He was clothed with a robe dipped in blood,
and His name is called The Word of God."
Revelation 19:13

Read Revelation Chapters 14 - 19

*I*n ancient times, a person's name was more than a title; it revealed one's character. Jesus Christ literally means, God is salvation (Jesus) and the sent One of God (Christ). At His second coming, our Lord will not come as a lamb for sacrifice, but as the *"KING OF KINGS AND LORD OF LORDS."* God's eternal character is revealed in our verse today, as He comes with glory and power to rule and reign over a once Christ-rejecting world.

To all who are of the household of faith, Jew and Gentile alike, we see the fulfillment of the promised return of the Messiah, Jesus Christ our Lord. What a thrilling picture this is! He is called Faithful and True, a testimony to His fulfillment of Scripture. His eyes are "flames of fire," and His robe dipped in blood symbolizes the complete knowledge of His fierce judgment. His garment depicts His rightful title: "King of Kings and Lord of Lords." Moreover, Jesus returns to earth riding a white horse which is symbolic of the righteousness of His mission.

Just as thrilling to the church is the fact that we will all join this mission to reclaim the earth! Having been given white robes at the marriage supper of the Lamb, we will also ride white horses following our Commander and King!

Prayer: Father, thank You for Your Lordship.

He Comes Quickly!

"Behold, I am coming quickly!
Blessed is he who keeps the words of the prophecy of this book."
Revelation 22:7

Read Revelation Chapters 20 - 22

*A*s we come to the end of the New Testament, how appropriate it is to end our journey with a new beginning. ***"Then He who sat on the throne said, 'Behold, I will make all things new.'" (Rev. 21:5)*** What a blessed hope we have in our Lord and Savior Jesus Christ! Not only will all things become new, but He will wipe away every tear. There will be no sorrow, no pain or death, for the former things have been "done away" forever.

We have so much to look forward to as we focus on God's eternal plan. That's why it's so important to have an eternal perspective. As we live in these last days, we should live each day as if it will be the day the Lord returns for His bride, the church. The time is near! We need to wake up and pay attention to God's Word for He is truly the Beginning and the End of all things. ***"And behold, I am coming quickly, and My reward is with Me, to give to every one according to his work. I am the Alpha and the Omega, the Beginning and the End, the First and the Last." (Rev. 22:12,13)*** We must remember the warnings that God gave in the days of Noah; remember Lot's wife! ***"He who testifies to these things says, 'Surely I am coming quickly.'" (Rev. 22:20)***

Prayer: Lord, thank You for being the Beginning and the End of all things.

Index

Matthew, pgs. 1-31

Mark, pgs. 32-45

Luke, pgs. 46-93

John, pgs. 94-135

John cont'd

Acts, pgs. 136-190

Romans, pgs. 191-219

1 Corinthians, pgs. 220-252